T0285263

HOC

RANTS &

HOCKEY
RANTS & RAVES

STEVE "DANGLE" GLYNN

HarperCollins*Publishers*Ltd

Published by HarperCollins Publishers Ltd

FIRST EDITION

HarperCollins books may be purchased for educational, business, or
sales promotional use through our Special Markets Department.

HarperCollins Publishers Ltd
Bay Adelaide Centre, East Tower
22 Adelaide Street West, 41st Floor
Toronto, Ontario, Canada
M5H 4E3

www.harpercollins.ca

Library and Archives Canada Cataloguing in Publication

Title: Hockey rants & raves / Steve "Dangle" Glynn.
Other titles: Hockey rants and raves
Names: Glynn, Steve, author
Identifiers: Canadiana (print) 20240441346 | Canadiana
(ebook) 20240441354 | ISBN 9781443469968
(hardcover) | ISBN 9781443469975 (EPUB)
Subjects: LCSH: National Hockey League—Anecdotes. | LCSH:
National Hockey League—History. | LCSH:
Hockey—Canada—Anecdotes. | LCSH: Hockey—United States—
Anecdotes. | LCSH: Hockey—Canada—History. |
LCSH: Hockey—United States—History. | LCGFT: Anecdotes.
Classification: LCC GV847.8.N3 G59 2024 | DDC 796.962/64—dc23

Printed and bound in the United States of America

24 25 26 27 28 LBC 5 4 3 2 1

*Dedicated to my son, Leo, and my daughter, Isla.
I wanted to dedicate my first book to you two as
well but you showed up late, a trait you definitely
inherited from me.*

Contents

Foreword

by Adam Wylde

Let me tell you about my friend Steve Dangle. Actually, he was Steve Glynn when I met him. Sir Oliver Mowat Collegiate Institute high school, 2002–2006. He was a good Catholic schoolboy and I came from the heathen/apostate/atheist school diagonally opposite his at the other end of the block. We went to school on the same street for a decade but didn't meet until high school, where—both lovers of being the loudest in the room—we found ourselves in drama class and a high school play together.

The subject matter of the play: infidelity, homosexuality, pregnancy, suicide, and regret.

If you're thinking, *This sounds a bit dark*, that's because it decidedly was. Our drama teacher, Ms. Kish, to whom we both owe a great debt of gratitude, was adamant that she was going to push every person in the cast to their absolute emotional limit. And she did. Our little play, which she wrote, went on to become a big hit at the Sears drama festival . . . a very prestigious high school thespian festival in Ontario.

As you can imagine this made us a hit with women . . . our moms, who were very proud.

What strikes me now thinking about it is how much Steve was always himself. He just walked around and would fire out these very clever, funny lines during the most serious moments.

Rehearsal was gruelling: every day after school and eight hours a day on weekends, for months. We were not fully mature enough to understand some of the themes we were playing . . . and when things got too serious, Steve always cut the tension and we'd all be doubled over. He was the release valve for all of us.

I love him. Absolutely love the man. I love working with him. I love being his friend. I love running a business with him. And I love observing him in his natural habitat . . . watching a Leafs game with nobody else around. Actually, it can be a room full of people and nothing changes; the lines shoot out of his head and into the air in a stream of consciousness like a kid throwing buckets of paint at the wall. They're uneven, raw, sometimes raise your eyebrows, and yet when they hit your ears and enter the processing part of your brain, a couple things happen:

1. You usually find yourself smiling at the ironic, sardonic, and sometimes flat-out wild things that he said, and
2. there's usually an element that you can instantly recognize . . . like you've heard it before, or that you've said it before, or that you were just about to say it but you couldn't quite find the words or the timing or the sheer depth of emotion (in the Leafs' case, despair). But you recognize it. You relate to it.

I've always thought that we gravitate toward people who to some degree or another say the things that the voices in our heads say. Or would say, if we'd let them. We see and hear ourselves in someone else . . . and sometimes that person says what we feel better than we can. I think it's the same reason we love certain bands or singers but can't relate to others. Some speak the language of the voices in our heads, and some do not.

What you're going to read in this book is a written account of the voice in Steve's head. The voice of one fan, but a fan who seems to have a propensity to say what we are all thinking. It's the same voice that you get every time he sits down to record a Leaf Fan Reaction, or record a podcast with Jesse and me. Steve's voice—quite loud to sit next to in real life—comes from an un-encumbered, filter-free place in his head that really thinks what he says.

He's not always right—nobody is. But he is always honest. What you are hearing is what he believes. He's not intractable—he'll change his mind if you can convince him—but he's usually had a long time to think about whatever he's saying. So if you read something and disagree, tell him—he loves a debate about hockey. After all, we're talking about a guy who spends his sum-mers watching Auston Matthews goal compilations on YouTube. Absolutely hopeless.

I want you to know that a lot of love went into this book. He wanted it to be great for you and I'm excited for you to read it. So let's get to it! Rants and raves from the guy who's known for doing it best . . . Steve "Dangle" Glynn.

—Adam Wylde

HOCKEY
RANTS & RAVES

Introduction

Hi, I'm Steve, and I really like hockey.

Some of my earliest childhood memories involve me ranting about hockey. The most consistent feedback my teachers gave me all throughout my education was that I talked too much. During almost any other time in human history, I would just be the guy at your work who spends too much of his time ranting about sports and not enough time doing that thing that was supposed to be done an hour ago.

Luckily for me, I came up during the dawn of YouTube and social media, where every putz or pigeon can blab on and on about the thing they're most passionate about, including hockey. I started a YouTube channel in 2007 where I could rant and rave about hockey, specifically the Toronto Maple Leafs, and over the past two decades it's grown to the point where a few hundred thousand followers want to hear what this pigeon has to coo about today.

From that YouTube channel came job opportunities with companies like the NHL Network, the CBC, and Rogers Sportsnet. My career has taken me to the Winter Olympics, the World Juniors, and the Stanley Cup Final, just to name a few events. My podcast, *The Steve Dangle Podcast with Adam Wylde and Jesse Blake*, has turned into a podcast network called SDPN, because one show to rant and rave about sports wasn't enough.

What gives me the right, as a hockey fan, to let words tumble out of my head and into a book? Great question.

Have I ever won the Stanley Cup? No, but my wife owns one, which means I own one, too. Hers has a lid, though.

Am I a great skater? Do I have a wicked shot? Have I ever played pro? No, I'm just some random guy who likes Doritos and happens to have a passion for puck. For whatever reason, that resonates with people. It hasn't made me a rich man, but sometimes my wife and I get organic bananas, and honestly that's close enough. Which reminds me—thanks for buying this book!

So what's in this book, anyway?

I'm lucky enough to live in a place full of people who love hockey and are dying to talk about it with you, especially when they find out you talk about hockey for a living. One time, after getting a colonoscopy, I was getting ready to leave when the doctor asked me what I thought about the Leafs that season. I walked out of the hospital wondering when I ever told the doctor what my job was and whether or not he discovered the Leafs had actually been the pain in my ass this entire time.

In my experience, hockey has certain hot-button topics sure to boil the blood of any passionate puckhead. Was any player ever better than Wayne Gretzky? Who's on your goalie Mount Rushmore? What would happen if you gave players from the past and present a time machine? What's the worst trade in NHL history? What do you think about fighting in hockey?

Throughout this book, my hope is that I can answer some of these questions once and for all. For the questions I can't answer, I'm going to give you as much ammo as possible for the next time the topic comes up, so you don't get caught with your head down.

There are times when you'll want to win an argument with three exclamation marks, but hockey is a big vibes sport. It's not always about winning an argument. Sometimes it's just about having a great time with your team, whether that's on the ice, on the bench, in the parking lot, on the train, in the office, or at the bar. Let's keep those vibes immaculate.

I wrote the words you're about to read in this book because I think they're right. Maybe next year I'll write a follow-up called *Never Mind: Why I'm an Idiot*. No matter what, I hope you have fun.

I don't care if you've won five Stanley Cups or if you just own one pair of socks with your favourite team's logo and holes in them. Trust me—you don't need a doctorate to have an opinion about a sport. Talking about hockey is one of my favourite things in the world. I want you to have as much fun with it as I do, whether you're laughing so hard it hurts or you scream until you're purple.

Get ready to nod, shake your head, laugh, and scream at a bunch of pages before we're done here. Hockey should be for everyone, and this book is for you.

Drop the puck.

1.
The Best Things about Going to a Game

Gosh darn it, I love going to a hockey game. I'm betting you do, too. The first hockey game I ever went to was on February 5, 1994. The Detroit Red Wings were visiting the Toronto Maple Leafs, in the old Maple Leaf Gardens. Did the Leafs lose? You bet they did, but I was five years old and thought it was the best thing ever.

I'm older now, and I still think going to a hockey game is the best thing ever. It's better than finding $20 in an old coat. It's better than pulling up to a red light just as it turns green. It's better than waking up and realizing you actually have three more hours before your alarm goes off so you smile and drift back into a peaceful sleep.

Going to a hockey game is still so special to me, even though I've been covering games for over a decade. I've tried watching games from the press box, and while that's fun (they usually have free ice cream), it's not the same as sitting in the stands as a fan.

You might think I go to dozens of games each season, but I'm lucky if I make it to half a dozen, and it's usually just two or three.

Do I lament not going to each and every game? No, because this way, it's still a treat. Christmas morning is magical because it doesn't happen every day. Still, I wish I was at a game right now.

I even love the parts that may not seem special but always are to me. Maybe to you, too.

GETTING TO YOUR SEAT

This isn't exactly exclusive to hockey. It could work across all sports and even apply to things like concerts or comedy shows. But just getting to your seat is an ordeal. In this day and age, if you want to go to a hockey game—or anything that's big and fun, especially in a major city—man, do they make you earn it.

Most professional hockey games start around seven p.m. locally. That provides hurdles right away. When do you get off work, around five p.m.? Maybe a little earlier if you can manage it? You'll want to go home first and at least change, because who wants to go to a game in your work clothes? I've never seen anybody wearing nurse scrubs to a hockey game. But will you even have time?

There's the potential nightmare of a commute, whether it's by train, subway, or the dreaded car—in that case you'll have to find parking, too. And are you meeting friends there? That can be like herding cats. Better budget some extra time for those guys.

Let's not forget about the most key gameday decision of all: When and where am I going to eat? If you decide to eat at the game, you're going to have to line up, and it's going to cost an arm and a leg. If you go to a restaurant instead, especially if it's right next to the arena, you're going to have to line up, and it's going to cost an arm and a leg. In this scenario, you don't eat dinner so much as you just kind of unhinge your jaw and inhale it, like you're Kirby or Snake.

You then arrive at the arena, funnel through the concourse, and then the metal detectors. You need to find your seat—is it this way, or no actually it's this way, I don't know. You get what you need at the concessions (and deal with that line), then maybe hit up the washroom (and deal with that line, too).

But then, that shining, shimmering moment. You walk through the tunnel, the Jumbotron appears, and with the *Jurassic Park* theme in the back of your mind, you breach the entranceway to the stands.

The cold in the air kisses you on the nose. You take in the brilliance of the ice. Maybe the players are warming up and you get to see your favourite one rifle a puck bar down and in. You think to yourself, *Oh yeah, they're going off tonight* like you're the world's foremost hockey scout.

Then at last you plant your butt into a seat that cost—how much did these cost again? No. You mustn't think of that. Don't ruin this for yourself. You sit. You smile.

You're here. You're finally here. The day you had at work, anything going on at home, the commute, the lines, the time crunch, the stairs—none of that matters now. Relax your shoulders. Unclench your jaw. Your team could get stomped into the earth's crust and play the worst game in franchise history tonight, but right now, in this shining moment, everybody's got a chance to win.

The pre-game show commences, and you promptly get to your feet and lose your mind along with everybody else. The lights. The highlight reels. The lasers. Heck, if you go to a Golden Knights game in Vegas, half the price of your ticket is to cover the pre-game entertainment. All of that, and the game hasn't even started yet. Then the puck drops and the real fun begins.

But if they could capture that feeling of when your butt first hits your seat at a hockey game, and sell it in a can, I'd buy a whole two-four, take two, crack them together, and chug them both at once, Stone Cold Steve Austin–style.

Maybe you don't pay for the seat after all. You pay for the feeling it gives you.

WHEN THE GUY WHO NEVER SCORES ACTUALLY SCORES

They say that superstars are the main attraction, and it's true. It takes all sorts to fill out a hockey team, but a small handful of players is the reason you show up. Sure, you would support your team no matter who was in the lineup that night, but you didn't part with your hard-earned cash thinking, *I hope our third-line right-winger tears it up tonight!*

No, you're there because Connor McDavid is going to get the zoomies and fly around the ice like the human incarnation of particles in the Large Hadron Collider. You're there because you might get to see Auston Matthews rip a puck so hard it could take out a tank. You're there because Igor Shesterkin might make such a ridiculous save that the shooter has an existential crisis, takes off all their equipment at centre ice, and starts their new career developing home security software because they're so tired of getting robbed.

There's just something about witnessing greatness and being able to say, "I was there." Maybe somebody you know can say they saw Wayne Gretzky score. Maybe they saw Alex Ovechkin do that thing on the powerplay where he just stands stationary for 90 seconds before Thanos-snapping a puck into dust. Can you imagine being able to say you were in the building when Sidney Crosby scored the golden goal at the Vancouver Olympics? Because I can—I was there! I still have the ticket stub, and I'll continue bragging about it long after I'm dead. I've already pre-ordered edible arrangements to be sent to everybody I ever knew (especially the Americans) that say, "I was there."

When you watch a star player do their thing, there's nothing in the world like it. But when some random guy scores, I might love that even more. I'm not talking about a third-liner scoring a goal. I get that a guy scoring ten goals in a season is unlikely to pot one the night you're there, but it's not *that* rare. Is it really the story you're going to tell your grandkids? "Pull up a seat, Johnny, and let me tell you about the time I saw something that had, like, a one-in-eight chance of happening." Who cares?

No, I'm talking about the once-in-a-lifetime moments. I can't decide which I like watching more: a rookie coming in and scoring their first ever goal, or a journeyman who's played hundreds of career games scoring his, say, third all time.

A rookie scoring their first goal is probably the bigger feather in your cap because, well, it only happens once. Even if that player goes on to be a star with hundreds of goals in their career, only a lucky few will ever be able to say they were in the building to see that first one, and even some of those folks were in the bathroom during the goal. Whether the rookies become superstars or not, it never gets old. You see the wide-eyed look of excitement as they realize they're living a childhood dream in real time. Their teammates go nuts, because who doesn't like watching a rookie bury their first one? A veteran player on the team rushes to the net to fish out the puck and hand it off to the team trainer, who throws some tape on it and writes, "First NHL goal" or "First PWHL goal." Players never forget their first, and if you're lucky enough to see it happen live and in person, you won't, either.

I saw Nick Abruzzese score his first NHL goal in a nothing

game at the end of the season when both the Leafs and Bruins were resting all their guys. Who cared? Well, Nick, for one. So did every fan in that building who was disappointed the star players weren't playing but got to see something special anyway.

When Matt Rempe, of all people, a six-foot-seven rookie with piston fists, scored the first goal of the Rangers' 2024 Stanley Cup Playoffs campaign, you could feel that the Madison Square Garden faithful were Hulking out for Rempe-mania, brother!

There's also something romantic about being in the building for a guy who, season after season, never scores but then finally finds the scoresheet. Think of your team's stalwart, zero-offence, stay-at-home defensive defenceman getting a goal. Or even better, your team tough guy.

Wade Belak was a tough guy for the Toronto Maple Leafs from 2001 to 2008. Even though he wouldn't get into the lineup every game, Belak had five seasons of more than 100 penalty minutes with the Leafs alone.

Belak scored a goal for Toronto on December 20, 2003. Go to the net, find the puck, bang it in, boom. Some call it simple, others call it essential. Fast forward four years, and that was still his most recent goal. Finally, after a 143-game drought, on December 4, 2007, Wade Belak scored for the Leafs, and in Toronto. The highlight of the goal is hilarious. The commentary team of Joe Bowen and Greg Millen sound like kids opening a birthday present. Belak's teammates mob him on the ice and come from the bench, too, to celebrate. The fans lose it so hard that the camera shakes like the building is on a fault line.

When a star player scores, even if it's impressive, you still kind of expect it. When you get to see somebody end a four-year goalless drought? That's on a whole different level. Think of a star player's goal-scoring as like the sun: You're happy when it's there, and it's literally the star of the show. People bask in it, love it, but often take it for granted. Think of a player who never scores like a solar eclipse. A goal is a goal in the same way the sun is the sun, but the rarity of the event is what makes it special.

Imagine being in the building for a John Scott goal. Scoring wasn't Scott's thing. The dude was six-foot-eight, 260 pounds, and his coaches were like, "Hey, how about you fight?" So he fought, and it turns out he was good at it.

Including playoffs, John Scott scored five goals in 290 career NHL games. If you went to an NHL game that John Scott was playing in, you had a 1.7 per cent chance of seeing him score that night. Compare that to his 38 regular season fights, which meant you had a 13.3 per cent chance of seeing Scott in a scrap.

Even more wild, only one of his five goals was on home ice! Would you believe me if I told you it happened on April Fool's Day? It did! April 1, 2015, when his San Jose Sharks hosted the Colorado Avalanche. The game was already 4–1 for San Jose when Scott backhanded the puck three-quarters of the way down the ice, in what was basically a clearing attempt, and it went into Colorado's empty net.

If you can ever find the highlight, watch it. Every single member of the Sharks has a smile from ear to ear. And why wouldn't they? This wasn't just any goal. Their big guy with a tough job just bagged one. Did they know that it was the first home goal he had ever scored? Maybe. Did the fans know? I doubt it. Did any of them know it would be the first and only time he would ever score at home? Not without a crystal ball they wouldn't.

Every time you go to a game, you might see something you'll be telling people about for the rest of your life.

BIG PENALTY KILL

This one rules. This is the good stuff.

A big penalty kill is hockey's purest form of David vs. Goliath. You hope for a powerplay and dread a penalty kill. For a powerplay to be successful, it just needs one moment for a goal to happen—a practiced passing play that takes a while to set up, or a lucky bounce. It could take the full powerplay or just five seconds.

A penalty kill, though? You're in it for the long haul. You're either coming out of this as heroes or failures. Obviously, failing to score on the powerplay is disappointing, but it's not so bad. You can take some pride in a few decent chances (hopefully you at least got that) and wearing down your opponent a bit. There's usually a feeling of "we'll get them next time."

Failure looks a lot different for the penalty kill. There are no brownie points for a penalty kill that gives up a goal. Every save, every blocked shot, and every puck battle won evaporates as soon as the other team puts their hands in the air in triumph. The player who blocked a shot with their rib cage may feel it for the next few weeks (especially when they sit, stand, lie down, or sneeze), but almost nobody else is going to remember it if the other team scores.

The irony is that the penalty kills that get cheered the hardest aren't even the ones that necessarily go well. Ideally, when the other team's powerplay attacks, you cut them off at the blue line and don't even allow them to breach your zone. If they do get in, the next-best thing is to win the puck away from them and clear it. Even that gets cheers from fans. Stop a shot and it's thousands of people oohing and aahing, but clear the puck down the ice and everyone cheers like crazy. Heck, you might even steal the puck and get a short-handed goal out of it!

An efficient penalty kill is a good penalty kill, but an absolute yard sale of a kill is the kind of performance fans remember. There's nothing better than being in the barn for one of those. The enemy powerplay crosses your blue line, backs up the penalty kill, and sets up their formation. They carry the puck and circle you like a pack of orcas around a seal trapped on a sheet of ice.

The powerplay takes a shot, but a hero defender fearlessly blocks it. They hobble for a moment with gritted teeth before rejoining the fray. Another shot is met by that same fearless player, who's now reeling but still willing to put their body on the line for the team. The puck gets worked around; another shot, and another block from the next penalty killer up. Finally, the powerplay gets a cross-crease one-timer on net, only to be robbed by the goaltender. The puck gets kicked into the corner, and the process repeats until the two minutes, or maybe more, have expired and the penalty has been killed.

The penalty killers return to the bench, hunched over, gasping for air, wincing, bloody and bruised, but victorious. Did that penalty kill go well? Of course it didn't! Yes, you achieved your ultimate goal of keeping the puck out of the net, but it took the maximum effort possible for you to get there.

And not a single person in that building, apart from perhaps the coaching staff, gives a damn about any of that. They're too busy rising to their feet giving that same chaotic, reckless, inefficient penalty kill a full-bodied standing ovation and yelling at the top of their lungs.

You went to the game, along with thousands of your fellow fans, expecting to cheer on your team's star sniper as they fired one bar down. At the end, the biggest pop of the night came from one of your team's penalty killers throwing themselves junk-first into a shot because it was what they had to do.

We revere the players with the best skill, but we adore the players with the best effort.

GAME-SAVER

Penalty killers can perform as bravely as they want, but if they're defending an empty net, even the league's worst offensive lines are probably going to score. You need your last line of defence: a goalie.

Sports thrive on scoring. You need runs in baseball, baskets in basketball, and goals in hockey. But gosh darn it, there's just something about a big save.

I'm sure it will surprise absolutely nobody who's ever seen one of my videos that I used to volunteer to play goalie in street hockey as a kid. Goalies are weird, so it was my natural calling. What else could possess you to voluntarily throw yourself in front of a hard, speeding projectile dozens of times per game and get mad if it actually misses you?

Like penalty killers, goalies go out on the ice planning to give up zero goals. If it were up to them, they would get a shut-out in every game they ever played. That's not how it works, though, is it?

Martin Brodeur owns the NHL's all-time shutout record with 125. The trouble with that is Brodeur played in 1,266 games. That means that over 90 percent of the time, the goalie with the most shutouts in the history of the sport failed in his ultimate goal of shutting out his opponent.

Goaltending can be a thankless job. Meanwhile, on a lot of nights throughout a season, your goalie is your most important player.

Fans have a super-weird relationship with goalies, too. We know goalies can't stop every puck they face. Most starting goaltenders and even some backups are going to face more than 1,000 shots per season. We have a sympathy for the difficulty of the job, and even more sympathy if the defence in front stinks. But then there's every goalie's least favourite phrase: sometimes you just need a save.

"Of course you needed a damn save there," grunted every goalie ever. "You need a save on every shot that makes its way on net. I promise I tried to stop it! You think it's easy? You do it, then!"

Goalies are not actually expected to be superhuman, but sometimes you'd like them to be. Sometimes you need them to be. Sometimes you need your goalie to forget they're made of flesh and bone and become Mister Fantastic from the Fantastic Four, stretching out and snatching the puck away from a certain goal. Sometimes you need your goalie to transcend consciousness and see into the future, like Doctor Strange, and know where the puck will end up even before the shooter does. Sometimes you need your goalie's groin to do whatever the hell it is that groins do to allow goalies to move like that.

Just like with the penalty kill, the best goaltending moments aren't necessarily born from perfect efficiency, but rather from chaos.

Nobody is expecting the big save. Every fan in that building is hoping for it, praying for it, but they know that it's madness to expect a miracle. The net is wide open, calling out to the puck, beckoning it, as the shooter goes for the easiest tap-in goal of their career.

Your goalie abandons all thought, all reason, and somehow, some way, tosses their body at the puck, hoping to get just a big enough chunk of the thing to keep it out of the net. In that one seemingly infinitesimal moment, a building full of thousands of roaring fans falls silent, almost breathless.

A brief pin-drop silence . . . and then the moment of realization. Spider-Man saved MJ from falling at the last second. The Flash got there just in time. Superman deflected the meteor just before disaster. The day is saved, and so is the puck.

The roar from a crowd when a goalie makes one of those saves simply can't be bought. The shock, the disbelief, the unbridled joy, and the complete inability to take your hands off your head or the smile off your face.

These saves can come at any time, but if they come in the final minute with your team up by one or, even better, in overtime? Curtis Joseph robbing Joe Nieuwendyk in Game 7 of Oilers-Stars in 1997. Braden Holtby in Game 2 of the 2018 Stanley Cup Final. Marc-André Fleury sealing a Penguins Stanley Cup victory in 2009. We go to games in the hope that we'll get to experience something like this. Although it should be mentioned that all of those saves happened on the road, in which case, disappointment was the mark of success on those nights.

OT WINNER

Who doesn't love a happy ending?

This one should be obvious. When you go to a hockey game, you want to see two things:

1. Something cool that will make you shout "Hooray!" or an appropriate synonym.
2. Your team winning

An overtime winning goal is a guarantee you'll get both.

You could sit there through an entire stinker of a game—no offence, no hits, just awful—and it's all made better by one moment. You could have been asleep for the entirety of a game up until the overtime winner and you would still have the same lasting memory as anybody else who went that night. Unless you see something truly historic, like a Gretzky record being broken, or a Zamboni driver recording several saves and an actual NHL win, the overtime winner is going to be the biggest, most consequential, and most exciting sequence from that entire game. And there are so many different types:

- Powerplay
- Short-handed
- Breakaway
- After a big breakaway save against the other team
- Snipe
- Clap bomb
- Off someone's butt
- Diving through the air

And most importantly . . .

- Anything that isn't a damn shootout

Even for an overtime that's been mostly a "which team is the best line-changer" contest, all is forgiven with a sudden-death winner at home. It also comes with a deadly music combo that I guarantee is better than anything you've got on your playlists: your team's goal song followed by your team's win song.

The chatter around the building? Truly elite banter. Yelling, cheering, jumping up and down, and then seamlessly transitioning to talking and thinking about this and only this for the entire next day.

If you're ever at a hockey game and your team wins in overtime, just remember me asking you this: How high are your eyebrows right now? Right?! They're all the way up there! Why? Because that's what happens when you're extremely happy!

Last place in the standings? Doesn't matter, got an OT winner.

First place? Add to that flex with an OT winner.

Exam tomorrow? If you can't think of the answer to a question, just think about the OT winner.

Boring meeting at work? Slap on that "I'm totally listening" face and think exclusively about the OT winner.

You can ride the high of an OT winner for days. The sky is bluer. If it's raining, you'll realize you forgot how much you love the rain. There's a snowstorm? Build a snowman to commemorate, you guessed it, that OT winner.

And if this happens in the playoffs? Forget it. Nuclear, gas, solar, wind—all those forms of energy are a waste of time. We should be allocating all our resources into figuring out how to bottle the feeling after watching your team win a playoff game at home in overtime. Straight rocket fuel. If we figured out how to harness the energy in LA when Alec Martinez won the Stanley Cup for the Kings in overtime, we could have gone to the moon and back in 60 seconds.

Of all the things about going to a hockey game that are the best, overtime winners are the best of the best. They're the purest form of saving the best for last.

If for some bizarre reason you've picked up this book, read it, and weren't sure if you should check out a hockey game, I hope this convinces you. Trust me, there are more than five things that are great about going to a hockey game. What else is there? How about you get out to a game and then tell me?

2.

It's a Business

No matter how much you love hockey, it's hard to deny the sport has a number of problems preventing it from gaining popularity.

The easiest problem to identify is how damn expensive hockey is to play. Whether it's the cost of equipment, enrollment fees, or, depending on where you live, scarcity of ice, if a sport is too expensive, kids aren't gonna play it. And if they can't play it, they're less likely to follow it.

There's a big problem at the other end of things, too. One of the sneakiest problems plaguing the NHL—and the popularity of hockey as a whole—is players who avoid big markets. Or, a little deeper, players who avoid the spotlight entirely. Just in case there's any confusion, the term "big market" doesn't necessarily refer to the population of a city but rather the amount of actual hockey fans in it.

Listen, I totally get it. You're in the NHL for a reason: you're an incredible hockey player. You made it through years of long road trips and early mornings, more social sacrifices than you can count, and offerings to the hockey gods of your very own blood, sweat, and tears during countless games. You didn't make it to The Show because you give an interesting interview between periods.

Let's say you're in your late twenties, which means you can finally cash in as an unrestricted free agent. You've busted your ass just to get to this point. You're big, so that means teams have to pay you more. And just for fun, let's say you're a defenceman who shoots right-handed, which, for some reason, means teams have to pay you even more.

You have two offers from two teams who finished with identical records last season. Both are offering you the exact same amount of money to play for the exact same number of years. The only difference: one team plays in a huge market where fans are obsessed with hockey and everybody will recognize your face and name wherever you go, while the other team plays in a smaller market where even their best players can still be mostly anonymous.

Why wouldn't you pick the team that allows you to have a more private and peaceful life? Do you want to get bothered when you're out for dinner with your family? Do you want people taking videos of you dancing at the club, like what happened to Ryan O'Reilly in 2023? Do you want people taking a paparazzi-style picture of you from outside a building, like what happened to Steven Stamkos in 2016?

Honestly, I can try to imagine, but I really don't know what it's like. It's difficult for me, some random overweight blowhard with a chronically bad back and the athletic resume of a two-toed sloth, to put myself in the position of a professional athlete. So let's talk a bit about Radko Gudas, a dude whose eyebrows have stronger muscles than I do anywhere.

Gudas is six feet, 208 pounds, which is big but not necessarily among the biggest players in the league. What separates Gudas from most of the rest of the pack is what he is willing to do to his opponents, which, in case you haven't seen him in action, is to plant his shoulder into the centre of their chest so hard that he blasts through the other side like the Kool-Aid Man.

Gudas is one of the toughest players in hockey today. If ancient warriors from thousands of years ago could travel forward in time and select one player from today's NHL to take with them back into the past and go to war with, they'd point right at Radko Gudas and say, "That one." Then Gudas would charge beard-first into battle, and any man foolish enough to cross his path would fall before him.

So it was incredibly surprising to me when, in the summer of 2023, hot off of signing a $12 million contract to spend the next three seasons in Anaheim, Gudas mentioned that media pressure steered him clear of signing in a bigger market: Canada, specifically.

"When I had the choice between Calgary, Edmonton and a team somewhere warm, Anaheim appealed to me more. But it wasn't about the weather, it was more about the role in the team, what they would want from me, and of course the financial side," said Gudas to iSport in Czechia, translated in *The Hockey News*.

Now, if Gudas had just stopped there, who could blame him? The guy likes warm weather better. Totally understandable! You want a better role on your team? Perfectly logical. More money? Who wants less money? Take it.

But he continued: "In Canada . . . [teams] differ in other things, such as the media . . . I don't know if I want to experience something like that every day."

If Gudas had been asked why he was signing in Anaheim, nobody with any common sense would have blamed him for saying, "Dude, I'm 33, I haven't scored more than three goals in a season since pre-Covid, and they just offered me $12 million to live next to the beach and Disneyland. Why the hell wouldn't I do that?"

And, of course, he'd be right. But he mentioned the media pressure.

I completely understand why a player would sign a multi-year contract to play in a place where the temperature is high and the pressure is not. Sounds like a great life. Twelve million dollars? Let me know where I can sign up for that, and I'll bring two pens in case the first one runs out of ink. I guess my question is, what does that say, then, about the perception of Anaheim, California, as a hockey market?

We know hockey works in California. Gary Bettman's NHL was once laughed at for trying to expand southward, and now look at it: the Kings have two championships, the Ducks have won one, too, and the San Jose Sharks have at least made it to the Stanley Cup Final in recent memory, which is more than we can say about the Toronto Maple Leafs, unless you happen to have vivid memories of the late 1960s. But when you avoid places for the media pressure, what does it say about the place you chose to sign with?

I don't want to put words in Gudas's mouth. First, because he'd probably bite my arm off from the elbow down, and second, because we don't know his exact reasons for signing in Anaheim beyond what he said in interviews. If I were an Anaheim fan, though, I think I might feel a bit slighted.

If you avoided places because of the media pressure, then it stands to reason that you chose to sign where you did because of the absence of pressure. As in the lack of coverage of the hockey team because not enough people care enough to want coverage of the hockey team.

Forget Radko Gudas. Nothing illustrates the problem better than this quote.

After Sheldon Keefe was let go as head coach of the Toronto

Maple Leafs, he quickly signed on to be the new head coach of the New Jersey Devils. Keefe was quoted in the *Toronto Star* as saying: "It was tremendous honour to coach the Maple Leafs. There's a lot that goes into that. I've had a number of well-established coaches in the league reach out to say that I should be happy now that I get to coach in the real NHL. Toronto is quite unique . . . it's not like the rest of the league."

What on earth is that supposed to mean? The real NHL?

What constitutes the real NHL? Well, to figure that out, we need to establish what Toronto is as a hockey market because apparently it's not in the "real NHL." Toronto is a big hockey market with high TV ratings, a regularly sold-out building, and a waiting list to become a season ticket holder that's decades long.

Is the implication there that people care less about hockey in other markets? And that their lack of caring is a good thing? If that's an accurate description of "the real NHL" then it should send a shiver down Gary Bettman's spine.

To be clear, I'm not ripping on Sheldon Keefe; he's not the one who said that. He's quoting "a number of well-established coaches in the league." Good to know that some of the league's most tenured coaches resent an abundance of fans, popularity, and any of those other pesky nuisances that keep the lights on.

The absence of pressure means the absence of caring and the absence of stakes. That absence is born from the lack of eyes and ears, and no butts in seats. If fans don't come to games, don't buy your jerseys, hats, shirts, chips, and popcorn; if fans don't watch your product on TV—that's death. The reason athletes make lots of money is because teams make lots of money.

But if you're avoiding having to deal with the people that make you a lot of money—which is an abundance of fans—why do you still expect to make all of that money? What's the plan there? Let stars like Sidney Crosby and Alexander Ovechkin do all the heavy lifting while you kick up your feet and chill?

According to *Sports Business Journal*, the average attendance for an Anaheim Ducks home game during the 2022–23 season was 14,953. That's the third-worst total in the NHL, behind the San Jose Sharks and Winnipeg Jets. Well, it's technically fourth worst, but the Arizona Coyotes basically played in a university rink, so they didn't count.

I'm not doing this to pick on the Ducks. I have no problem with them. It's one thing if you sign in a smaller market in the hopes of creating a bigger and more passionate fanbase. That's noble and awesome and the league needs more of that. But if peace and quiet is the goal, then a bigger and more passionate fanbase isn't the goal. Let's just go back to the Covid bubble, then, if that's the goal. I mean why not, right? We wouldn't have any of those pesky fans to deal with, at least.

Part of this argument falls somewhat flat because obviously the money exists regardless of the intensity of Anaheim as a hockey market, since Gudas signed a $12 million deal. Sure, that's a lot of money for a normal person, but take a look at the NBA, which also has an 82-game season. According to SalarySwish.com, the basketball equivalent of CapFriendly.com, NBA teams had salary cap hits between $131.5 million and $206.8 million in 2023–24. In the NHL, with teams made up of larger rosters, those cap hits were between $72.9 million and $97.6 million.

Nathan MacKinnon was the highest-paid NHL player during the 2023–24 season, at $12.6 million. Do you know how many NBA players had a higher cap hit than him? The answer is 128.

In 2021, the NHL signed broadcast rights deals with both Disney, which owns ESPN, and Turner Sports, which owns TNT.

According to NYTimes.com, those deals pay the NHL roughly $400 million and north of $225 million annually, which is a big number and lovely. On the other side of the coin, as I'm writing this, the NBA is rumoured to be about to sign for $76 billion over 11 years, or roughly $6.9 billion per year.

What I'm getting at is that NHL players need to not just embrace the spotlight but rather seek out the spotlight, because in the greater picture of North American professional sports, they're barely even in it. Financially, the NHL and NBA are in two completely different conversations.

When an NHL team signs you to a contract, they're not signing you to play hockey for them, they're signing you to sell their product. Yes, playing the game is a big part of selling their product, but not all of it. You can't sign with a team and then actively hope for a lack of pressure, which is a lack of attention, which is a lack of fans, in an industry that's powered by paying customers, and expect the product to grow.

I'm not saying all this to be a bootlicker for the billionaire franchise owners out there across all sports. Those guys grind everyone around them for every dollar, but when it's time for them to build a new arena, they cry poor to the government and demand taxpayer money. If the government gives them a hard time, the owner huffs and puffs and threatens to move the team. Generally speaking, lots of owners kind of stink.

What I'm getting at is it's in the players' best interests to build up the NHL to a point where there are literally no markets small enough to escape media attention or fanfare because the sport is so popular. Remember, it's part of the NHL's collective bargaining agreement that players get 50 per cent of hockey-related revenue generated by the league. Under this system, the more money the NHL makes, the more money the players make.

There's a saying in the English language, I'm not sure if you've heard of it: You can't have your cake and eat it, too.

If you want peace and quiet, nobody should ever blame you. And is millions of dollars a year such a bad way to live? Anybody reading (or writing) this would gladly take that deal if they could. But just to be clear, when there are bench players in the NBA making more than Nathan MacKinnon, Connor McDavid, and Auston Matthews, the highest-paid players in hockey, this is part of the reason why.

In a lot of ways, professional sports is show business. No matter how good an actor or actress is, if nobody's watching their movies, the roles are gonna stop coming in. Is that fair? No, but that's business.

There's nothing wrong with wanting some peace and quiet, but there's more to playing the game than just playing the game.

3.

Leafs Lament

Listen up, because I'm only gonna say this once. If you'd never heard of me before reading this book, I have a YouTube channel where I talk about the Leafs after every game, win or lose. I've been doing this since 2007, so for a long time there was more losing than winning, usually resulting in me pulling out my hair and screaming into the camera. So much losing, in fact, that when Auston Matthews and company arrived in town, joining the Leafs as hotshot prospects, and the team started having some regular season success and making the playoffs, people were genuinely asking me what I was going to do now.

What am I gonna do now? I've been making videos about this miserable, sad-sack laughingstock of a team for a decade, through every year they tanked—either intentionally or not—and you think I'm stopping now? Hell no! This is it! This is the light at the end of the tunnel, baby!

Little did I know what the hockey gods had in store.

With that out of the way, we can say that you, the reader, fit into one of two groups of people:

You're a Leafs fan who's going to sit there and read every word of this chapter with your eyes pried open because you're a long-suffering fan who treats reading about the

Leafs' many misfortunes as a twisted kind of therapy. That, or you've become such a masochist over a lifetime of cheering for this evil cartoon of a team that you've lost the basic human skill of achieving joy through regular means. The only way you can get your rocks off anymore is by mentally clubbing yourself in the feelings by reliving your worst moments of sports fandom.

You hate the Leafs and relish in their failure. The misery of that team, and more importantly, their fanbase, sustains you in the same way that sun and rain sustain our crops. Leafs haters used to think they loved watching my postgame videos when the Leafs lost a regular season game in January that dropped them to 25th in the standings. Once the Leafs began achieving regular season success, Leafs haters discovered that those measly, barely meaningful losses were simply snacks, the finger food of schadenfreude. Now they get to treat a Leafs fan's misery like a cow destined for wagyu beef, raising it and massaging it until one day a guy wearing a Patrice Bergeron Bruins jersey enters the slaughterhouse just in time for Game 7 of the first round.

In the nearly two decades that I've made videos about this team, there are four losses that I hate the most, all for completely different reasons. One is a cherished memory of a historic night, now ruined. One is the most painful of the lot for how long it took to happen and who it happened against. The third loss was what it was like to be the team in a Disney movie that the protagonist is playing against. The fourth was a historic loss that may have broken our brains forever.

Whether this chapter is therapy for you or borderline spank bank material, these are the most embarrassing Leafs losses since 2004.

LEAFS VS. SENS: AUSTON MATTHEWS'S FOUR-GOAL DEBUT

I know, right? Starting with an unusual choice for one of the worst games ever, but I bet I can talk you into it. Considering how many absolutely crushing playoff defeats the Leafs have suffered in recent years, surely the first regular season game of the 2016–17 season doesn't belong in this conversation. After all, that season came with zero expectations, and ended with a scrappy gang of borderline children battling their way into a playoff spot in dramatic fashion.

And it all started with one night, one magical night when Auston Matthews, a budding superstar the Leafs nabbed with their first number one overall pick in over a quarter of a century, scored four goals in his NHL debut.

You've all seen the highlights a thousand times, to the point where you can probably picture all four goals without me even describing them to you. But I'm gonna do it anyway.

The first goal was a great effort from Zach Hyman and William Nylander, two kids in their own right, winning a puck battle down low before shovelling it to an open Auston Matthews in front, followed by the now-quintessential Matthews raised knee and fist pump while he got absolutely mobbed by his teammates.

The second goal was Matthews playing keep-away with Mark Stone and Mike Hoffman before charging into the zone, pantsing Erik Karlsson of all people, stripping him of the puck, and ripping it five-hole on Craig Anderson at a speed that bent the fabric of space and time.

The third goal was a sick setup from Morgan Rielly to a wide-open Matthews. Matthews pointed at Rielly to signify that he liked his pass. Rielly pointed back at Matthews and screamed like someone who sold a kidney for front row tickets to a Taylor Swift concert. The only difference was this game happened in Ottawa, and Taylor Swift would never go there.

The fourth goal was a two-on-one in the dying moments of the second period, the completion of a beautiful pass from William Nylander. Matthews, his arms presumably too exhausted from the previous three goal celebrations to even react, basically just stood there as his teammates went completely berserk.

It was a night of wild excitement and immense joy. I'm not ashamed to admit I came very close to crying. My wife says I full-on cried, but I don't remember. I was too busy crying.

By now you're confused because that game sounds awesome, right? It was literally a record-breaking debut for a kid who would go on to become a 60-goal-scorer more than once, a league MVP, and the cornerstone of the entire franchise. How could this magical night end up in a worst-of conversation, especially while talking about a team that churns out traumatic playoff losses like *Saw* movies?

Because they friggin' lost.

The game went to overtime. Why did it go to overtime? Because even though the Leafs got a record-breaking performance out of their youngest player, the rest of the team allowed four goals while contributing no other offence in support.

Jake Gardiner loses a battle for a rebound with Bobby Ryan, there's goal one. Erik Karlsson cranks one, it deflects off everything, there's goal two. Goal three actually gave me chest tightness as I re-watched it in preparation for writing this chapter. Derick Brassard breezes by a pursuing Martin Marincin, who took a penalty on the play by trying to slow down Brassard in a way that resembled trying and failing to slam a screen door, and Brassard tucked it five-hole on Frederik Andersen (a trend that made me grow greys in my twenties). The fourth goal was Marincin trying to whip the puck around the boards to Nikita Zaitsev. Mark Stone gets to it first and gives it to Kyle Turris, who was so wide open the Sens could've built their new arena in the space between him and the nearest Leafs defender. I cannot believe this team made the playoffs.

Then in overtime, which was three-on-three, Matthews loses Turris, who ends up scoring the OT winner.

Stop me if I've mentioned this already, but *Matthews scored four goals in his NHL debut and the Leafs still lost.* He had four goals on six shots, was a plus-three, and was on the ice for the OT winner against.

I still like watching the highlights of all the goals. I still remember it as the arrival of the new, exciting, and youthful Toronto Maple Leafs. I still look back on it and crack a smile. Then, after a moment, that smile falls as I remember they lost. It doesn't help that it was against the Senators, either, does it? Sens fans bring that up at every opportunity, and why wouldn't they? It's the Battle of Ontario, baby! Turn that knife. It's hilarious the Sens won that game and even more hilarious the Leafs lost. I'm surprised there isn't a mural of Kyle Turris's OT winner on the side of the Parliament building.

If you're a Leafs fan, you can enjoy the memory of Matthews's four-goal game. I'm just saying the fact that they lost that game is a lot like someone cutting a fart in the middle of you walking up the aisle on your wedding day. You can still have a great time at your wedding and you'll still have all the pretty pictures, but every time it comes up for the rest of your life, everyone's going to bring up the fact Kyle farted.

Kyle Turris and the Ottawa Senators took what should have been the happiest day for Leafs fans in over a decade and wrecked it. I hated that the Leafs lost at the time, and now that some years have passed, I hate it even more, like a stain on a brand-new white shirt that you know will never fully wash off.

LEAFS VS. HABS: IT WAS A 3–1 SERIES

Is this the most embarrassing Leafs loss in recent memory? It's difficult to say because there's so much competition. I can say, from a personal level, it was easily the most agonizing. Pure, un-adulterated torture.

In Greek mythology, Sisyphus was a cursed figure, damned to push a massive boulder up a hill for all eternity. Every time he got near the top of the hill, the boulder would roll back down, and Sisyphus would have to begin the torturous process again. In so many ways, that is being a Leafs fan, and nothing embodies that quite like the Leafs' humiliating choke against the Montreal Canadiens.

Blowing a 3–1 series lead in the Stanley Cup Playoffs is rare, but it can happen in ordinary ways. For example, you could lose three games in a row by scores of 2–0, 3–1, and 4–2, in any order. But the Leafs? No, no. They can't just lose any old way. They've always got to add a little Leafs razzle-dazzle. As the saying goes: it's the hope that kills you.

Due to Covid travel restrictions, the NHL opted to have a seven-team all-Canadian division. The Leafs dominated it. In 56 games,

Toronto had a record of 35 wins, 14 losses, and 7 losses in overtime or the shootout: 14 more wins than losses. Toronto also had
the fifth-most goals in the league, with 187, and the seventh-best
goals-against in the league, with just 148: a goal differential of
plus-39.

The Montreal Canadiens, on the other hand, struggled. The
Habs' record was 24 wins, 21 losses, and 11 losses in overtime or
the shootout: eight more losses of any type than wins. Their goal
differential was negative nine.

Yes, the Montreal Canadiens had Carey Price, once the best
goalie on Planet Earth, but he had struggled with a downright human .901 save percentage that season. Even if Price were to step
up his game, there was basically no reason to expect Montreal to
win that series.

Was there reason to expect the Leafs to lose? Well . . . I mean,
yes, purely in that they were the Leafs. There was no *logical* reason to expect the Leafs to lose. Toronto had better offence, better
defence, better depth, and even Jack Campbell had had a spectacular season in net up to that point. If the Leafs were not the Leafs,
a team that had routinely struggled and flat-out choked in the
playoffs, you would call them the favourite to win that series. Also,
what a way to finally win your first playoff round since 2004: by
beating your most historic rivals in your first Stanley Cup Playoff
series against one another since 1979.

Admittedly, the series began under extremely unusual and
grim circumstances. In a pure fluke accident, Leafs captain
John Tavares was knocked over by Habs defender Ben Chiarot
and fell head-first into a streaking Corey Perry's knee. Tavares
was knocked unconscious, sustaining several injuries. As the
team's medical staff rushed onto the ice, the silence in a building completely devoid of fans (also due to Covid restrictions) was

absolutely deafening. Injuries happen in hockey, but rarely one as chilling as that. After a lengthy delay, the game resumed under the haze of what had happened.

With the game tied 1–1 in the third period, Canadiens forward Paul Byron was sprung on a partial breakaway. Byron fell to his knees but stuck with the puck and fired it up and over Campbell. It was a spectacular goal, and it would prove to be the game-winner. Montreal leads the series 1–0.

For the next three games, the Leafs regained their composure despite their captain's absence, and dominated the series. After falling down 1–0 early in Game 2, Toronto would tie the game within five minutes, en route to five unanswered goals and a 5–1 victory to tie the series.

Game 3 was much tighter, with all three goals coming in the second period, but the Leafs defended a one-goal lead for the entirety of the third period to win the game 2–1 and take a 2–1 series lead.

Game 4 was bliss. After a goalless first period, the Leafs scored early in the second, followed by another pair of goals just over two minutes apart. Former Montreal Canadiens player Alex Galchenyuk led the Leafs with a goal and two assists as they blanked the Canadiens 4–0 and took a 3–1 stranglehold in the series.

How many wins do you need to win a playoff series, boys and girls? Four. Sisyphus was just about to get that boulder to the top of the hill . . .

The Leafs, to put it in soccer terms, completely bottled it to start Game 5. Joel Armia dominated with two goals in three minutes, followed by Jesperi Kotkaniemi putting Montreal up 3–0 early in the second. Zach Hyman got Toronto on the board less than two minutes later, and despite being down 3–1 heading into the third, Toronto had life.

Leafs defender Jake Muzzin scored a pair of goals, the second of which came from a beautiful pass from Galchenyuk, and the Leafs had mounted a comeback to force overtime. Do you understand how massive winning this game would have been? Beating the Montreal Canadiens in five games is one thing, but erasing a 3–0 deficit in the deciding game to do it? That's ripping out your mortal enemy's heart and showing it to them. And it would have been the Leafs' first playoff series win in nearly two decades. The Leafs ride the momentum of that into the second round against the Winnipeg Jets—who the Habs killed, by the way—then you're in the final four and all bets are off.

But that didn't happen.

Less than a minute after overtime began, Galchenyuk had another beautiful assist—straight to the other team. Habs forwards Cole Caufield and Nick Suzuki tore loose on a two-on-none breakaway, and you pretty much couldn't get two Habs you'd like to face less in that situation. Suzuki buried it to win the game and keep Montreal alive.

Ah, no worry. The Leafs will pull it off in Game 6. After all, Montreal just got lucky with their best flurry of the series during the first period and capitalized on a stupid mistake in overtime. There's no way that happens again, right?

Game 6 arrives, and the Montreal Canadiens kicked the Toronto Maple Leafs up and down the ice at will. The Habs were playing their best hockey of the series, maybe even of the entire season up to that point, and the Leafs were hollow husks of what they had been mere days before. Jack Campbell miraculously shut the door until the third, when Corey Perry and Tyler Toffoli scored power-play goals barely over one minute apart to give Montreal a 2–0 lead.

Once again, the Leafs, as if startled awake to find themselves in a hockey game, managed to tie it. Veteran forward Jason Spezza scored his third goal of the series, followed by defender T.J. Brodie's first goal, with barely over three minutes to go. Once again, we head to overtime.

The Canadiens partially lifted restrictions for Game 6 and allowed their fans to fill a small, spread-out fraction of their building's capacity. The only thing those fans could have been thinking during that overtime was that their first game of the season would be the Canadiens' last. As if snapped out of a trance, the Leafs remembered who they had been in the regular season and dominated the Habs for nearly every single moment of that overtime. The fact Toronto didn't win that night was a combination of Carey Price practically turning water into wine and the Leafs proving, once again, that they had absolutely, positively zero dog in them.

After dominating Montreal for over 15 minutes, the Leafs made their mistake. The Habs pressured Leafs defender Travis Dermott into spinning in a circle with the puck. That resulted in a giveaway. Paul Byron gets the puck to Jesperi Kotkaniemi, who rifles it past Jack Campbell. The few Habs fans in attendance go completely bonkers, and we're going to Game 7.

The 45 hours or so between the end of Game 6 and the beginning of Game 7 was like a two-day funeral where the person being memorialized was technically still alive. Sure, the Leafs *could* win Game 7, but everybody—Leafs fans, Habs fans, and neutral fans watching purely for the schadenfreude—knew the series was over.

Sitting down to watch this game, I had the "let's get this over with" energy of doing my taxes. There was a small, naive part of me with foolish, near childlike innocence that defiantly said, "You'll see, you negative bum. They're going to win Game 7, and it'll just be a funny bump in the road. Remember when the Vancouver Canucks nearly blew a 3–0 series lead to the Chicago Blackhawks in 2011 but ended up winning Game 7 in overtime? They still call that overtime winner from Alex Burrows 'Dragon Slayer.' We're going to witness the same thing here. Who cares how the Leafs win? They're going to win."

From puck drop to final horn, the Leafs spat on the name of hockey.

The score was 0–0 heading into the second period, but three minutes later, gritty Habs winger Brendan Gallagher fired a *bleu-blanc-et-rouge*-berry muffin at Jack Campbell that any goalie collecting an NHL paycheque should stop 11 times out of ten. Later that period, on the powerplay, Corey Perry scored to make it 2–0. You know what sucks? Losing. You know what sucks more? Losing to Corey Perry.

Tyler Toffoli would score on an empty net in the third period. Leafs forward William Nylander spoiled Price's shutout with 96 seconds to go, but Canadiens fans completed their 3–1 series comeback and haven't let Leafs fans live it down ever since.

As a Leafs fan, I can't decide what's worse: the Habs fans gloating about ripping the heart out of Leafs Nation, or the Habs fans who have come up to me to express genuine condolences about my stupid hockey team. The only thing that hurts more than the wrath of a rival is their authentic, genuine pity.

If the Leafs had had John Tavares in the lineup, would things have gone differently? I'm biased, but yes, I think so. Still, Alexander Kerfoot, who replaced Tavares as Toronto's second-line centre, was second on the Leafs in scoring with six points. If ifs and buts were candy and nuts, my therapist would live in a smaller house.

It's an annual tradition for fans of a struggling team to declare that they're done, forever, but sometimes I wonder how many members of Leafs Nation left the blue and white behind for good that day.

DAVID FRIGGIN' AYRES

First, we need to go back in time, to March 29, 2018. The Chicago Blackhawks are hosting the Winnipeg Jets. The game was never really close, with the Blackhawks going up 4–0 at one point, taking a 5–2 lead into the third period, and then scoring early to make it 6–2. Then the unexpected struck.

Blackhawks starter Anton Forsberg was supposed to play that night, but suffered an injury. That's not a problem, though, because the Blackhawks still have another goalie in Collin Delia. At least, it wasn't a problem until later that night, when Delia, too, suffered an injury. With no backup goalie on the bench, and a four-goal Blackhawks lead, 36-year-old emergency goaltender Scott Foster had to enter the game.

Naturally, every hockey fan, whether hardcore or casual, immediately stopped what they were doing to watch the game. Hilariously, that also applied to Foster's men's league team, which stopped playing its game to watch his NHL debut on the TVs at the arena.

During his 14:01 of ice time, Foster faced seven shots and stopped all of them, including a beauty save on Paul Stastny served up from Patrik Laine. Facing a shot every two minutes would add up to 30 shots in a full game, so it's not even fair to say the Jets took it easy on the Blackhawks. They might not have been giving their maximum playoff-style effort, but they had chances to score, and were denied. Scott was a hero in Chicago and the rest of the hockey world, probably even in Winnipeg, that night and the next day.

What happened with the Leafs and David Ayres was very different and made for an even better story, unless you're a Leafs fan with aspirations of achieving normal blood pressure.

February 22, 2020, the Leafs host the Carolina Hurricanes. A lot of the context heading into that game got lost in the Covid-19 pandemic, which would shut down the NHL a mere 19 days after Ayres's historic night, but the Leafs were in a playoff hunt. It's important to note that the hunt wasn't actually going that great. The team was far from guaranteed a playoff spot with about a month and a half remaining in the season.

The Leafs had lost back-to-back games by a score of 5–2, first to the Buffalo Sabres and then the Pittsburgh Penguins. Immediately after, on February 20, 2020, the Leafs hosted the Penguins in Toronto with a chance to get a little payback and show they still had some fight in them.

Jake Muzzin cranked one home right off a faceoff to give the Leafs a 1–0 lead just under eight minutes in. A mere two minutes later, and sitting on a two-man advantage, Auston Matthews set up William Nylander, again right off the faceoff, and despite bobbling the puck a bit, Nylander whistled it past Penguins goalie Matt Murray. During the second period, Alexander Kerfoot sent Kasperi Kapanen on a perfect breakaway, and he sniped it home to make it 3–0. Finally, in the third period, and yet again off the draw, Mitch Marner floats the puck on net, Zach Hyman buries the rebound, and it's 4–0.

At the time, I was calling the game the Leafs' most complete win of the season. They held the Penguins to a mere 24 shots and a measly two shots through the entire third period. Frederik Andersen got the shutout, Kapanen even fought future Leafs legend (sarcasm) Jared McCann, and everyone went home happy.

I think it's important context for the David Ayres game that the Leafs went into it coming off a genuinely impressive team win, at home, in a shutout. Nobody screws with their own fanbase's head like the Leafs, especially in the chaotic 2019–20 season.

Two days later, the Carolina Hurricanes come to town. With their emphasis on skill and gritty, determined play, and their belief and investment in analytics, the Carolina Hurricanes were a team that the Kyle Dubas–era Toronto Maple Leafs always held up as representing a standard to aspire to. A team that really got it. And the Hurricanes won a lot of games.

The first period against Carolina did not go quite as smoothly as the previous game against the Penguins. With the Leafs getting outshot by a margin of 15–8 on home ice, you might count them lucky for not being down at least a goal in the final minute of the first period. That was until Kasperi Kapanen flew into the offensive zone with the puck, slammed on the brakes, and passed the puck to an open Jake Muzzin. The big, bearded Leafs blueliner threw the puck on net, and Alexander Kerfoot put it home. Despite being outshot 17–11 on the period, the Leafs ran away like thieves with a 1–0 lead after one. It's such a genuinely infuriating footnote of this game that the Leafs were winning after the first period. Under the surface, though, another little subplot was percolating.

A mere six minutes into the game, Hurricanes starting goalie and former Leaf James Reimer left the game with an injury; Leafs forward Zach Hyman had knocked over Hurricanes defender Jaccob Slavin, who fell into Reimer. Petr Mrazek, another guy who would find himself in a Leafs uniform at some point, would have to enter the game for Carolina. This meant that Carolina would have no backup goalie sitting on their bench. That is, until David Ayres arrived. Hold that thought.

The second period begins, and the Leafs' luck runs out in a big way. About six minutes into the second, after about 48 or so rebounds (I lost count), Lucas Wallmark ties the game for Carolina. Four minutes later, a couldn't-be-more-wide-open Nino Niederreiter blasts it past Andersen to make it 2–1 Hurricanes. Less than a minute after that, the Leafs, with the defensive prowess of a wet napkin, let Warren Foegele saunter across the goalmouth to tuck it in and give Carolina a 3–1 lead. That's when the game got spicy and David Ayres's life changed forever.

The puck ends up along the half boards in the Hurricanes' zone. Leafs enforcer Kyle Clifford, who hadn't even been with the team that long after being acquired along with Leafs backup goalie Jack Campbell, is making an absolute beeline after this puck with the grace of a freight train. Clifford's no slouch—he was on the ice for the LA Kings' Stanley Cup–winning overtime goal in 2014 and also picked up an assist. But he was known more for running guys over and thumping anybody who had the idiotic idea to say anything about it afterward.

With no defender in a position to get to the puck quickly enough, Petr Mrazek goes way out of his net to play it. As in top of the faceoff circle.

Clifford, stick still extended because he's clearly trying to play the puck, can't stop. Clifford was never one of the best skaters on the Leafs, but I doubt Mitch Marner, William Nylander, or Auston Matthews would have been able to stop in time. The result was Clifford running over Mrazek like the goalie was an old sedan that broke down on the train tracks.

A chaotic scrum ensues while Mrazek is sprawled on the ice. As chaos reigns, David Ayres, the backup goalie in attendance at Scotiabank Arena, starts getting texts to his phone to get into the game and that he was going to do great. He didn't even know yet that Mrazek had been hit when he started getting these texts.

Details about Ayres start hitting the airwaves. He's a former Junior B goalie, although his time in Junior B came long before February 2020, seeing as Ayres was now 42 years old. And he wasn't exactly in peak health. A number of years prior, Ayres had received a life-saving kidney transplant from his own mother. Of course, there was the part that everybody couldn't help but talk about that night and ever since: he was the team's Zamboni driver.

Which is a half truth, really. Ayres did operate the ice-resurfacing equipment at Ricoh Coliseum, now Coca-Cola Coliseum, the home of the Leafs' farm team, the Toronto Marlies. It's important to note that Ayres was also the Leafs' practice goalie, and it was common for him to face, in his words, something like 300 shots in a single practice. Those aren't your buddy's beer league muffins, either. These are NHL shots. One practice, Zach Hyman cracked Ayres's mask with a one-timer. Still, would you bet money on him winning an actual NHL game? No, because you're not out of your mind.

Here's the thing, though: David Ayres won a frickin' NHL game that night.

Kyle Clifford got a charging penalty for his "hit" on Peter Mrazek, which, screw it, I'm still mad about. Mrazek was a mile out of his net and being careless, Clifford was going for the puck, and I will happily die on that hill. Tell my family I love them.

On the ensuing powerplay, Teuvo Teravainen scored for Carolina to give the Hurricanes a commanding three-goal lead in the second period. Just one small problem that I think I mentioned earlier: their goalie was a 42-year-old Zamboni driver.

You might have forgotten, but Goliath was kicking David's ass at first in this one. Leafs captain John Tavares scored with a shot past Ayres just 19 seconds after the Hurricanes made it 4–1, bringing the Leafs to within two goals. To be fair, every great NHL goalie in history gave up their first goal at some point. Just 94 seconds later, Leafs forward Pierre Engvall scored to make it 4–3 and bring the Leafs within one.

And this is why I started by talking about Scott Foster. When the Blackhawks needed to turn to Foster in 2018, they were up by four goals, and more importantly, they were using their own hometown emergency backup goalie, or EBUG, in their own rink, relatively late in the third period. The Hurricanes having to turn to David Ayres was completely different.

Ayres walked from the visitor's locker room, down the tunnel, onto the Hurricanes' bench, and out onto the ice wearing a red-and-white Carolina Hurricanes jersey. However, he was also wearing a blue-and-white blocker, a blue-and-white glove, blue-and-white pads, and a goalie mask that actually had the Toronto Marlies' logo on it.

After Ayres took to the ice, Hurricanes coach Rod Brind'Amour could be seen on camera shaking his head in a way that clearly said, "What the hell is going on?" This dude was the Leafs' hometown emergency backup goalie, a guy who makes money working for the Leafs organization, literally wearing the logo of the Leafs' farm team, stepping into an actual NHL game that counted, for— and I can't stress this enough—the other team!

As Sportsnet insider Elliotte Friedman tells the story, he was getting messages from people around the NHL who were furious this was even allowed to happen. This wasn't the happy-go-lucky story of Scott Foster in Chicago. The Leafs were directly benefiting from taking out both of their opponent's goalies and were in the midst of erasing a three-goal deficit in a game with important points on the line by shelling one of their own employees on a nationally broadcasted game.

This wasn't fun. This wasn't cute. This was an enormous issue that could have affected the standings, playoff positioning, and millions of dollars around the league. And then what happened?

The third period begins, and anyone watching wants to see one of two things:

1. The Leafs come back and win this game, giving birth to an enormous controversy leaguewide.
2. The Leafs fuck this up.

The Leafs chose option two. Or rather, Carolina chose. It depends who you ask.

Warren Foegele scored 53 seconds into the third period to put Carolina back up two goals. It was off a Leafs defensive zone giveaway with net-front defence that would make your dad's Facebook password look strong. Less than three minutes later, after another defensive zone giveaway, the Leafs look like they've given up a goal to Erik Haula, who actually hits the crossbar. With everyone diving for the puck like it's a freshly cracked-open pinata, Martin Necas puts the Hurricanes back up three goals.

But don't worry! It's no problem. The Leafs can still come back. Dude, they have a 42-year-old guy who works for them in the opposing net! It's cool.

Before the period began, Ayres had faced three shots. The first two shots from John Tavares and Pierre Engvall went in before Ayres made his first NHL save on Auston Matthews, which is a wild thing for any human being to be able to say they did. After Foegele made it 5–3, Matthews and Marner had a shot each two seconds apart, both stopped by Ayres, before Necas made it 6–3 Carolina. Matthews gets stopped again with 15:44 to go in the game. Don't worry, the Leafs still got this.

Here's a fun detail I forgot about: the Leafs got a holy smoking honest-to-god powerplay! On that Leafs powerplay, Carolina outshot them 2–1 and Ayres stopped the one he faced, which was actually a pretty good one from Zach Hyman. Each fact about this game is more unbelievable than the last. Or, I guess if you've followed the Leafs your whole life, completely believable. Either way, it's hilarious.

After Ayres made a save on Alexander Kerfoot, the Leafs head to the penalty kill with 10:29 to go in the game, and that's where it starts to sink in. Leafs fans around the world, slack-jawed and wide-eyed, all mutter to themselves, "They're about to lose this game." Fans of every other team, eyebrows up near their hairline with a smile wider than the Joker's, laugh to themselves, "They're about to lose this game!"

The Leafs had two shots in the final ten and a half minutes: a wrister from Jason Spezza with 3:47 to go and a whole-grain bagel of a shot from Kyle Clifford—why did it have to be Kyle Clifford?—in the final second of the game to seal the win for the Carolina Hurricanes and David Ayres.

That's the funny thing: even though the Hurricanes won the game, it didn't mean that David Ayres had to get the win, as well. Ayres entered the game when his team had a 3–1 lead. Because the Leafs reached three goals, however, Ayres became the goalie of record and earned an official NHL win. David Ayres began and ended his NHL career that night with as many NHL goaltending wins as once-prized Leafs goalie prospect Justin Pogge, although I guess you could give Pogge the tie-breaker since he had an overtime loss on his record, too.

What followed was absolute madness. I went downstairs that night and screamed the most bloodcurdling, genuine screams into my camera and uploaded it to YouTube. To this day, it's my only video after nearly two decades making them to cross one million views. How much money did that one video make? I'll put it this way: enough to cover the therapist's bill.

The next morning, wanting to think of anything except the fact that my favourite hockey team lost to one of their own damn employees, I woke up to a text from my cousin telling me his Friday night beer league goalie won for the Leafs last night. I'm lucky I bought a good phone case.

Videos spread far and wide of the Hurricanes dousing Ayres in water the moment he entered the locker room. Ayres was invited onto *The Today Show*, *Fox & Friends*, and *The Late Show with Stephen Colbert*, among something like two dozen other appearances. The Hurricanes even invited Ayres down to Carolina for a home game, which obviously sent the faithful in Raleigh into a frenzy.

Remember Elliotte Friedman getting angry texts from around the NHL about the unfair injustice of the Leafs scoring goals on their own Zamboni driver? He reported that, by the end of the game, those same people were laughing.

As the story goes, then–Leafs general manager Kyle Dubas put off plans to make certain additions to the team at the 2020 NHL trade deadline, which just so happened to be two days later. And why would he bother trying to add to that team? Were they about to go on an epic Stanley Cup run? No! They just lost to a 42-year-old Zamboni driver who works for them!

About a year or so later, still in the midst of Covid-19, I finally got to meet David Ayres; we were shooting a video on the outdoor rink in the backyard of Sportsnet's Jeff Marek. He told me how those pads he wore that night actually once belonged to Toronto Maple Leafs goalie prospect Kasimir Kaskisuo. I still remember sitting with him while he was getting his gear on ahead of the video we were shooting and him telling me about how his knee was bugging him that night. I tried not to show it, but in my head I was screaming, *And his knee was bugging him!*

At the end of the day, David Ayres winning that game with the Carolina Hurricanes is a thousand times better than if the Leafs had won that night. Even most Leafs fans can surely appreciate that. Even though it made for a great story, as soon as that final buzzer hit, all Leafs fans knew one thing: we are never going to live this down.

LEAFS VS. BRUINS: GAME 7, FIRST ROUND, 2013

It was 4–1.

Nothing tops this. Nothing. Not even losing to your own Zamboni driver.

Since their last Stanley Cup win in 1967, the Toronto Maple Leafs have kind of been known for losing. It certainly doesn't help that every Canadian team that's been here and never left (sorry, Winnipeg) has been to at least one Stanley Cup Final since the Leafs' last trip there. It also doesn't help that every other team in the Leafs' division has been to at least one Stanley Cup Final since the last time the Leafs made it there. But there's one loss that stands out above them all.

I hate so, so, so many things about the Leafs' infamous Game 7 choke against the Boston Bruins, but besides not being able to ever live that game down, what I hate most is that the 2013 Leafs were actually scrappy underdogs.

After the end of the 2011–12 season, the NHL decided it loved reruns and went into the third lockout of Gary Bettman's tenure as NHL commissioner. Side note: Gary Bettman is already in the Hockey Hall of Fame. Life is pain, and how am I not bald yet?

Once that lockout wrapped up and the NHL decided to resume hockey in January 2013 with a shortened 48-game season, the Toronto Maple Leafs decided to pull off a tried and tested method for letting your fans know the team they love is about to be good: they fired their general manager right before the season began. Wait, what?

The Leafs fired cantankerous necktie-hater Brian Burke and promoted Dave Nonis to GM. The team hadn't even played a playoff game since, hilariously, their final game before the previous NHL lockout, in 2004. Again, Gary Bettman is in the Hockey Hall of Fame. One day the sun will explode and we'll all be dead.

The 2013 Leafs were two things: tough and not spectacular at hockey.

The Leafs averaged 26.3 shots on goal per game that season, which was the third-lowest average in the league. They averaged 32.3 shots against per game, tied for the third highest. And they were outshot by an average of six shots per game, tied for the worst discrepancy in the league that season.

Almost every night, the Leafs would get outshot. Almost every night, one of the Leafs goalies, whether it was starter James Reimer or backup Ben Scrivens, would have to stand on his skull and brain with a litany of saves to keep the team alive. More nights than not, the Leafs would weasel out of getting outplayed with great goaltending and high-percentage shooting. And if anybody on the opposition had anything to say about it, one of Colton Orr, Frazer McLaren, Mark Fraser, or Mike Brown would beat the brakes off of them.

It was all so dumb, but you have to admit it was kind of fun. The analytics crowd kept trying to rain on the parade by saying the Leafs' success was unsustainable, that they were a paper tiger, that their luck would run out. After 48 games, however, the Leafs had finally returned to the Stanley Cup Playoffs, where they would face the Boston Bruins.

The main problem was that the Boston Bruins were pretty good at hockey, also had a good goalie (who the Leafs gave them, by the way), and were tough as nails. The Bruins had the likes of Shawn Thornton, Adam McQuaid, a prime Milan Lucic, and Zdeno Chara, who could probably eat a human thigh in one sitting, femur and all. Boston also had youngsters like Tyler Seguin (who the Leafs also gave them), Brad Marchand, and some dude you may or may not have ever heard of named Patrice Bergeron.

In Game 1, the Leafs weren't in it for long. After they scored early, Boston replied with four straight goals, held the fort, and stood up to Toronto when the Leafs got grumpy late in the game. Game 2, the Leafs actually showed a little fight, Joffrey Lupul had himself a game, and the series was tied 1–1. In Game 3, the Leafs' first home Stanley Cup Playoff game in nine years, the blue-and-white got slapped 5–2. That made Game 4, also in Toronto, that much more important.

Naturally, Game 4 goes to overtime, Dion Phaneuf goes for a hit that was certainly an interesting choice, the Bruins attack, and score. Already there was talk of, "Well, it was nice to at least get back into the playoffs for a change." I mean the series is over, right? There's no way the Leafs are even going to force a Game 7, let alone win the series.

Well gosh darn it if James Reimer doesn't drag the Leafs to a Game 7 by stopping 72 out of 74 shots over the next two games, despite getting outshot by 15 and only getting four goals in support. Hey! We're going to Game 7 in Boston! This is fun!

A lot of players are haunted by what happened in that game, but for me, one of the biggest "what ifs" belongs to defender Cody Franson. After Boston scored first, Franson scored two goals from the back end to give the Leafs a 2–1 lead that they would take into the third period. Scoring two goals in a Game 7 your team won could get you a reputation as a "clutch" player for the rest of your career!

Now, if you didn't know what happened, the first 5:29 over

that third period was euphoria for Leafs fans. Phil Kessel, the often-booed once-Bruin who couldn't buy a goal against his former team in the regular season, bagged his fourth goal of the series to make it 3–1. Just over three minutes later, Nazem Kadri picked the perfect time to score his first goal of the series, and ho-ly cow.

The Bruins are leaking oil here, there, and everywhere, the players are looking dejected on the bench, and fans in the stands are thinking, *There's a chance I might have made a very expensive mistake.* I was in Maple Leaf Square that night in a sea of thousands of Leafs fans. Their song—"Na Na Hey Hey Kiss Him Goodbye" by Steam—still haunts me to this day.

The whole fanbase thought they had won. Why wouldn't they? The Leafs had a 4–1 lead! No team in NHL history had ever choked on a three-goal third-period lead in a Game 7. This series was over.

Nathan Horton scores near the halfway mark of the period to give the Bruins life, but as the minutes pass by, the Leafs still have a two-goal lead. This team that got peppered and outshot into oblivion all season long can weather this storm for another few minutes.

Milan Lucic scored at the 18:38 mark to bring Boston within one, but again, the Leafs just need to hang on. Surely, they can do that for 82 seconds.

Eighty-two lousy seconds.

The Bruins needed just 31.

Patrice Bergeron tied the game, and TD Garden might've needed a new roof. Complete elation in Boston, utter shock and despair for Leafs fans everywhere.

Then overtime and, ugh, any Leafs or Bruins fan can hear the goal horn in their head if they think hard enough. Jack Edwards with the call: "Bergeron scores! Patrice Bergeron! With the point of the dagger at their throats, they rip it out of Toronto's hands, and kill the beast! The Boston Bruins have won it after being three down in the third!"

Leave it to the Leafs, the flipping Toronto Maple Leafs, who went from scrappy underdogs with no business being there in the first place, to comeback kids, to some sort of beast holding a dagger (does it have paws or hands?), to the single biggest choke in Stanley Cup Playoff history at the time. A sincere thanks to the Vegas Golden Knights for blowing a three-goal lead to San Jose in 2019, joining the Leafs in the "we blew it" club. But the Golden Knights ended up winning a Cup after their debacle, so the fans don't need to care about it anymore.

It's been a tough time as a Leafs fan at the bar, at a friend's house, or even just online ever since. If "It was 4–1" memes were a mudslide, we'd all be underground by now.

—

While I would argue that the Leafs losing to their own Zamboni driver is more embarrassing than coughing up a lead in a Game 7, blowing a third-period 4–1 lead to the Boston Bruins in Game 7 in 2013 has done more damage to the psyche of the Leafs' fanbase than any other game ever.

Losing to your own Zamboni driver is cartoonishly bad—the kind of slapstick thing you might expect to happen in a corny movie from the late nineties. I saw a lot of people compare losing to an emergency backup goalie to losing to Air Bud, the movie golden retriever who got really good at basketball. In reality, what happened that night was more like the plot of *Mystery, Alaska*, a 1999 film where a team full of random players led by Russell

Crowe for some reason play a shockingly tight game against the New York Rangers. But you know something about that movie? The team full of random guys lost, and David Ayres won by three friggin' goals. Should I have given a spoiler alert? Sorry, but it came out 25 years ago.

What's funny is that, in some ways, your favourite NHL team is more likely to lose to their own emergency backup goalie than they are to blow a 4–1 lead in Game 7 of a playoff series. Technically, an emergency backup could be called upon at any minute in any game if both goalies get hurt, whereas you might go all season long without playing in a Game 7. Heck, before losing to Boston in the 2013 series, the Leafs had gone nine years without playing in any playoff game.

I've been pretty open about going to see a therapist from time to time, and believe it or not, the Leafs are actually not a frequent topic of conversation. There is one thing I've learned in therapy that can be applied to the Leafs, though, and in the worst way: irrational fears.

Basically, an irrational fear is something you're afraid of that has little to no chance of actually happening. For example, if you're walking down the street, it's not impossible that you'll be eaten alive by a bear. Could it happen? Sure. Is it likely? Of course not!

Take all these stunning, monumental Leafs losses together, and doom always feels just around the corner. When it comes to the Toronto Maple Leafs, there are no irrational fears.

It's not like the Leafs have had an abundance of accolades over the last half century or more. The number one chirp to any Leafs fan is simply shouting "1967!" at them, indicating the last time they won the Stanley Cup, which, I don't know if you know this, wasn't recently. Over the years since that distant championship, the Leafs have earned their fair share of scars.

When referee Kerry Fraser missed Wayne Gretzky's high-stick on Doug Gilmour during the Leafs' 1993 playoff battle with the LA Kings, that wasn't exactly something fans who are old enough to remember were willing to let go of. Some still haven't. But missed penalty calls and bad penalty calls are a staple of most sports. Every football fan, basketball fan, and heck, every other hockey fan has at least one official's decision—or indecision—that still haunts them to this day. Because of that, Kerry Fraser's missed call in that infamous Leafs-Kings playoff series is ordinary. It's normal.

When the Leafs blew a 4–1 lead in the third period in Game 7 against the Boston Bruins in 2013, that was not ordinary. Teams blow leads and teams mount comebacks, sure. But not like this. That night, the Boston Bruins became the first team in NHL history to mount a comeback and win a Game 7 after trailing by three goals in the third period. What a heroic, historic, awesome night for that team and fanbase. Of course, that also means that night, the Leafs became the first team in the entire history of the NHL to have a three-goal lead in the third period of a Game 7 and lose the game.

This was, without a doubt, the biggest before-and-after moment for the modern Toronto Maple Leafs, and it's one of the biggest on-ice before-and-afters in the NHL in recent memory. For something like a century, a Game 7 loss like this was always a possibility, but had never actually happened. This was the Leafs going for a leisurely stroll on a city street and being mauled and eaten intestines-first by a grizzly bear. For Leafs fans, no lead has ever felt safe since.

That very next season, with a new goalie in net and everything, the Leafs blew a 4–1 lead to the Pittsburgh Penguins and lost. At least it wasn't the playoffs.

A lot of people forget this, but a few years later, with the hope of rookies Auston Matthews, Mitch Marner, and an entirely new squad, it happened again. Do you remember? Everyone remembers the first game of that season: Matthews scores four times and the Leafs still lose—classic. In the second game, the home opener, Marner scores his first career NHL goal and the Leafs win. What about the third game?

At the height of the debate between Leafs fans and Winnipeg Jets fans about whether Auston Matthews or Patrik Laine was better, the Leafs went to Winnipeg, got a commanding 4–0 lead, promptly blew that lead, and Laine won the game for the Jets with an overtime goal that completed a hat trick. If you're a Leafs fan who lives in Manitoba, there's no way that wasn't the worst day of your entire life.

The Leafs blew a 3–0 lead in Game 3 of a 2020 playoff series against the Columbus Blue Jackets in front of a crowd of literally zero, before erasing a 3–0 deficit against the Blue Jackets and winning Game 4 in overtime, only to lose the deciding Game 5 with their worst performance of the series. Again, there is no such thing as an irrational fear when it comes to the Toronto Maple Leafs.

They even blew a 5–1 lead to the Ottawa Senators and lost in overtime during the vaunted 2021 season in the Canadian division. Did it have to be Ottawa? Canada has been shut down for over a year, all I can do is screw around on my phone, and that night the Leafs single-handedly made social media unusable for millions of people for at least a week.

But none of those games, none of those blown leads, none of those complete choke jobs, were worse than Game 7 in 2013. Honesty, I'm not sure any of those games happen without what happened in 2013.

"That's ridiculous! Those games were years apart! The team

had completely changed!" No, some of the players from 2013 stuck around. They played with new players, who then played with newer players, and so on. There's no way it never got spoken about. After all, the scariest horror stories are non-fiction.

Now, it has been more than a decade since that infamous night in Boston. Has enough time passed for those demons to be exorcised from the fanbase's psyche? There's always hope in youth. Kids who were seven or eight years old the night the Leafs blew that 4–1 lead can vote now and are heading off to college. Does a loss as traumatic as that one even register with a fan if you can barely even remember it?

If the Leafs had beaten Boston in another playoff series, maybe then you call it even. After all, nobody seems to remember that in 2010, the Bruins blew a 3–0 series lead to the Philadelphia Flyers, followed by blowing a 3–0 lead in Game 7, just not all in the third period, before losing the series to Philly. Do you know why we don't really talk about that? Because Philly didn't end up winning the Stanley Cup that year, and the following season, the Bruins stomped the Flyers to a pulp during a four-game sweep in the second round of the 2011 Stanley Cup Playoffs en route to becoming Stanley Cup champions. You can exorcise your demons by defeating them. Did the Leafs do that with Boston?

No! They made the demons stronger.

In 2018, after the Leafs erased a 3–1 series deficit against the Boston Bruins to force a Game 7 just like they had in 2013, the Leafs took a one-goal lead into the third period, just like they had in 2013. Did the Leafs hold that lead? Of course not, but at least this time the Leafs had the common courtesy to get slaughtered and lose before the game even reached overtime.

Then, in 2019, the Leafs taking on the Bruins once again, they have an opportunity to win the series in six games. Do they? No, because during that Game 6, the Leafs couldn't catch water if they fell out of a boat, leading to yet another Game 7 in Boston, where the Bruins tore out the hearts of that entire Leafs roster like a finisher in *Mortal Kombat*. At least it wasn't even close this time.

Even though it wasn't against Boston, you know what did feel great as a Leafs fan? Toronto erasing a 4–1 deficit during their 2023 playoff series against the Tampa Bay Lightning and winning the game in overtime, before going on to win the series and advancing to the second round for the first time in nearly two decades. Oh, so *that's* what all the fuss is about! It's amazing when the team you cheer for pulls off the inspiring comeback instead of showing up for a winner-take-all game and shrivelling up like a banana peel that's been left in a hot car.

That win against Tampa definitely felt good. That was as big a serotonin boost for me as any movie, concert, or comedy show I've ever been to. But . . . it wasn't against Boston. Oh, I'll absolutely take it, no take-backs. But Boston.

Fun fact: during the writing of this book, the Leafs actually got a shot at redemption against Boston, fell down 3–1 in the series, forced Game 7, earned a third-period lead in that Game 7, and blew it in overtime again. The Leafs are Bill Murray in *Groundhog Day* if every spring somebody showed up and kicked his ass.

Bruins fans had it easy. They suffered their gut-wrenching loss in 2010, only had to wait one year to get their revenge, and won the Cup on top of it. That's the good stuff. That's the kind of sports victory you could ride the rest of your life. Leafs fans? No. We didn't get the automatic relief that comes with revenge. We've had to do what's harder: just move on. How do you move on?

The corny answer is time. The real answer is you never really do.

4.

My Basement Is Better than Yours

It's tough out there for nerds.

To me, the worst part about being a nerd, or at minimum having nerdy tendencies, is having to constantly defend myself, taking crap for the stuff I like. Few things are more annoying and buzz-killing than somebody yucking your yum. Like, this is obviously something I'm really excited about, or proud of, or even just interested in, and you're bugging me for it right out of the gate.

There are few things that I get dragged for more than my sports collectibles, specifically my hockey collectibles. In fairness, my collection is a bit bigger than most. I have an entire room in my basement dedicated to hockey. You might be thinking, *Hey, I've got a hockey room* or *man cave* or whatever you want to call it. No. You have a few nice things you've chosen to display, maybe a picture frame here or there. You might have even framed a jersey or two, which is totally cool, by the way.

The room I have—"The Blue Room," as I call it—is my YouTube studio, and it is absolutely covered ceiling to floor in figures, pictures, jerseys, and anything else you can think of. You know those old McFarlane hockey figures and, in more recent years, those hockey figures from Imports Dragon? At my last count, I have over 80 of those, and nearly all of them are hung up on the Blue Room wall. And above those hockey figures is a picture of the player. Every. Single. One of them. Side note: They've started making McFarlane figures again. They haven't paid me to say that, I'm just beyond jacked about it.

I have more autographs than I can count. After several years of giving away jerseys or auctioning them off for charity, I still have over two dozen hung up in the Blue Room. There are figures in boxes and figures on shelves. There are enough pucks to keep your beer league stocked for an entire season, even if you've got a guy who couldn't hit a soccer net. I could give you at least a full starting lineup's worth of sticks, too, if you don't mind using autographed twigs with no curve. Tickets, programs, stuffies, and patches, and that's still just the tip of the iceberg.

Maybe you have a bit of a collection and people give you grief about it. Maybe you're tired of living in shame and you want to embrace your inner pack rat. Well, I'm here for you. There are good reasons to embrace your collection of memorabilia and continue to grow it.

IT'S RARE

This is a classic reason for collectors. Everybody knows somebody who has the rarest version of something. Even though it's clearly worth a billion dollars, they're not gonna sell it. Imagine how much more they'll get if they hold on to it!

It's so hard to find rare items, too. I guess that's kind of the point, isn't it? I can't tell you how many times people have shown me a mint condition Jaromir Jagr or Mats Sundin rookie card, and I don't have the heart to tell them they're basically worthless, in terms of financial value. Why? They're not rare. Hockey card manufacturers printed millions of these things in the late 1980s and early 1990s, and that diminishes their value. If you want to sell one, you'd be lucky to get a couple bucks. The upside is everyone gets to have one (or half a dozen).

At the opposite end of the scale, once at a card expo I saw a Wayne Gretzky rookie card valued at $55,000 Canadian. I've never even been behind the wheel of a car worth that much, let alone possessed a treasured piece of memorabilia worth even 5 per cent of that. I've driven home from the hospital with a newborn baby, and I was less apprehensive doing that than I was standing near a Wayne Gretzky rookie card gently sitting behind glass.

I have a replica Felix Potvin mask that's actually signed by the Cat himself. Not one of those little McDonald's helmets— although I have a couple of those, too—but a life-size replica I received as a gift. There are plenty of those little McDonald's Potvin masks kicking around, but there aren't many big ones like mine. It's basically my prized possession, possibly ahead of my wedding ring. In fairness, one of them costs more, and it's not my wedding ring.

I have a Bryan McCabe figurine from when he was with the Leafs. Is it any old figurine? Nope! It's the rare variant of McCabe where he has no helmet and that cool mohawk hairdo he used to display in warmups.

Nothing beats a one-of-a-kind piece of memorabilia, though, and I have one. I didn't even get it through working in hockey. My buddies used to work for an audio/video equipment business, and they would install stuff like TVs and sound systems in people's houses. One day they got to work at the home of famous Toronto Maple Leafs play-by-play announcer Joe Bowen. From his time in hockey over the years, he has more items than he can count.

He had a novelty poster featuring Wendel Clark that spoofs the posters for *Risky Business* and *The Good, the Bad and the Ugly*. Clark, wearing a cowboy hat, overlooks the Toronto skyline. The poster was signed by Clark addressed to Joe Bowen. Joe gave it to my buddy, my buddy gave it to me, and now I have the kind of one-of-a-kind item you could never buy in a store. Well, maybe you could if I sold it, which I'm never going to do and you can't make me.

Something doesn't have to be a one-of-a-kind item for you to take pride in its rarity. But if you find something special—whether from a flea market, Craigslist, eBay, or even a garage sale—grab that thing! Hell, if the items you got as a kid survived into your adulthood in good condition, they might be rarer than anything you could find in a store. The amount of times I've found battered and tattered cards from my childhood—rookie cards, too—makes me physically ill.

A rare piece of memorabilia isn't just a time capsule. It's a survivor. Whether it managed to survive your childhood or you bought it at a shop, you have to cherish it. You are now its caretaker. If you don't do it for yourself, do it for the collecting community at large. Have you ever told a collector about an item you used to have or ruined? They recoil like they've been stabbed in the heart.

You don't have to have a huge collection with a million items in it. If your little piece of history is rare enough, it's worth it all on its own.

IT'S SPECIAL TO ME

Yeah, this one's good. Go straight for the guilt trip.

Oh, you think this thing I have on display is stupid? Cool, let me hit you with a story about why this thing means something to me even though you just called it dumb.

Now, maybe your group of friends won't be deterred by your little sob story and instead go at you harder, like sharks smelling blood in the water. So what? Screw 'em! It doesn't matter if anybody else likes your memorabilia because, to quote a famous meme, "She is very gorgeous to me!"

I've had the pleasure of giving many people a tour of the Blue Room. Sometimes someone will remark about how many figures there are. Then I tell them that if you look above each and every figure I have, you'll find a photo of me with that player. I'd be lying if I told you I didn't get a kick out of the shocked reaction, which happens almost the same every time. They stop, take another look at the things they already looked at, and appreciate each figure for what it actually represents: a memory and a story.

I'll never pass up an opportunity to talk about asking Johnny Bower two interview questions at the Hockey Hall of Fame. With the final syllable of his first answer, his dentures popped out. As I stood there in shock, he popped them back in, looked me in the eye, and said, "All right, what's question two?" Then I took a photo with him a few minutes later while he was having a beer. Legend.

I've got photos with Wayne Gretzky, Sidney Crosby, Mats Sundin, Grant Fuhr, Marc-André Fleury, and literally dozens of others, all of them with a corresponding figurine hanging on the wall. Am I going to tell you each and every one of those stories? Hell no, I'm gonna try to milk that into another book!

However, as with all collectors, there are items that have so far eluded me. There are three players that I have figures for in the Blue Room but not a companion photo of me with that player.

The first is Connor McDavid, who I've yet to meet. I was at his final OHL game, which saw his Erie Otters fall to the 2015

OHL champion Oshawa Generals in Oshawa. I managed to get a last-minute press credential because I lived down the street at the time and I knew the OHL's head media guy. The main story should have been that the Oshawa Generals won an OHL championship on home ice, but the real focus was Connor McDavid playing his last game in junior hockey. After the game there were so many reporters I couldn't even get a sniff of McDavid's final scrum.

I was standing right there and couldn't even hear what he was saying. Then, at the end of his scrum, with everyone looking down to tweet out what he had said, he walked away and immediately hugged a man I didn't recognize. I snapped a quick pic on my phone. It turns out it was his father.

It's a great photo that I got by fluke and because I was too slow getting into the initial scrum. A bunch of outlets picked up and shared the photo. That was awesome. But until I get a photo of the two of us, my collection can never be complete.

The second is Alexander Ovechkin. I've never met him, either. I have, however, done a book signing in Washington, DC, with a bunch of Capitals fans. I coordinated the event with Ian Oland and the other fine folks at the Washington Capitals blog *Russian Machine Never Breaks*. We took a massive selfie as a group, and it's a memory I'm still very fond of. Maybe one day I'll get to meet Ovi.

Last is Auston Matthews. I have met him, several times, actually, but the photo hanging above his figure isn't from any of those meetings.

In Game 3 of the Toronto Maple Leafs' first-round matchup against the Boston Bruins in 2018, the game was tied up 2–2 in the second period. A sophomore Auston Matthews scores, the place goes ballistic, and we head to second intermission.

While standing in the concourse I met up with some people to talk hockey. Just then, a couple burst into our circle and ask, "Can we get a picture?" I look up and it's Auston Matthews's parents! They were easily recognizable. For the first couple years Matthews was a Leaf, they were on TV basically every time he scored, which was a lot, by the way. Apparently they had seen some YouTube videos of mine where I yelled about their son. Someone snapped a photo, and it's still hanging in my room.

I'm aware that because of my line of work I've been blessed to meet more NHL players than the average person. As a result, my hockey collection has some pretty rare gems in it. But the principle remains the same: memorabilia comes with a cool story to tell.

One of my photo/figure combinations is a photo I took with Darcy Tucker when I was 19 or 20 and he was signing photos at the Toronto Zoo. Steve, did you go to the Toronto Zoo just to get Darcy Tucker's autograph? No, I was actually on my lunch break, because I used to work there. That photo with Tucker at the zoo means the same to me as any of the other photos on my wall that I've accumulated over my career in the sport. That's how it should be.

Do you have a photo with a player? Hang it up! It's not just a cool photo but a story to tell. Do you have a program or ticket stub from a game you went to? Display it with pride! Sure, you can probably find the highlights on YouTube, but what fun is that? Tell your story from your perspective. Do you have a puck you found lying on the ground? Put it in a glass case and tell everyone you caught it bare-handed as it was screaming toward some adorable baby's face, and you saved that infant's life.

If you have something that means something to you, share the story. It might keep your visitor from picking on the next person who shows them their collection. And if someone is worth sharing a story with, they'll enjoy it just like you do.

IT LOOKS COOL

What do you mean, "It looks cool"? Steve, that doesn't seem like a very good excuse to spend money on sports memorabilia.

Screw you. Yes, it is.

Does your friend, family member, or significant other roll their eyes at your cool display of goalie masks? Who cares? Do these things you're displaying need to be rare? No! Do they even need to mean something to you? Still no! It's good enough if they simply look cool.

How many houses have you walked into with a goofy "Live, Laugh, Love" picture on the wall? Oh yeah, my hockey pictures are so childish, but your little "Sea, Sand, Surf" canvas above your toilet is a truly breathtaking display of your maturity and superiority. Give me a break! In case you think I'm picking on you, my wife and I have a "Sea, Sand, Surf" canvas and neither of us surfs. I'm pretty sure we just have it because it's green.

While we're talking about home decor choices, nobody wants to see giant blown-up pictures from your wedding. They want to see Sidney Crosby throwing his gloves in the air after scoring the golden goal for Canada at the 2010 Olympics in Vancouver.

Would you rather see awkward photos from a pottery class your friends took on their honeymoon or Kawhi Leonard arching a Game 7 buzzer-beater over Joel Embiid's head and making him cry?

No, no, it's cool, I have this great photo of my favourite team in the whole world winning a dramatic game in heroic fashion as literally thousands of people lose their collective minds, but I'd rather see . . . what is that? Is this a work photo? You actually hung a flipping *work* photo? Like from an office party? How are you not in jail?

Sometimes you'll get a bit of an attitude from folks who think you're a bit too into sports. "Oh," they start sarcastically. "How many touchdowns did the Leafs get at the sportsball game?" Kick that person out of your house, block them on all forms of social media, and install *Home Alone* booby traps to thwart them in case they ever come back.

Some people hang up random pictures of the outdoors in their indoors. Some people cover their home with pictures of their pets. Others hang those big blocky letters that say "BE GRATEFUL" diagonally or whatever. Cool, do whatever you want! Just don't look at me sideways when I make a coffee table out of hockey sticks I found in my Nona's tomato garden.

I WANT IT

"Why do you have that?" I just wanted it, okay?

You don't have to justify your fandom to anybody. I mean, I guess there are limits. If you drop $10,000 on a full uniform and gear set of autographed Carey Price stuff, your significant other is within their rights to ask if you've lost your mind. Nine thousand would have been far more reasonable. Beyond extreme examples like that, you don't have to justify your collection of cool sports stuff to anybody.

Is being a hockey fanatic, or being "obsessed" with any sport, any dumber than any other hobby? I'm not going to bother you about that reality show with all the young, hot people who get isolated from the rest of the world, get stuffed to the brim with alcohol, and compete for love. Which reality show am I talking about? Exactly.

Or people who like that show with the celebrities who have cameras following them around as they go about everyday life and

have totally non-scripted conversations and get into definitely-
not-completely-made-up conflicts with each other. Which show
am I talking about? Exactly! Leave me alone about my Canucks
pillow, all right? It's comfy and it helps me sleep.

We all do things because they make us happy. Why did you
order that pizza? It's going to help you compete in the Olympics?
No, you got it because pizza is awesome. Why do you listen to the
music you like? I dunno. It sounds good? Other people might not
think so, but you're in luck, because guess what? You're not other
people!

Whether it's the shows you like, the music you listen to, the
pets you have, or the people you love, you don't have to justify that
to anybody.

If you want that poster of Vince Carter at the 2000 Slam Dunk
Contest, hang it right next to the family photos. If you found an
autographed painting of Joe Carter rounding the bases at the
SkyDome after hitting the World Series–winning homerun for
the Blue Jays with "Touch 'Em All, Joe!" written in rhinestones,
hang that bad boy right next to the front door. And if you found
the full set of those holographic NHL Pogs they released some-
time in the nineties, you could display them proudly in a circle
around your high school diploma. You could also just, like, give
them to me instead.

Without realizing it, people do all kinds of stuff somebody
somewhere finds weird. Is watching the same show or reading
the same book over and over again weird? Is going to the gym or
running for hours at a time weird? Is working on your car weird?
Do you really like petting and walking your dog? Whoa, what a
weirdo!

Are any of those things actually weird? No, I don't think
so! That's just my opinion, though. And if somebody else does

consider your hobby weird, then you can welcome them to en-joy the lovely and underrated hobby of minding their damn business.

Get as many gosh darn collectibles as you want, for what-ever reasons you like. Remember, you're not a dork, you're a connoisseur.

TURN IT OFF

I've always found that watching hockey is like drinking three cups of coffee: you can enjoy it while sitting down, but be careful because it might make you shit your pants.

Hockey, like any professional sport, is not part of the relaxation business. It's fun, but it's stressful. Is my team going to win? I hope they win. Are you gonna score first? I hope they score first. Did they score first? I hope the other team doesn't tie it. Is something good happening? I hope something bad doesn't happen to ruin it.

I know there's some psychiatrist reading this right now going, "Actually, that sounds like anxiety, Steven," and you know maybe they're right—but a lot of sports fans know these feelings all too well.

So if hockey is so stressful, then why watch at all?

Hope.

Hope is why we watch. We hope they score, we hope they make saves, we hope they win. Whether your team is a contender or compost heap fodder, when you watch a hockey game, you have no idea how it's going to end up.

There's a beauty in that, an optimism that shines through even the thickest calluses on your psyche.

That all being said, and this might be a wild thing to say for somebody who yells and screams about sports on camera, into a microphone, and in print: maybe sports aren't good for everybody all of the time.

Sports should 100 per cent be accessible to absolutely everybody, but what I'm saying is this: Have you ever sat with somebody while they're watching a hockey game and thought to yourself, *I'm not entirely sure my friend is enjoying this*?

You know what we do this with a lot? Video games.

"Oh I like to play this game to relax a bit."

"Yeah? What's the game about?"

"Well, it's a war strategy game where absolutely every click of a button matters, speed and precision are paramount, it's lightning-fast but at the same time battles can last for hours and hours, and also the whole time some stranger from half the planet away is hurling slurs at me, and at the end of it I'm screaming because I either won or died."

"Cool."

I know people who probably shouldn't watch every single game. I can say with unashamed honesty that there were a few years in my life where I shouldn't have been watching every single Leafs game. I used to host Maple Leafs playoff streams on Sportsnet, and they would hook me up to a heart rate monitor. There's a screenshot online of my heart rate hitting 128 beats per minute. Commander

Chris Hadfield, who is a Leafs fan and also an astronaut who has been to actual space, saw that and responded that his launch pulse was "two-thirds Dangle." I was a guy who needed to be on drugs, and it turns out my doctor fully agreed!

Not even including playoffs, your favourite NHL team plays 82 games per season. That's so many games! Missing the occasional hockey game, or any game for that matter, will not kill you. In fact, it will probably have the opposite effect. It won't make you a fair-weather fan if you miss a few games to prioritize your mental health, physical health, or anything else that isn't the hockey team you cheer for.

The biggest compliment anybody can give me as somebody whose career is ranting about hockey is that something I made was cathartic. *Merriam-Webster Dictionary* calls catharsis purification or purgation of the emotions (such as pity and fear) primarily through art. Sports are supposed to make you feel good. If they don't, and I can watch for you and get mad on your behalf so you don't have to be mad yourself, that's a good shift on the ice for me.

As somebody who covers hockey for a living, I might be committing sacrilege by telling you these things. I need people to watch my hockey content, and if they don't, I'm not allowed to order all the chicken fingers I want. But I'll sacrifice those chicken fingers if it means you're not gnawing your own fingers off.

5.

Chel

If you've never played a hockey video game, then this rant might be a bit strange to you. If you have played a hockey video game before, you're probably saying, "All right there, grandpa, just call it Chel."

From a young age, I knew I wasn't going to be a good hockey player. Even worse, after getting slapped for 33 goals against in a game of *NHL 96* by my older neighbour Brian, I knew it was unlikely I would be any good at these games, either.

Then, one Christmas, Brian got me *NHL 99* for PC. Eric Lindros on the box, baby. The Big E and EA Sports all in one.

Year after year, I played new versions of this awesome *NHL* video game, getting better and better as I got older. Years of digital overtime winners, slobber-knocking fights, and Stanley Cup wins I still remember, where I was the long-awaited prophesied son finally bringing the Cup back to Toronto.

Then, one day, we all decided: This is too good. Why don't we let people ruin it? And that's how online gaming was born.

I know what you're thinking: *Here we go! He's gonna let the game developers have it!* Listen, the EA Sports *NHL* franchise isn't perfect. I got a great kick out of the fact that for a while the top-ranked team in *NHL 22* was called "This Game Cost 125" and EA had to display the name on the leaderboard. But the game developer isn't who I have a problem with. It's you. The next *NHL* game could have a $40 billion budget, blowing *Grand Theft Auto* and *Red Dead Redemption* out of the water, and be the best video game of all time, and people would still find a way to screw it up.

The online version is actually the greatest thing EA Sports has ever developed on the hockey side. For those of you who don't know, EA Sports Hockey League is an online version of the *NHL* games where you play one individual position—centre, for example—with as many as 12 players for the two teams. Yep, that means someone is playing goalie the whole time. It's fantastic. And you can play a bunch of games back to back all night with the same group, or find some new players, whatever you want. The dream is to play the Drop-In mode with a group of hockey fans from around the world in an environment that's competitive and fun for all.

But that's not what happens, is it? People find creative ways to ruin everything. If you've ever tried to enjoy the game online, you'll recognize these worst kinds of players in Chel.

HEADSET FRED

This dope comes in many shapes, sizes, and levels of annoyance. Let's do an exercise: Ask yourself right now, "What is a gaming headset for?" Take all the time you need!

If your answer was anything other than "talking to the people I'm gaming with," you should be arrested.

Maybe I'm in the minority on this one, but it always creeps me out: dude's on headset when nobody else is . . . and he uses it anyway. Like, we're all sitting there, trying to have a fun game, and buddy's just chatting away to himself. It's one thing when it's the occasional "Oh!" or "Aw!" at a scoring chance, but this guy's just having a fun little conversation with himself about how bad our breakout is and—you're not gonna believe this—how we should give him the puck more.

It's a fine line. For some reason, I think it's way less weird to talk to your TV when nobody can hear you, but it's absolute serial-killer stuff to have a one-way conversation about your team when you know we can all hear despite none of us being on headset. If we're not on headset, that means we don't want to talk.

These dudes never backcheck, by the way. That's generally the case with any annoying online player, but there's a solid 99 per cent chance Headset Fred is flying up the wing without passing, firing a complete trickle of piss wide from the rockstar zone, and not doing a damn thing about the ensuing two-on-one against. Then they huff and puff into the mic when we get scored on, like it's our fault? Jail. Straight to jail, always.

THE GOON

In a way, The Goon is the easiest Chel player to understand. It's not that they wish ill on you, it's that they wish ill on everybody. They get a genuine joy from hitting everything that moves at all times, no matter whether it ruins the game for you or even their own team.

The Goon is what happens to the kid in your school who spends their summer frying ants with a magnifying glass if nobody bothers to tell them to knock it off. Out in the real world, they're average, unassuming, and inconspicuous. The second they fire up their console, they're six-foot-nine, 255 pounds of spite. It's not that they're taking their anger out on you, it's that your anger gives them the kind of pleasure that really ought to land them on a watchlist. Heaven help you if you start a game and realize every player on the opposing team has their height and weight stats maxed out. Whether you end up winning or losing, if a fun game is what you're after, you ain't about to find it with The Goon.

HITTING HERO

The Hitting Hero is a close cousin of The Goon. They're still out there trying to blow up the competition, but not because they're an ill-meaning monster. They've deluded themselves into think-ing they're genuinely good at the art of hitting.

I'll put my hand up and say this one is me. You've been playing well, your team is up one goal with two minutes left in the third, and all you gotta do is shut it down until the final horn so you can emerge victorious. Keep it calm, keep it cool. The other team attacks in a two-on-two situation. As the defender, all I have to do is stay with my man and calmly poke the puck away.

Except that's boring and I don't really feel like it, so how about I try to blast this guy out of his friggin' skates. But it doesn't work, does it? The guy blows by you—you idiot—and you've gifted the other team a two-on-one. All of a sudden everything is in slow motion. You're praying your defensive partner cuts off the pass, you're praying the goalie makes a miraculous save, because you know the second that puck tickles the back of the net it's all your fault . . . and it's in. They scored.

If you win in overtime, maybe everybody forgets about it and you all laugh later. If you lose? Don't you dare throw a hit for the rest of the night.

PENALTY PETE

Speaking of players prone to disaster in the final minutes of play, how about ol' Penalty Pete? Here you are again, up by one, two minutes to go, and the other team is barrelling down. Luckily, your Hitting Hero learned their lesson from last game and they're on their best behaviour. You know who's not on their best behaviour? Penalty Pete.

Did they get a bit too excited and take a charging call? Or completely whiff and hit the wrong player for an interference penalty? Let's stop pretending: they pressed the stick-lift button knowing damn well it only works 10 per cent of the time. The rest of the time, it's a one-way trip to the box for high-sticking or slashing.

While they wait to see what happens on the replay, they're positively flabbergasted, absolutely beside themselves, and simply cannot believe the way their fair and honest play was misinterpreted by a computerized referee. But we're all watching the replay as this guy performs major dentistry on the opposing player, and yes, they've taken the same dumbass penalty countless times before.

The powerplay starts, the powerplay scores, and the entire party sits there daring Penalty Pete to say anything other than nothing.

TOMMY TRAPPER

Video games are getting more realistic every year, and there's nothing wrong with that. There will always be room for whacky, cartoony, slapstick-style games, not unlike Threes Eliminator in the *NHL* franchise, and there will always be room for the growing hyperrealism modern gaming has to offer.

That being said, if you play the defensive zone trap in *NHL*, there's a ridiculously high chance you watched *The Wolf of Wall Street* and thought Jordan Belfort was the good guy. I can't reveal how I know that, just trust that my methods are highly scientific. Are you breaking any rules when you play the neutral zone trap in hockey? No. But I know beyond the shadow of a doubt you ratted on everyone for everything in elementary school, you enormous narc.

BILBO RAGGINS

Boo to the puck-raggers out there, the miserable dudes who take the puck and dick around with it, wasting time as precious seconds tick off the clock while you try to tie the game.

We're not talking about a few seconds here or there, either. More like 20 or 30 seconds of everyone's life, which simply never happens in real hockey, unless there's some dude in your beer league with a fetish for getting his car keyed. "Get good!" these complete goofs might shout, trying to have fun before the clock expires, as you chase them down in a futile effort and tear your hair out from the root.

NHL 24 got around these trolling tactics by making it a penalty, and the only people unhappy about it are people who don't deserve any happiness ever. Any Bilbo Raggins players out there sore about it? To borrow a phrase: get good.

BACKWARD BILLY

Some of the biggest worms are the losers who start a sentence with "If this was real hockey . . ." Well, it's not, you actual walking diaper garbage. There is, however, one small group of Chel players you would never in a million years see in real hockey who I hope are cursed with one-ply toilet paper for the rest of their lives: the backward-skaters.

It's one thing to protect the puck from a defender, or throw a little spice on a deke. It's a completely different animal when you get some guy who definitely has a poster of the Joker in his room—the Joaquin Phoenix Joker, not the Heath Ledger one—who takes the puck from goal line to goal line going backward the entire time so you can't get the puck off him. I watched a world championship game of Chel years ago that was played almost exclusively backward by both players, and I kept waiting for Chris Pronger to take them to the world's worst chiropractor. These guys are the worst.

TIKTOK JACQUES

The simplest offenders are the TikTokers who get on their phones during every whistle, blasting whatever the hell song snippet is trending this week for the rest of the team to enjoy, and completely missing the ensuing faceoff. Bonus points if that jackass is your team's centre and you're starting every shift chasing the puck down.

"Steve, don't you make this kind of content for a living?" No . . . okay, well, yes, but what if you only watched it when we're not on the penalty kill?

Besides, you're not watching me between whistles, are you? No, you're watching some dude tell you volcanoes were invented by aliens and the pyramids are made of cheese. Unplug for five minutes so you can stop being a plug, you absolute plug.

CAPTAIN AMERICA

Then there's the heroes who decide it's time to save the day and put the team on their back. Did anyone ask them to do this? No, but that's what heroes do. Playing their position? Backchecking? Passing the puck *once ever*? Those are the types of menial tasks beneath such superhuman Adonises as themselves. Who needs X-ray vision when you're gifted with the superpower of a limp shot from just inside the blue line screaming eight feet wide of the net?

Was this hero in the last *Avengers* movie? No, because they were too busy scoring a pair of goals for their team while simultaneously being directly responsible for five or six against. Be a Pro is a single-player game mode that exists—please play that instead! Sure, the virtual coach in the game might scream at you, but who cares, because at least that guy isn't real.

MARTIN BRODEUR

You're not Martin Brodeur, so stay in your net. Stay in your net. No, no, shut up, shut the hell up, just stay in your net. If you're—oh my god no, *please* shut the hell up. If you're a goaltender, tend the goal. "I'm helping!" No, you're not. Maybe one time you did. The other 40 ended up in our net, where you should have been. Stay in your net.

THE RACIST GUY

If we're being honest, we know racism and gaming have had a long and miserable history. If you can find a platform with anonymity and the ability to talk or type, guaranteed it has a bunch of dumbasses being racist, misogynistic, homophobic, transphobic, so on and so forth. Some of them try to be subtle with it, dropping in little dog-whistles when they can. Others will just make their team name some variation of one of many slurs so they can sneak past the game's filters.

Anybody and everybody should be hoping these clumps of pond scum get caught, have their EA accounts permanently banned, their console automatically bricked so it stops working forever, and their credit card on the account cancelled, and that their internet provider just cancels their service.

Don't be a dick, you dick.

FAILING BAILER

Here's the scenario I like to picture: two people in a job interview.

Boss: Your resume is extremely impressive.

Guy interviewing: Thank you.

Boss: It says here you went to the best school in the country and graduated with honours.

Guy: That's correct.

Boss: It says here at your last job you helped make your previous company umpteen billion dollars.

Guy: That's correct.

Boss: It also says that you volunteer at a soup kitchen once per week, including Christmas Eve and Christmas morning.

Guy: That's correct. So, do I get the job?

Boss: Just one more question. When you're playing a full 12-person game of EASHL online and your team falls behind 1–0, what do you do?

Guy: I pause and leave the game immediately.

Boss: Get the hell out of my office. You absolute monster. Security!

Seriously, why do people do this? Did you log onto this online sports game thinking you were going to be winning at all times, always? The other team scored one goal, and that made you fill your diaper up to the waistband?

It's one thing if you're down 12–0 in the second period and decide you have better things to do with your time. But bailing after the first or second goal? Your console should spontaneously combust.

SAMMY SABOTAGE

These people actually exist. They log on, they get into a game with 11 other living, breathing, human beings, and they wreck everybody's good time on purpose.

I'm not talking about people who join the game and use annoying tactics to win. Do I like those people? Of course not, but at least they're competing and actually trying to play and win.

Sammy Sabotage? The moment the puck drops, this guy will immediately begin trying to score on their own net. They'll intentionally put themselves offside, making it impossible for their team to play. Lord help you if they join the game as the goalie.

This has happened to me a bunch of times. And what's really crazy is they'll be screwing up the game on purpose *and* talking smack to the entire rest of the team on headset.

I spend way too much time thinking about people who do this. I don't think about them because I'm mad. It's more like I want to study them sociologically for the benefit of all humanity. What is this person's life? When they log off, what do they eat? When they wake up tomorrow morning, are they going to work? What on earth could a person like this do for a living? Imagine the nightmares their co-workers have to endure. Or, do they act completely normal at work before coming home and ruining the good time of dozens of random gamers around the world every night?

I bet Sammy has a driver's licence. It would explain a lot. That dude who never lets you merge even though you've been signalling? That nut who tailgates everybody? That absolute bog monster who brake-checks people on the highway? I think we might have finally found out what they're doing when they're not driving.

Does this person have a significant other? Children? We must warn them!

KID WITH A CREDIT CARD

Alright, so EASHL isn't your thing. That's fine. You grew up playing the *NHL* games in their classic mode where you control the whole team. Maybe your skills as a rink general are better suited for controlling every player on the ice because your brain is the size of a watermelon.

Well, do I have the game mode for you: Hockey Ultimate Team. It's real simple! As you play, you get cards with different players on them, and those are the players on your team. The more you play and the more you win, the better the cards become, and the better your team becomes.

The best part? HUT is ranked, meaning if you're just starting out, you'll be all the way down in Tier 10 playing against other users that are at your level. Except there is one asterisk: you can buy packs of cards.

I didn't know this when I started playing HUT. I'm down in Tier 10, playing my first ever game. My top line is a junior player, some depth guy from the Czech league, and Ryan Reaves. My goalie might honestly be a made-up person. Meanwhile, the random person I'm playing against has a top line of Pavel Bure, Pavel Datsyuk, and Gordie Howe. Top D pair of Larry Robinson and Cale Makar. Their goalie tandem is Patrick Roy backed up by Voldemort.

There's nothing more humbling than getting your ego stomped into a paste by some 12-year-old with their parents' credit card. Is there a way to prevent this from happening? No, probably not, and even if you tried, you'd be the enormous dork getting barbecued by every teenager on the internet for being the most mad-online person who has ever existed. The solution is obviously to get good and, until then, get absolutely wrecked.

ANYBODY WHO BEATS ME AT *NHL*

Okay, wow, big whoop. You beat me at Chel. Good for you. Are you proud? It's just a video game. Who cares? I bet this is the highlight of your whole day, you loser.

You definitely cheated, too. I *know* you cheated. If you like cheating at video games to pass the time, then that's on you.

Am I mad? I'm not mad. You wish I was mad, lol. I'm chilling, bro. Nothing fazes me. You're mad that you beat me. What do you mean, that doesn't make sense? You don't make sense. Shut up.

Crying? I'm not even crying, bro, I'm just crazy congested and I was chopping onions before I logged on. Whatever, bro, I'm just gonna play another game and definitely not shut my console off and swear under my breath every time I walk by it for the next three weeks. Damn it.

6.

Hockey Time Travelling

Which player, across all eras, is the best? It's a classic, evergreen argument in sports.

Most major sports and many leagues have been around for a century or more, which means there's 100 years of star players to fight over—human beings you could point to, from one era or another, and say, "This player is the best in the world."

I wonder if they knew how we would talk about them in the future. To this day, you can walk into any bar in Burnaby, any pub in Pictou, any tavern in Toronto, or any saloon in Saskatoon, and somebody's gonna be bickering over whether Gordie Howe would kick Brad Marchand's ass (or something).

The great thing about this debate is you could have it forever and pretty much never be wrong, unless you say you're wrong. Publicly, no hockey debate has to have a declared winner. Privately, obviously, you were right. It should go without saying, shouldn't it?

There are a few things we should all agree upon, though, when it comes to these debates across eras. If we're going to do this, we've got to do it right.

DON'T CHOP DOWN THE TREE

This is a common tactic, and a bad one. It railroads debates, and worse, it resembles politics. What do all the major candidates in every political party everywhere do? Usually, most of their hot air is spent trying to blow down their opponent's house. That's not to say criticisms aren't relevant. If your opponent is running on the platform that eating babies is delicious, I think you're well within your rights to ask a couple of questions. But we're talking about hockey here.

Do you really want to start with two legends of the sport and go over every imperfection, every blemish, and every screw-up? Wouldn't you rather list accolade after accolade, accomplishment after accomplishment, and reminisce over all those highlights?

If you admire both trees, by the end of the debate you have a greater appreciation for both athletes. You might even go home to watch their highlights, or watch them right on your phone with your buddies at the bar. Or, screw it, ask if the TV at the bar has YouTube and throw them on for everyone to see. That's a joke, by the way. Don't do that.

Preferring Mario Lemieux to Sidney Crosby doesn't make either of them a bum. Same goes for Wayne Gretzky and Connor McDavid. I don't want to know why my guy stinks, I want to hear why your guy is so great.

If you take the low road, by the end of the conversation you might be convinced both players are overrated, the sport sucks, all sports suck, and you should just go home. "On second thought, no, you're right. Patrick Roy and Martin Brodeur were actually complete sieves who couldn't catch a paper ball if they were made of tape. Actually, I think hockey might just suck."

Stop ruining this for the rest of us.

CHAMPIONSHIP TRUMP CARD

You ever play the card game President? It also goes by the name Asshole, but I'm not sure my publisher will allow that. Did they leave it in? That's hilarious.

Anyway, the rules are very simple. One player puts down a low card, a three being the lowest. The next player puts down something like a four or a five, depending on what they have in their hand. Eventually you get to the face cards, jack, queen, king, before hitting the ace, a two for some reason, and then the highest-ranked card of them all, the joker.

But sometimes, after a three or four, the next guy decides to plop down a joker before anybody else gets the chance to play. That's what you look like when you use championships as your primary argument about which player is best, especially when you're talking about an individual athlete in a team sport.

Championships are absolutely relevant to a player's legacy. If you're comparing a couple of players who have a similar number of games played, similar number of goals, assists, points, and even have the same individual trophies, eventually you'll get to the tie-breaker: How many championships do they have?

That's what championships are supposed to be in these arguments, a tie-breaker. Using championships as the be-all and end-all in a conversation about individual athletes is like playing tag with a kid who refuses to admit you tagged them. We all grew up knowing one of those kids (and you know gosh darn well if you were one of those little snot-noses).

Using championships in an argument about individual players doesn't require any critical thinking or any thought at all. All you need to do is find out how many championships somebody won and how to count that high, which any first-grader could pull off. Wayne Gretzky wasn't better than his brother Brent because he won four Cups. Imagine asking somebody who was better between Sidney Crosby and Alex Ovechkin and they answered you with "Chris Kunitz. Why? Because he won as many Cups as those two clowns combined!"

Championships matter but they can't be all you've got. It's like standing there naked except for a Burberry scarf. Sure, it's a nice scarf, but nobody's gonna want to sit next to you.

TIME TRAVEL DOESN'T EXIST

I don't care how many videos your stoner friend has sent you, it's impossible to time travel. You can't send Alexander Ovechkin back to wreak havoc on the NHL in the eighties. You also can't have a 25-year-old Gretzky travel into the future to shake hands with his current older self before playing a game with his linemates Connor McDavid and Leon Draisaitl. These conversations can definitely be fun, but they stop dead if you go about them the wrong way.

In the wake of Ovechkin's pursuit of Gretzky's all-time NHL goal-scoring record, people will use time travel to tear down the eighties. Think about it: Ovechkin is a six-foot-four, 240-pound goal-scoring automaton "allegedly" made of flesh and bone, designed to fly up the ice with the puck and pancake any mortal foolish enough to try to stop him.

Imagine if Ovechkin, or any star in the game today, got to feast on the goalies of the eighties. I'm too young to have watched that era live, but seeing old footage of it is genuinely funny if you grew up with today's game. Somehow nearly every goalie looked like his pads weighed half a ton when wet, probably because they did, while simultaneously looking like he could be knocked over by an ill-timed burp.

Go back even further and try to imagine one of Ovechkin's clap-bombs soaring at a goalie with no mask. Actually no, I've got a better idea. How about you don't picture that, because it's easy enough to google drawings of what the inside of a human skull looks like.

You can't even argue the tougher players in the eighties would have ended Ovechkin before he got close to the record, because Gretzky managed just fine at more than 50 pounds lighter than Ovechkin. Part of Gretzky's success might be because he skated around with a few armed guards on the roster at any given time. So then imagine if Gretzky still had the likes of Dave Semenko and Marty McSorley but he was also built like a mid-size SUV.

By now you're probably like, "Whoa, Steve. All you've done is put down older eras in the time travel argument. Are you saying that today's players are better than any other players from hockey history?"

Yes, I am saying that. Hockey is better now than it ever has been. I'm saying that in the most respectable way possible, though. Let me explain.

Hockey gloves used to look like oven mitts and went most of the way up your elbow. Today's gloves are made of bulletproof material but weigh less than a napkin. Hockey skates have actual boots on them now instead of some soft and bendy leather nonsense. Have you seen today's sticks? They bend! Like, they're literally designed to flex to help players turn vulcanized rubber into laser beams because they're not made of trees anymore. Why? It's the future! Technology evolves!

Today's players had the fortune to be born when they did, after the greats who came before them. Could Gretzky have scored

92 goals in one season against today's goalies? Well, with what he had in his prime in 1985, no, not likely. But give him today's super-light gloves, supersonic boots, and Jedi-sword hockey sticks, who knows? Maybe he would have scored even more.

The past teaches the present. The greatness of old players inspired the new ones. We haven't even talked about the sacrifices players had to make off the ice so that players could earn their fair share from greedy owners and quit their day jobs to focus on hockey.

You can only beat the team in front of you, and you can only play in the era you're in. You can have a debate about athletes and time travel; it's actually kind of fun. Just as long as you know everybody involved is pulling fantasy scenarios out of their butt.

DILUTION

This is one I have a hard time wrapping my head around as somebody who was born more than two decades after the NHL expanded from six teams to 12 in 1967. It's a bit of a micro-argument for a very specific era, and I'm not a big fan of it. Bobby Orr's legacy is especially impacted by this tactic because his best years immediately followed the NHL's first expansion boom.

The idea is that when the league had six teams, they were the best six teams in the world, with the best six teams' worth of hockey players. In one season, the number of teams doubled, and with it, so did the number of hockey players.

On one hand, that's like the NHL magically going from 32 teams today to 64 teams tomorrow morning. During the 2023–24 season, 924 skaters played, as well as another 98 goalies. Doubling that means 1,848 skaters and 196 goalies. I'm sure there are a bunch of guys outside of the NHL right now who could play pretty well in an NHL game, but I'm not sure there's like 1,000 of them.

The big problem I have is that expansion had to happen, and the games still counted. If you talk about dilution, you're basically throwing a massive asterisk on everything Bobby Orr ever did, even though the players who played at the exact same time as him couldn't even come close to putting up the numbers that he did.

Why stop at Orr? Do you know when the NHL expanded to 21 teams? If you guessed Wayne Gretzky's rookie season, you'd be right! Same thing as Orr—do we put an asterisk on Wayne's numbers even though he was leaps and bounds ahead of every peer who made their NHL debut around the same time?

It's not a completely invalid thing to bring up, but to me, dilution just dilutes the conversation.

THE GAME HAS CHANGED

Piggybacking on the time travel conversation, only a few things about hockey have stayed the same over the years. The most important is that you're supposed to put the puck in the other team's net.

Today you hear a lot about the new hooking and slashing rules that prevent defending players from getting their stick into an attacking player's hands, even if it's not done in a painful or malicious way. Then somebody raised on the hockey of the nineties talks about how you used to be able to hook a player and ride them up the ice like you were Santa's sleigh and they were Rudolph.

Then somebody who watched hockey in the eighties chimes in, followed by the seventies, and sixties, until eventually some guy yells, "Back in my day, murder was legal!"

The conversation usually devolves into something about how today's players would be too soft to survive the rigours of old-time hockey. That might even be true! Those guys were born into an era when bench-clearing brawls were a regular occurrence, and in some cases, the police actually had to run onto the ice to help stop a fight. I couldn't believe it the first time I saw it; I thought I was watching a movie. An uncle of mine somehow found a game where the Leafs and Habs basically committed a big ol' bunch of crimes against each other until they just kind of got tired of it. I still don't know how it didn't take at least five business days to finish a single game.

Here's a little factoid to add to the argument that's sure to piss off your dad: Gordie Howe's first Hart Trophy as league MVP was in 1952. Only eight out of the 143 skaters to play in the NHL that season weighed 200 pounds or more; that's barely over 5 per cent of the league. A 207-pound Harry Watson was the heaviest human being in the NHL that season. For comparison, during the 2022–23 season, 439 out of the 951 skaters to play, or 46 per cent of the league, weighed 200 pounds or more, and 267 of them weighed more than the heaviest player in 1952.

No, I'm not saying being bigger makes you tougher, a better fighter, or more durable . . . but I am saying that a little bit. Today's NHL players may not be the meek little lambs they're portrayed as in these kinds of arguments.

On the other side, someone will always point out how old-school players lacked the skill for today's game and would get turnstiled so badly they'd go flying into the sky, eventually breaking free of the Earth's gravitational pull and returning every 50 years or so as a sweater-and-sock-wearing comet.

Let's be honest, you're both right. If you sent a current player into the past or a past player into the future, they wouldn't quite fit. Maybe if these players were born in different eras and were raised with the rules of that era, they would adapt. Who knows? As a famous Italian chef once said, "If my grandmother had wheels, she would have been a bike."

Imagine all the questions a goalie time travelling from the past to the present would have. What's all this equipment? What the hell is this trapezoid behind the net? Who the hell is the opposing goalie and was one or both of their parents a mythical giant? Also what the hell is the butterfly and why is the other guy always down on his knees?

It's unfair to do an apples-to-apples comparison of eras because, in some ways, they're not even the same sport. The basic idea of scoring more goals than the other team is the same, but so much has changed. Should hockey's record books include lacrosse players so that we can have something like "Most goals scored by a guy with a stick?" Hey—a bat is kind of like a stick. I won't rest until Babe Ruth takes his rightful place in the Hockey Hall of Fame!

You don't need to use random made-up scenarios to get your point across. Players can only play the opponent they have in front of them, and until something changes, that opponent isn't about to pop out of a time machine.

7.

The Worst Things

Hockey games are the best. That's why we drop a whole mortgage payment just to go to one. But what happens when the thing you expect to be the best turns out to be the absolute hair-pulling, eye-gouging, nightmare-making worst?

There are few things quite as disappointing as going to a sporting event that sucks. You look forward to it so much—all day, all week, or all month, depending on when you bought the tickets—and then your team stinks up the joint. I've never gone to a hockey game and seen my home team win and thought, *Man, this really wasn't worth the money.* If it's a brutal game and my team dies an agonizing death over two and a half hours of pure misery, I become a chartered accountant and start thinking about all the things I could have spent my precious money on other than my dumb hockey team.

Look, normal losses are going to happen—that's sports. The things that really ruin a game, that make it the absolute worst, are inexcusable. That's what makes them so hard to take. Indulge me as I rant about the things that suck most about going to a hockey game, including what you can change and what you can't.

STUPIDLY BAD SEATS

In Greek mythology, the character Icarus was given wings made of wax and feathers. He was warned, or you could say coached, not to fly too close to the sun or his wings would melt away. Icarus did not listen to his coach, flew too close to the sun, his wings melted, and he crashed into the ocean. This is why you listen to your coach.

Partially obstructed seats certainly suck. Like, why is there even a seat here? But sitting too close is actually worse. You might be thinking, *There's such a thing as sitting too close at a sporting event? Gee, must be nice!* I can assure you it's not.

You're on the website, you see that tickets are available right behind the benches, and you think, like Icarus, *I'm going to fly to heights I've never reached before!*

This exact thing happened to me at a junior hockey game with the Oshawa Generals of the OHL. My friends were visiting me in Oshawa, we were hanging out having fun, and I wanted to show off a bit. We went on the website to look for tickets to the game and there were none to be found, except a row of seats right behind the home team's bench.

Should it have struck me as odd that there was an entire unsold row at an otherwise sold-out sporting event? Yes, it should have. But I was too blinded by the light to see the flaw in my own hubristic plan.

We arrived at the game shortly before puck drop, sat down in our seats, and took in the scene. The players are right there and larger than life. Coaches go over last-minute preparations and plans. Equipment managers use screwdrivers on players' helmets while they're still wearing them, which will never not look funny.

Then the fateful words, "Please rise, if you're able to, and remove your hats for the singing of our national anthem." All the players stand up, and I realize I've made an enormous mistake.

Half of these players are taller than us, and the ones who aren't are still wearing skates. We look to centre ice, peering through a sea of heads, necks, shoulders, and sticks in an attempt to see the anthem singer. If I can't see them, how am I going to see the puck?

If you get courtside seats at a basketball game, you're seeing all the action unobstructed with no boards or glass blocking you. Hell, you'll probably pick up a couple of rebounds and maybe even get an assist. Shaq dives into the stands, he knocks over your beer, you get a signed jersey or something. It's awesome! Hockey, not so much.

They dropped the puck, and we couldn't see a gosh darn thing besides a blue flash being chased by a red flash. Then the players on the ice disappeared from sight behind the players on the bench. If it weren't for the reactions of the people behind us, who could actually see the puck, we would have had no idea what was going on.

I think we lasted four shifts before deciding to get up and just walk around the arena all game instead.

Luckily for us, junior hockey tickets aren't the most expensive. If you make this mistake at an NHL game, then heaven help you, because depending on where you live, you could've bought a gently used car instead.

To be fair, in my experience, some pro hockey rinks have their seating elevated a bit more so that you can actually see over the players on the bench. The ones that don't, well, you'll get an awesome look at the nameplates.

There are some perks to sitting up close. You might get on TV for a split second. You can text your mom, "Hey I got on TV!" and she can reply, "That's so nie" because she missed the *C* button. Mostly, you'll hear from your friends saying, "I saw you, loser" with poop emojis and crushing you with memes in the group chat.

With seats up close to the glass, if something cool happens down at your end, you'll have an awesome memory. You could also see exactly zero goals or no action at all because everything is happening on the other end of the ice. It's like listening to a game on the radio without the commentator.

Middle of middle is what you want, if you can get the tickets in time. The best seats in the house might be top of the lower section of seats, dead centre ice. You're close to the action, you don't miss any of it, and there's a greater-than-zero chance you actually get a puck.

Listen to your coach. The ideas that bring you closest to the sun aren't always the brightest.

WHEN YOUR TEAM GETS DEMOLISHED

When you witness your team get completely caved in on home ice, the process goes something like this. The road team goes up 1–0, and the crowd lets out a collective groan. Whether your team is doing great in the standings or they're at the bottom of the league, there's still a part of you that thinks, *They'll get it back. Go, team!*

You wait for your team to score the tying goal, but gee, the other team sure does seem to be getting a lot of shots, and a lot of chances. That's okay, hit 'em with the ol' rope-a-dope! The road team is just wasting their energy, and they'll tire out at some point soon, right?

Then they score again. All right. It's not ideal, but it's 2024.

Teams erase 2–0 leads all the time. And hopefully they erase 3–0 leads, too, because the other team just scored again.

No matter how positive you try to be, this is a bad situation. There's no sugar-coating being down three goals on home ice. Can your team mount a miracle comeback? You'll have to wait a little bit to find out, because now it's the first intermission.

You spend the whole intermission exchanging looks with people and making that cringe face where you smile with your teeth but it's an upside-down smile. Everyone's muttering a myriad of curse words, and some are saying them much louder. For a second you think, *Dude, there are kids here,* and then you see little Johnny and can tell that if he wasn't worried about getting in trouble, he'd be saying them, too.

Best case, you'll overhear someone somewhere say something encouraging like, "They can only go up from here!" Part of you begrudgingly admires that attitude, and gosh, you even start to believe it. Whenever you drop your hard-earned money on a hockey game or any sporting event, you're spending that money hoping you're going to see something special. As you sit back down in your seat, you decide you're ready to witness that special thing and cheer on your team . . .

Until your team blows a tire off the opening faceoff, immediately gives up a two-on-one, and the puck is in the back of your net.

Sometimes a road team scores a goal that breaks your spirit, and this is dangerously close to being the one. You can't even trick yourself anymore into thinking the first period was just a string of bad luck. The riveting Miracle on Ice speech you were imagining your coach giving in the locker room at intermission has clearly fallen on deaf ears and maybe, just maybe, you're in the middle of watching your favourite team get their asses kicked.

But then, magic! Your team finally grabs the puck, pulls themselves up by their bootstraps, attacks, gets a few chances, keeps the pressure on, and finally puts one in the net and gets on the board.

You know what? They might not come back and win this thing, but darn it, they're going to try. Even if your team loses, you're still going to be entertained. The ice is about to tilt in their favour and they're going to make a game out of this, whether they win or not. Let's go, team!

Then the dagger. Your team rides the momentum briefly, but the puck comes back the other way, and it's in the back of the net once again. And that's where it all breaks down.

You had hope. You allowed yourself to have hope like an idiot, like a big naive rube idiot. You let your guard down, you let yourself believe, and your team strung you along for the ride just high enough to let you crash down to Earth.

You think about how much money you spent on the tickets. You dwell on how long it took you to get there that night. You remember you have work in the morning. No matter how much sleep you get, this game is going to clock you over the head like a whisky hangover, and you're going to be marionetting your body around all day trying to get by.

Maybe worst of all, you realize how much time is left in the game.

So what do you do? Do you cut your losses? You've already spent the money either way. Do you just leave the arena to end the suffering? No, that would make you a quitter. What if you stay for the rest of it? No, there's like 90 minutes left before the final horn. What if they make a magical comeback? No, they're not going to. Unless they do!

In the time you've struggled with this debate inside your own head, the road team has scored again. Even the road fans are starting to feel bad and toning it down, except for one guy who's enjoying his night more than his own wedding, and he just so happens to be sitting in your section and oh god dude will you please just shut up.

The only redeeming quality for the rest of the game is the collective bonding with other fans you can only achieve through each other's misery. Look at us: just a big, dumb gaggle of dummies who love this stupid hockey team. Why do we do this to ourselves? What's that? You'll buy me a beer? No, no. Here, I'll buy you a beer. No? Tell you what, let's head to the concourse together and we'll each get ourselves two beers. One time I saw my favourite team lose 7–3 in a playoff game—on the road. What can you even do except stand there like King Leonidas at the end of *300* and embrace the thousands of arrows in the form of chirps hurtling toward you. Best case, someone will feel bad enough for you to buy you a pity beer, which is pathetic, but still beer.

Over time, the mere fact you went to this game and stayed for the whole thing becomes something you wear in front of other fans like a badge of honour. I have friends that still brag, or lament, that they saw their team lose 9–2 live and in person. I've never asked them how much they spent on the tickets because I like them too much.

The beauty of sport is you never know what's going to happen. The pain of sport is you never know what's going to happen. You know what went viral in the fall of 2023? A photo of a little boy with a sign that said "My first Sharks game" with a scorebox beneath at the bottom left of the screen that showed that the Sharks were losing 8–0. If it makes you feel any better, the Sharks actually ended up allowing ten that night. The sign also said "Today is my birthday!" I hope the team gave that kid a U-Haul truck full of merch.

WASHROOMS

This is a universal topic among all sporting events, but every person I asked, "What's one of the worst things about going to a hockey game?" said the washroom.

An NHL intermission is around 20 minutes long. Have any of you, ever once in your entire life, gotten up from your seat at the horn for the end of a period, gone to the washroom, gotten food or a drink, and gotten back to your seat in time for the start of the period without throwing out a few Tom Wilson elbows?

Maybe I shouldn't be lumping together in the same category hitting up the concessions and going to the washroom, but there's a huge difference between the two.

One is an experience where you can calmly evaluate options (read the menu), decide what you want, and even change your mind three or four times. You also get to enjoy the delicious aromas before it's even your turn, and at very least, you know there's food and drink at the end of it.

I can only draw from my personal experience in the swamps known as the men's bathroom. This lovely experience starts in a line that usually spills out of the door, and you're immediately blasted in the face by a smelly waft that's the by-product of the inaccuracy of dozens of other men. It's finally your turn, and you can actually feel the clock ticking; the patience of the guy behind you is directly dependent on how bad the home team is getting rocked in their own barn.

Do you have something in your hands? No, not that, I mean like a phone, a beer, or something else? Good luck finding somewhere to put it that's not covered in what I can only assume is the goopy birthplace of a virus that Covid-19 checks under its bed for at night.

Instead of having to touch faucets and stuff, we now have

sensors so we don't spread nearly as many germs. Isn't that a great idea? In theory it is, sure! But what ends up happening is one or all of the tap, soap dispenser, and hand dryer start getting wishy-washy about you washing your hands.

Person: Hi, I'd like some soap.

Soap Dispenser: No.

Person: Uh, okay, I'll start with some water.

Faucet: Here is exactly 0.9 seconds' worth of water.

Person: What the—

Soap Dispenser: Here's that soap you ordered. You wanted it all over the counter, right?

Person: Dude.

Hand Dryer: Hi, there! There's actually a tiny ecosystem that lives in here and I'm just gonna blow it all over the place.

Person: Looks like I'll just have to do the ol' wipe-on-the-jeans dry.

Faucet: I haven't even given you anything yet!

I could get killed by the CIA or a bunch of rich dudes or who-ever "The Man" is for telling you this, but screw it, I'm gonna do it anyway. A few years ago, I started getting invited into the press box as well as box suites to gaze down upon the commoners below.

Most places I've been have individual bathrooms. Like, you go in and it's just you, a sink, and a toilet. *That* is how the other half lives while the rest of us pack in and rub shoulders while two dudes take a pee on either side of us while trying to have a conversation with the plastic lip of their beer cup bitten between their teeth.

I know some dudes can go in a trough—a literal, zero-hyperbole metal trough—and be totally cool with it. I'm not ashamed to admit that it's my damned nightmare. This might be a hot take, but multi-billion dollar arenas and stadiums where tickets and food cost a mortgage payment should have clean, spacious bathrooms.

If one of those things you're holding is food, I have bad news: you went to the wrong thing first. Why did you go get snacks first when you knew you had to go potty? There's a famous photo from the olden days (hockey Twitter circa 2012, or whichever year) of a dude at a game standing at a urinal doing his thing with, I'm not kidding, a container of nachos under the urinal. Everyone involved in that scenario is a psychopath, from the guy splattering his own nachos with collateral damage to the dude whose first instinct when he saw that was to say to himself, *Oh damn, I need to take a photo of a stranger peeing in a public bathroom right now.* That's watchlist stuff. Jail! Immediate jail! Under the jail! Build a prison under the prison!

We can't control what happens during a game, and we can't control how other people are going to act at a game, either. Unless you're comfortable seeing the game in a diaper, all you can control is how you treat the place.

I will say this, though: every year, sports teams show off their latest food items and drink spots. There's always a few teams like

"We've got a brand new three-foot hot dog" or "Try our new gravy fudgesicles!" No, no. Don't distract us with all that window dressing. Show us what you've done with the bathrooms.

If you're going to sell deep-fried nonsense that turns regular human beings into fleshy time-bombs in a building that cost taxpayers more than the sun, show us a bathroom you would offer to kings and queens, with golden toilets and urinals that sing when you use them. Well, that and, most importantly, sinks that actually work.

We can't forget the nightmare scenario of going to the bathroom while wearing the visiting team's jersey. Dude, I'm not going to think less of you as a fan if you take that thing off before going in. I know most people are cool, but some folks are nuts. I've heard horror stories of getting shoved while standing at the urinal, getting yelled at. Some people pay good money for that kind of treatment, but not at a hockey game. I hope women's bathrooms are better than the unholy hellscape that is the men's.

If you want to avoid the *Mad Max*-esque dystopia of visiting the washroom during intermissions, you can go during commercial breaks or between whistles. But this route amounts to making peace with the fact you're going to miss some gameplay. Honestly, it's probably worth it.

The other strategy is to dehydrate yourself like food destined for the space station. Stop having water three hours before the game and eat salty popcorn until your tongue feels like Velcro. You'll go and have the best in-arena experience of your life, assuming you don't faint. For legal reasons, I'm kidding.

I don't blame hockey teams for the state of their bathrooms; I blame us and our barnyard animal tendencies. One of the best things about going to the game is enjoying the company of other people, and it's also one of the worst.

WHEN YOUR TEAM'S TOUGH GUY GETS DUSTED IN A FIGHT

If you don't like fighting at a hockey game, I get it. That being said, people lose their actual minds for a hockey fight. To quote Theo Von, "I'm not judging you, but I'm just saying everybody else is gonna."

I would have become a New York Rangers fan for one night just to experience the night a rookie Matt Rempe dropped the gloves with certified NHL heavyweight Matt Martin at centre ice during an outdoor game and held his own like it wasn't literally his first career NHL game. Go watch the clip on YouTube and tell me the Rangers fans in attendance aren't showing symptoms of rabies. Pure prehistoric pandemonium. What was the score? Who cares! The Rangers' team tough guy for the next generation just went to centre ice and rocked a player for one of their biggest rivals. If you could bottle that feeling and inject it, you'd test positive for anabolic steroids.

Then there's the other side of the coin. The list of undefeated fighters in the history of combat sports is very short. Even the great Muhammad Ali lost to Joe Frazier before later beating him. Hockey isn't officially a combat sport, but as long as fighting is only a five-minute major, I think the comparison holds.

Almost nobody who fights even semi-regularly at the NHL level goes their entire career without getting got. When it happens at home? Oh, dude. When the home team's tough guy drops the mitts, everybody gets to their feet and starts screaming. The commotion before their beloved warrior loses makes the silence that comes afterward that much more pronounced.

Then that weird realization sinks in for an entire audience of thousands of people: we just watched the baddest man alive get humbled in their home rink. What do you do? What do you say? If the fight is close, you can fake it, cheer your guy on, then kind of mumble to your friend, "I think he might've got beat up."

We can say that fighting has no effect on the actual gameplay. If we're being honest, that's probably true a lot of the time. Very often it's two guys grabbing at each other's collar, wrestling a little bit, throwing a couple of weak punches directly at the other guy's helmet, and the refs separate them while the home crowd pretends something actually happened there. When the fight is a decisive loss, you can't tell me it isn't felt by everyone in that arena.

The next day, whether the team won or lost, people will ask, in a way that's typically reserved for a viewing at a funeral home, whether you saw the fight. The main difference is that with a funeral, you don't usually respond with, "Yeah, well, they'll get 'em next time."

Fighting can be either a shot in the arm or a punch to the gut that ruins your night.

THE CHOKE

Earlier we spoke about watching your team get obliterated. This is much worse. It's a combination of two of the most lethal things in all of sports fandom: hope and embarrassment.

Any team can lose. In a sport with a season of 50 or more games, depending on the league you're watching, you can't expect your team to go undefeated. It's not necessarily embarrassing watching your team lose on a "regular" night. Less than ideal? Absolutely. Annoying? Of course! You wanted to see a win. But not all losses are chokes.

You've been watching your team kicking butt all night long.

There have been more ups than downs, and now here they are winning the game, probably by more than one goal, and probably in the third period. All that's left is for these beauties to shut this thing down and bring it home.

The clock ticks away and oops! Uh oh, the other team scored. All right, we're a little less comfortable now, but we've still got this. Put on a brave face and enjoy as your team walks the brick road to victory.

You look up at the clock and become a mathematician, trying to figure out the likelihood of the other team scoring two goals in 90 seconds. Then 80. Then, oh. Oh no. They scored again.

It's not just that the other team has roared back to within one goal, it's that a loss now inexplicably feels inevitable. You start to question. Am I just being a pessimist, or is it because my team has gotten outshot 15–1 over the last five minutes and everyone is visibly breathing out of their butts after every whistle?

You can't quite explain where any of this came from, for either team. Why is the other team battling determinedly onward like ancient Roman legionaries, and why is your team wilting like a bag of lettuce you left in a hot car? Watching your team choke is awful. Knowing the choke is about to happen is worse.

Of course the other team ties it. Of course they win it in overtime. Of course you paid to be there.

If you saw this happen on the road, best of luck to you. You're in an arena full of thousands of people who feel like they just ran with Rocky Balboa up the steps of the Philadelphia Museum of Art. Sure, it was a bunch of professional athletes who pulled off the comeback, but the win felt so good for those fans that they start saying "*we* did it" because it genuinely feels like everybody in the building—at least those with the right jersey on—had a piece in the miracle we all just witnessed. And there you are wearing an Ivan Drago jersey. What a nightmare.

You could have seen your team lose any day in any way, but you had the pleasure of seeing this absolute choke show without a Heimlich maneuver in sight. No lead will ever feel safe again.

———

Listen, ultimately, going to a hockey game is the absolute best. These things, however, can make your special night out at the rink the absolute worst.

8.

Goalie Mount Rushmore

This could be a bar argument with your buddies every single weekend this month, and each time you have it, you could all give different answers.

Deciding the "Mount Rushmore of" whatever has been a staple of sports arguments since the creation of Mount Rushmore, which was apparently 1927–1941. That's not a thing I knew offhand—I had to google it.

It's the best kind of "greatest of all time" argument because it doesn't force you to pick one person. Players can be equally great for different reasons, across different eras, and you can value those reasons differently depending on what you've recently read, or seen, or even what you've eaten that day. With a Mount Rushmore of something, you get to pick four.

I'm going to repeat that because this is my number one biggest pet peeve in all of sports fandom: you get four picks. That's it. Don't give me five, six, or in some special cases that should come with a permanent ban from any self-respecting group chat, three. Mount Rushmore has four presidents on it, so when you have a Mount Rushmore sports argument, you're picking four.

For bonus points, can you name those four presidents? The correct answer is: none of those dudes played in the NHL, so who cares.

Which brings us to the Mount Rushmore of goalies. I'll be honest: I reached out to dozens of former NHL players, hockey insiders, broadcasters, and even just regular old hockey fans to ask them what their goalie Mount Rushmore looked like. While there were a lot of overlapping answers, nobody had the same list of four.

Let's settle the debate. To make our own mountain, we have to figure out the criteria.

- Peak: If we're talking about the best of all time, then we have to be able to look back at how they played when they were at their absolute best. When they were the best goalie in the league (if they ever were), did they squeak by their competition in a way you could still contest today, or did they completely blow their competition out of the water? Did this player, even if it was just for a fleeting flash in the pan, produce performances that were truly magical?

- Longevity: This one is tough, and in some ways, a bit cruel. Most professional athletes don't retire because they got bored. Usually, a player's body just can't do it anymore. Whether it's from wear and tear over time, an injury that changed everything, or illness. There's a massive element of luck when it comes to longevity. Still, some of the truest greats of all time, in any sport, managed to find a way to stay great along with their incredible luck not to get injured too badly.

- Accolades: There's no "I" in "team," but there is one in "Vezina," and that's the award you get when you're voted the best NHL goalie in any given season. If your pick was never awarded this, how are you going to argue that goalie should be one of the all-time best? You're allowed to like a goalie, they can even be your childhood idol, but if they don't have the hardware, they can't sit at the table with the best to ever do it.

- Championships: This one is controversial and perhaps even more cruel than longevity, but I'm going to hold strong on this one. A goalie can have an incredible peak, could have dominated in the best league in the world for two decades, and could have won every individual trophy there is to place on the mantel. But every summer that goalie trained, every season played, and every playoff war waged—it was all an attempt to win a championship. You can make it into the Hockey Hall of Fame without winning the Stanley Cup; the Hall inducts four players every year. The Mount Rushmore of goalies? No, no. We're making a list of the four best *ever*. That's it. Gold medals at international competitions do count for something, no doubt. But a ring on the finger and the name on that Cup are a must. No GOAT conversation can have a player in it who didn't win the ultimate prize at least once.

Now that we've nailed down the criteria, we can start figuring out who to put on our goalie Mount Rushmore. You've probably started putting together a list in your own mind. I'm going to tell you my four, but I'll be honest, right now as I'm writing this chapter, I don't have the list finalized in my head. And that's why I've come up with something to help you.

When it comes to the best goalies of all time, there are only seven guys in this conversation. That means you can pick any four you want, but if they're not from the following list (in no particular order), you're wrong and your Mount Rushmore of goalies is wrong.

PATRICK ROY

STATISTICS

Record (Regular Season): 551–315–131
Record (Playoffs): 151–94
Regular Season Wins: 551 (3rd all time)
Playoff Wins: 151 (1st)
Career Save Percentage (Regular Season): .910
Career Save Percentage (Playoffs): .918
Shutouts (Regular Season): 66 (16th)
Shutouts (Playoffs): 23 (2nd)
Saves (Regular Season): 25,800 (4th)
Saves (Playoffs): 6,559 (1st)
Vezina Trophies: 3 (1989, 1990, 1992)
Other Trophies: Conn Smythe Trophy (1986, 1993, 2001)
Stanley Cups: 4 (1986, 1993, 1996, 2001)

Before he became an NHL head coach with a propensity for banging down panes of glass to scream at Bruce Boudreau with greater volume, Patrick Roy was drafted in the third round, 51st overall, by the Montreal Canadiens in 1984. He was actually the fourth player the Habs picked that year, behind Petr Svoboda (fifth overall), Shayne Corson (eighth overall), and Stéphane Richer (29th overall). Fun fact: all four of those players ended up playing over 1,000 NHL games (4,267 total). All in all, not a bad draft class.

Though Roy played 20 minutes of one game in the 1984–85 season, his rookie year in the NHL was the next season, at just 20 years old. Heading into that 1985–86 season, the Habs had gone six consecutive years without winning a Stanley Cup. That might not sound like much, but it was actually the Canadiens' longest stretch without a Cup since 1947–52. Yep. That's a real stat. Put the book down and look it up if you don't believe me.

In that stellar rookie season, Roy went 15–5 in 20 Stanley Cup Playoff games, with a 1.93 goals against average and .923 save percentage, en route to becoming not just the youngest goalie but the youngest player to ever win the Conn Smythe Trophy as playoff MVP.

Roy's goaltending resume is cartoonishly good. He won four Stanley Cups—two each in Montreal and Colorado—and won playoff MVP in three of them. Hilariously, the only Stanley Cup win where Roy didn't win playoff MVP was the season his coach in Montreal famously hung him out to dry for no good reason; on the bench, while the game was still happening, Roy demanded a trade, and he went to Colorado to win it all powered by pure, unfiltered spite.

Not to say Patrick Roy wasn't one of the best goalies of all time in the regular season. Roy's 551 regular season wins puts him third all time in that category, behind only Martin Brodeur and Marc-André Fleury. It's just that playoff Patrick Roy was a whole other animal.

Roy has more playoff wins than any goalie in NHL history, with 151. Brodeur is second in that category, with 113 playoff wins. That's bloody 38 more wins Roy has over his closest competition. For perspective, 38 playoff wins is two whole four-round Stanley Cup runs with six wins to spare.

Roy also has the most saves in Stanley Cup Playoff history with 6,559. Brodeur is a super distant second with 4,830, which is 1,729 saves behind Roy. If the gap of 1,729 saves between Roy and Brodeur was a completely separate goalie, it would still be 41st in all-time playoff saves. That's stupid.

In the 2001 Stanley Cup Final, Roy went head to head with Martin Brodeur as the Avalanche went to battle against the New Jersey Devils. Despite facing 178 shots in the 2001 Stanley Cup Final, a whole 32 more shots than Brodeur faced, Roy allowed just 11 goals to Brodeur's 19, the Avalanche won Game 7 by a score of 3–1, and Roy got his fourth and final Cup.

There's a decent argument to call Roy the best playoff goalie of all time. There's a massive asterisk, though. Roy's worst error, the Statue of Liberty–size mishap against the Detroit Red Wings in 2002, cost him and the Avalanche a shot at back-to-back Cups. In a tight series, Roy made a spectacular save in a tied game. Instead of simply covering the puck, he goes to raise his glove to the crowd, before accidentally dropping the puck for a wide-open tap-in for Detroit. The Avs go on to lose the series, the Red Wings go on to win the Cup, and the Avalanche wouldn't win another Cup until 2022, long after Roy's retirement.

Even though I absolutely hate this cliché, every goalie is going to have some goals they'd like to have back. Remember, I'm arming you for this debate, whether you're for or against Roy going on your goalie Mount Rushmore. Just know that if you talk bad about Patrick Roy, he can't really hear what you have to say, on account of the four Stanley Cup rings he has plugged in his ears.

TERRY SAWCHUK

STATISTICS

Record (Regular Season): 445–336–171

Record (Playoffs): 54–47

Regular Season Wins: 445 (8th)

Playoff Wins: 54 (19th)

Career Save Percentage (Regular Season): stat not tracked

Career Save Percentage (Playoffs): stat not tracked

Shutouts (Regular Season): 103 (2nd)

Shutouts (Playoffs): 12 (10th)

Saves (Regular Season): 16,678 (39th, despite stat not being tracked for the first 6 seasons of his career)

Saves (Playoffs): 2,328 (26th, again, despite missing his first 6 seasons)

Vezina Trophies: 4 (1952, 1953, 1955, 1965)

Other Trophies: Lester Patrick Trophy (1971), Calder Memorial Trophy (1951)

Stanley Cups: 4 (1952, 1954, 1955, 1967)

Before the likes of Patrick Roy, Martin Brodeur, and Dominik Hasek, the "best goalie of all time" conversation revolved around Terry Sawchuk. Heck, Sawchuk's last NHL game came before Ken Dryden's first, that's how old-school he is.

Sawchuk is the subject of one of the most iconic photos in the history of hockey, highlighting his scars from a career throwing his bare face in front of pucks on purpose. He also has one of the best resumes in the history of goaltending.

Sawchuk won four Stanley Cups. Three of those were with the

Detroit Red Wings, where he played most of his days, including back-to-back rings in 1954 and 1955. The fourth Cup was the legendary 1967 Stanley Cup with the Toronto Maple Leafs, where he split goaltending duties with another legend in Johnny Bower.

Terry Sawchuk became the first man to reach 100 shutouts in a career, setting the record at 103. That record stood for over four decades until Brodeur broke it 42 years later, in December 2009.

Before Sawchuk came along, George Hainsworth held the shutout record at 94. One important note: 49 of Hainsworth's shutouts, more than half of the shutouts he had in his career, came before the legalization of the forward pass in all three zones.

You can scoff at Sawchuk's numbers as a symptom of playing in a six-team league, but he went toe to toe with other giants of goaltending like Jacques Plante and Glenn Hall for most of his career. That, and nobody was particularly close to Sawchuk's shutout record for years. Sawchuk has 19 more career shutouts than Glenn Hall and 21 more than Plante.

It's been over half a century since Terry Sawchuk's final NHL game, and his numbers still hold up. It's up to you to decide if they hold up enough to earn him a spot on your goalie Mount Rushmore.

DOMINIK HASEK

STATISTICS

Record (Regular Season): 389–223–82, with 13 overtime/ shootout losses

Record (Playoffs): 65–49

Regular Season Wins: 389 (17th)

Playoff Wins: 65 (13th)

Career Save Percentage (Regular Season): .922

Career Save Percentage (Playoffs): .925

Shutouts (Regular Season): 81 (tied for 6th)

Shutouts (Playoffs): 14 (tied for 6th)

Saves (Regular Season): 18,648 (24th)

Saves (Playoffs): 3,037 (14th)

Vezina Trophies: 6 (1994, 1995, 1997, 1998, 1999, 2001)

Other Trophies: 2 Ted Lindsay (1997, 1998), 2 Hart (1997, 1998)

Stanley Cups: 2 (2002, 2008)

The dead puck era of the NHL doesn't get that name because it was fun to watch. It was slower, skewed to defence, and full of hooking and holding that would be called in each and every game in today's league, except for maybe an elimination game. In that NHL, the Dominator was must-see TV.

In the same way that Connor McDavid is a must-see today for his ability to score, you knew that when you tuned in to a game with Dominik Hasek, especially during his prime with the Buffalo Sabres, he wasn't just going to make routine saves. No, that was for mere mortals. Hasek would defy the laws of physics and the conventions of the human body in a way that would make you think the Czech Republic's number one export was pretzels.

Dominik Hasek would throw his body at pucks as if he was in a hostage situation and if he let just one puck get by him, some dastardly villain would blow up Gotham City. Hasek would hit you with the two-pad stack, you'd get a second chance, and he would fling his entire upper body the opposite direction and deny you with the back of his glove, the front of his blocker, or both if he had to. Nobody in the history of hockey has perfected the absolute chaos of making saves accidentally-on-purpose like Dominik Hasek.

The Chicago Blackhawks selected Hasek in the tenth round of the 1983 NHL Draft, 199th overall. Read that again if you need to, but there's no typo. Not only that, Hasek was the 17th goalie picked in 1983. Buffalo picked two goalies ahead of Hasek—Tom Barrasso and Daren Puppa—who combined for 1,206 NHL games. That could be worse. Both Boston and Calgary picked two goalies apiece ahead of Hasek in 1983, except none of the four of them played an NHL game. Besides the fact that goalies are often chosen with lower picks, in part because their development can be a bit harder to predict, this was 1983. According to EliteProspects .com, Hasek was just the 15th Czech-born player ever drafted into the NHL and the first ever Czech goalie drafted. The next Czech goalie to be drafted into the NHL wouldn't come until the Minnesota North Stars selected Roman Turek in 1990, which is seven years after Hasek was picked and still, somehow, before Hasek's first career NHL game. Wild.

The wildest thing about Hasek is he was a late bloomer of sorts. Despite being drafted in 1983, Hasek didn't make his NHL debut with the Blackhawks until five games into the 1990–91 season, eight years later. The next season, he was the backup to the Blackhawks' other hot young goalie, Ed Belfour. In his third NHL season, Hasek was traded to Buffalo for Stéphane Beauregard and a fourth-round pick, and he had an 11–10–4 record with an .896 save percentage in just 28 games.

And then in the 1993–94 season, as if flicking on a switch, Hasek decided, "Actually, I think I'm the best goalie in the world now."

Hasek won six of the eight Vezina Trophies as the NHL's best goalie between 1994 and 2001. His save percentage from the 1993-94 season through the 2000–01 season was a preposterous .928, which was the best in the NHL among goalies with more than two starts. The closest goalie with more than 100 games played over that stretch was Patrick Roy, with .915. During that stretch, Hasek's save percentage grew to .929, still better than Roy's .926. Nobody was even close to the Dominator.

Despite Hasek's six Vezinas in eight years, it's possible he could have won an inhuman eight in a row. In both 1996 and 2000, the only two seasons during that stretch where Hasek didn't win the Vezina, he had the highest save percentage among goalies who garnered at least one Vezina vote, but lost out due to a combination of injuries and a lacklustre Sabres team. The six Vezina Trophies Hasek *did* win tie him with Bill Durnan for the second most in NHL history.

Hasek became the first and only goalie to ever win back-to-back Hart Trophies as the league MVP. To me, this is where Hasek becomes undeniable in the all-time conversation. When Hasek won best goalie and league MVP in back-to-back seasons, he did so in an NHL where both Patrick Roy and Martin Brodeur were already well-established players. Brodeur had already won his first Stanley Cup and Roy had three. Roy and Brodeur have two of the best resumes in the history of goaltending, but Hasek was consistently better than both of them for most of a decade. That's dominance.

Hasek and the Czechs stunned Canada in the semifinal of the 1998 Olympics in Nagano, Japan, and then shut out the Russians in the gold medal game to bring the entire Czech Republic to its feet. Finally, in 2002, the season after Hasek's run of six Vezinas in eight seasons, he finally won his first Stanley Cup, in Detroit. He was also with Detroit in his final season for the 2008 Stanley Cup win, though largely as a backup.

The coulda-woulda-shoulda conversation can be a slippery slope, but most would agree it's more than fair with Hasek. He dragged the 1999 Buffalo Sabres to a berth in the Stanley Cup Final even though they only scored 59 goals in 23 playoff games that year (2.56 goals per game). Would Hasek have won at least one championship with Brodeur's Devils? My money is on yes. Would he have won at least one championship with Roy's Avalanche? I think so.

Is one Stanley Cup as a starter and another as a backup enough to be a part of the "best goalie of all time" conversation? Hasek's individual accolades might just put him over the top.

Bonus point for you, if you're ever having this debate with a Leafs fan and just want to bother them: Hasek won the first ever NHL shootout as a member of the Ottawa Senators in October 2005. Eric Lindros gave the Leafs the lead with 91 seconds to go, Daniel Alfredsson tied it just 29 seconds later, and then Hasek and company won it in the first ever NHL shootout.

GLENN HALL

STATISTICS

Record (Regular Season): 407–326–164
Record (Playoffs): 49–65
Regular Season Wins: 407 (11th)
Playoff Wins: 49 (Tied for 23rd)
Career Save Percentage (Regular Season): stat not tracked
Career Save Percentage (Playoffs): stat not tracked
Shutouts (Regular Season): 84 (4th)
Shutouts (Playoffs): 6 (Tied for 28th)
Saves (Regular Season): 24,611 (6th; the NHL did not track
    this stat for the first 8 games of his career)
Saves (Playoffs): 3,285 (9th)

Vezina Trophies: 3 (1963, 1967, 1969)
Other Trophies: Conn Smythe Trophy (1968), Calder
    Memorial Trophy (1956)
Stanley Cups: 2 (1952*, 1961)

* Hall did not play in the NHL during the 1951–52 season or
playoffs, but the Red Wings had his name engraved on the Cup as
their practice goalie that year)

This man started 502 games in a row. He won a bunch of awards and championships, too, but really, the whole argument for Hall could be: he started 502 games in a row. You can play with the phrasing and say, "He started 502 consecutive games" or whatever—but *the man started 502 games in a row.*

This is Glenn Hall, in his own words, from his profile on the NHL's website for the 100 Greatest NHL Players during the league's centennial season in 2017: "You have to be lucky to have a run like I had, and I was. Of course, you have to be a little bit crazy to play where I played, and I plead guilty on that count too."

You might scoff at Hall's streak by saying, "Yeah, but that was back in the day." Sure, he set that record a long time ago, but nobody else came close. Though the seasons Hall played were a bit shorter than they are today, he played in all 70 games in a season for seven consecutive seasons. During that stretch, which ran from the 1955–56 season through the end of 1961–62, Terry Sawchuk, Jacques Plante, Gump Worsley, and Al Rollins played all 70 games in a season just once each. Ed Chadwick of the Toronto Maple Leafs was the only other goaltender to do it more than once, and he only did it twice.

Since the 2012 lockout, do you know how many times a goalie has played 70 or more games in a single season? Four. That's it.

All three of Braden Holtby, Jonathan Quick, and Tuukka Rask did it in 2014–15, Cam Talbot did it during the 2016–17 season, and it's never happened since. These days, if a starting goalie, even a really hot one, starts getting around 60 games, we start ripping the coach for overworking them, or ripping the GM for not getting enough support in net.

Glenn Hall was a busy bee, to say the least. During that stretch from 1955 through to the end of 1962, Hall played 62 more games than any other goalie, faced nearly 1,200 more shots, and made nearly 1,100 more saves. Despite the workload, Hall had a .915 save percentage during that stretch. The only comparable two starting goalies during that time frame were Jacques Plante of the Montreal Canadiens (.921) and Johnny Bower of the Toronto Maple Leafs (.918). It's worth mentioning that Bower played less than half as many NHL games as Hall did during that stretch.

Hall wasn't out there just collecting a paycheque. He won the Calder as rookie of the year in 1956 and the Vezina Trophy in 1963, 1967, and late in his career in 1969. Hall even won the Conn Smythe as playoff MVP in 1968 despite the fact that his St. Louis Blues got swept by the Montreal Canadiens in the Stanley Cup Final. The reason for this is probably that Hall faced a whopping 151 shots in those four games while his counterpart, Gump Worsley, faced just 91. That's Hall facing 37.75 shots per game to Worsley's 22.75. Despite that, Hall's Blues only lost each game of the Final by just one goal, including overtime.

I'm sure I'll mention this a few times throughout this book, but from a purely historical context, the Habs basically ruin every statistic. They were so ridiculously good that losing four straight playoff games to them by just one goal is actually an accomplishment.

The knock against Hall being on the Mount Rushmore of goalies could be that during his seven-season stretch of playing every single game with Detroit and Chicago, he won more than half of his team's games only once, with 38 wins in 1957–58. If that stat seems wrong, just remember that ties still existed back then. He also had a whopping 91 ties during that stretch. You could argue that those games would have been more impressive as wins. You could also argue that without Hall, those 91 ties would have been losses.

While Hall might lack the whopping accolades of the other goalies on this list, he does still have his fair share. How you value Hall likely comes down to how much you value him playing 502 consecutive games—a record that will never be broken.

Side note: Man, some nerdy billionaire needs to pay a staff to go back in time and get all kinds of advanced stats and analytics from this era. Glenn Hall would be a wild case study.

JACQUES PLANTE

STATISTICS

Record (Regular Season): 437–246–145

Record (Playoffs): 71–36

Regular Season Wins: 437 (9th)

Playoff Wins: 71 (10th)

Career Save Percentage (Regular Season): stat not tracked

Career Save Percentage (Playoffs): stat not tracked

Shutouts (Regular Season): 82 (5th)

Shutouts (Playoffs): 14 (tied for 6th)

Saves (Regular Season): 20,889 (16th, despite this stat not
    being tracked for the first 3 seasons of his career)

Saves (Playoffs): 2,790 (19th)

Vezina Trophies: 7 (1956, 1957, 1958, 1959, 1960, 1962,
    1969)

Other Trophies: Hart Memorial Trophy (1962)

Stanley Cups: 6 (1953, 1956, 1957, 1958, 1959, 1960)

It's going to be difficult to talk about Jacques Plante's statistical accomplishments because I can't wrap my head around the fact that NHL goalies didn't use to wear masks. Right now you might be laughing off that fact, like, "Yeah, it was crazy back in the day." No. It wasn't just "back in the day." By the time Jacques Plante decided to become the first NHL goalie to regularly wear a face mask, the NHL had already been a league for 42 years.

That means for more than four decades, goalies were just standing there in front of vulcanized rubber pucks and getting blasted in the face. If we accept 1959 as the birth of the face mask in the NHL, then that means the goalie face mask had only been in the NHL for less than half of the league's history until 2002. That's the year youngsters like Tim Stützle and Seth Jarvis were born.

Andy Brown was the last goalie to not wear a face mask, in 1974. That was only 50 years ago! That means half of the NHL's history has featured maskless goalies. Wild.

Jacques Plante, after getting stitched up, had to argue with his coach, Toe Blake—mid-game, no less—just to be able to wear the thing. He was quoted on NHL.com: "'I told Toe I would only return if I could wear the mask, so there was no choice,' said Plante, who started wearing the mask during practices following an operation to deal with his sinusitis. 'He never wanted me to wear [it] because he thought it would make me too complacent.'"

It would make him too complacent? With *what*?

Beyond Plante's work pioneering the idea that getting your face broken kinda sucks and should be avoided, he was also a pretty good goalie. Plante had seven Vezinas, five of which were in a row from 1956 to 1960. You might be wondering, "Seven? Holy cow! What's the record?" It's seven. Plante holds the record for most Vezinas with seven. Plante also won six Stanley Cups, including five in a row that just so happened to be from 1956 to 1960.

If you're one of those people who grade the older players on a curve, maybe you dock points for Plante's career largely being in a six-team league. Is that fair? It's not like that's Plante's fault. At the same time, it seems relevant that there are 26 more teams today.

The question is: If Jacques Plante is on your goalie Mount Rushmore, does he go up there with or without the mask?

MARTIN BRODEUR

STATISTICS

Record (Regular Season): 691–397–105, with 49 overtime/
    shootout losses

Record (Playoffs): 113–91

Regular Season Wins: 691 (1st)

Playoff Wins: 113 (2nd)

Career Save Percentage (Regular Season): .912

Career Save Percentage (Playoffs): .919

Shutouts (Regular Season): 125 (1st)

Shutouts (Playoffs): 24 (1st)

Saves (Regular Season): 28,928 (1st)

Saves (Playoffs): 4,830 (2nd)

Vezina Trophies: 4 (2003, 2004, 2007, 2008)

Other Trophies: Calder Memorial Trophy (1994)
Stanley Cups: 3 (1995, 2000, 2003)

Being completely honest, for these next few paragraphs, prob-ably more than any others in this book, I wish I could see your reactions. Listen, Martin Brodeur being in this conversation shouldn't be controversial, but you might be surprised by how much it is.

Martin Brodeur has the most wins in NHL history, with 691. Patrick Roy is 140 wins behind him, with 551. If the gap between Brodeur and Roy was a goalie on its own, it would be tied for 152nd in NHL wins all time—ironically, with Trevor Kidd, the only goalie selected ahead of Brodeur in the 1990 NHL Draft. Send this paragraph to a Calgary Flames fan you don't like.

Martin Brodeur holds the NHL record for shutouts with 125. Terry Sawchuk is second all-time with 103 shutouts, which is 22 behind Brodeur. If the 22-shutout gap between Brodeur and Sawchuk was its own goalie, it would be tied for 116th all time with the likes of Billy Smith and Kirk McLean, one behind Ron Hextall, two behind Mike Richter, and just three behind Hall of Famer Grant Fuhr. After Brodeur and Sawchuk, only one other goalie has hit 90 shutouts, and outside of five additional guys, nobody has even reached 80.

If hardware is your thing, Brodeur has it. Like many others on this list, Brodeur won the Calder as rookie of the year. He won four out of five Vezina Trophies between 2003 and 2008 and could have potentially won five out of six if it weren't for the gosh darn 2004–05 lockout.

Here's where I have to pull the "I was there" card. For the most part, Roy, Hasek, and Brodeur were the goalies I grew up watch-ing throughout the 1990s. Even though Brodeur was absolutely spectacular, if you gave me a choice out of the three of them to play one game for a hockey team that had to win to save my life, Brodeur would be third. For me, the conversation is Roy or Hasek, then Brodeur.

What people often forget in the conversation with those three is the age gap between them. You could argue that both Roy and Hasek were better than Brodeur when all three of them were in the league at the same time, but you could also argue that's because they should have been. Roy and Hasek were both born in 1965; Brodeur was born in 1972. The fact that Hasek was a late bloomer, along with the fact he played well into his forties, might trick you into thinking Hasek and Brodeur are the same age. Nope.

Roy got the best of Brodeur in the 2001 Stanley Cup Final. Hasek finally got his Cup in 2002. After that, Brodeur ran the show with a Cup in 2003 and a streak of four Vezina Trophies in five seasons. With Roy and Hasek basically aged out, the Vezina Trophy could have just been renamed after Brodeur.

One of the other knocks on Brodeur is that he played behind one of the best defence pairings in NHL history in Scott Niedermayer and Scott Stevens, strengthened further still by the smothering trap style that would define the dead puck era.

Can the coulda-woulda-shoulda conversation work in reverse? Would Brodeur have won three Cups if he were a member of the 1990s Buffalo Sabres instead? My money is on probably not, but we'll never know. Then again, even as his regular season save percentages began to fall off, Brodeur and the Devils still made it to the 2012 Stanley Cup Final with no Stevens or Niedermayer in sight.

Strong peak, longevity, records, individual accolades, and championships. You don't have to put Martin Brodeur on your goalie Mount Rushmore, but his presence in the conversation is undeniable.

Some of you are probably reading this right now thinking, *You're nuts if you leave Brodeur off the goalie Mount Rushmore!* You'd be surprised, especially with younger hockey fans, anecdotally. Brodeur played more recently, and when he did, he was older and nowhere near as dominant. As with the goalies that came before Brodeur, sometimes the legend of a player keeps evolving long after they're done playing.

KEN DRYDEN

STATISTICS

Record (Regular Season): 258–57–74

Record (Playoffs): 80–32

Regular Season Wins: 258 (62nd)

Playoff Wins: 80 (7th)

Career Save Percentage (Regular Season): .922

Career Save Percentage (Playoffs): .915

Shutouts (Regular Season): 46 (tied for 34th)

Shutouts (Playoffs): 10 (tied for 12th)

Saves (Regular Season): 10,213 (107th)

Saves (Playoffs): 2,953 (16th)

Vezina Trophies: 5 (1973, 1976, 1977, 1978, 1979)

Other Trophies: Conn Smythe Trophy (1971), Calder
    Memorial Trophy (1972)

Stanley Cups: 6 (1971, 1973, 1976, 1977, 1978, 1979)

Some of the arguments for goalies on this list will skew to a strong peak. Ken Dryden has the most juiced-up, undeniable peak of any goalie, ever. The difference is that even though Dryden's peak burned white hot, it was the blink of an eye in hockey terms.

Among the goalies we've talked about, you might have noticed Dryden doesn't even come close to the all-time best in regular season wins; with just 258, he's only good enough for 62nd.

For Dryden's legacy, percentage is everything. Dryden won just shy of 65 per cent of the regular season games he ever played. He lost barely over 14 per cent of his career regular season games. He had 17 more career ties than he had career losses.

Going up against Ken Dryden in the playoffs was basically a death sentence. He won 80 of his 112 career playoff starts, which is over 71 per cent. If that sounds good enough to win a Cup or two, you're close—he won six: 1971, 1973, and four straight from 1976 to 1979.

Dryden only lost back-to-back games in the playoffs seven times in his entire career. You know what's even crazier? He lost those seven back-to-backs over the course of six different playoff series and ended up winning four of them. Even his losses are impressive.

Did I mention Dryden did this while studying law? He even used that to his advantage. Prior to the 1973–74 season, Dryden discovered that despite being one of the most dominant goalies in the league, he certainly wasn't paid like it. A contract dispute with the Canadiens ensued, and Dryden simply retired and went to work at a law firm in Toronto.

Can you imagine if, after winning the Stanley Cup in 2020, instead of going for a repeat, Andrei Vasilevskiy got into a contract dispute with the Tampa Bay Lightning and was just like, "That's fine, I'll just start articling for a law firm." That's what happened.

Without Dryden, the Canadiens lost in six games to the New York Rangers in the first round of the 1974 Stanley Cup Playoffs.

As you might have figured out by now, Dryden came back to hockey, returned to the Habs' net, and after a warmup season in 1975, went on to dominate the league with four straight Cups.

Ken Dryden and the Montreal Canadiens went 48–10 in the playoffs during their run of four straight Cups in the late 1970s. I mean, if you cheered for whoever the Habs were playing, why even show up to the rink? Why even bother to buy a ticket, throw on a sweater, ride on transit, or sit in traffic when your team has less than an 18 per cent chance of winning?

Dryden lost one game out of 13 in the 1976 playoffs. His loss total doubled the next year with two. It tripled in 1978 with three. In 1979, Dryden won his sixth Stanley Cup and his fourth straight, but he also lost four games out of 16. I guess with such a dismal downhill track, he thought, *Ah, heck, I might as well retire again.*

In his retirement, Dryden took up the casual hobby of, let me check my notes, becoming the president of the Toronto Maple Leafs for six years before serving as a Member of Parliament in the Canadian government from 2004 to 2011.

The only thing you can knock in Dryden's bid to be on the Mount Rushmore of goalies is that he played fewer than 400 regular season games. With the exception of Dominik Hasek, Dryden played less than half as many games as every other goalie on this list played. He played less than one-third of the games Brodeur played. Even Hasek played 338 more games than Dryden.

One thing about Dryden's retirement I'm not suspicious of but I do think is kind of funny: he retired the season before Wayne Gretzky entered the league. How would Ken Dryden have performed in the high-flying, high-scoring 1980s with the dynasty New York Islanders and Edmonton Oilers? Would Patrick Roy and the Canadiens have won a Cup in 1986 if Dryden was still in the picture? Would the Habs have even drafted Roy? Maybe Dryden retired right on time.

Oh, I almost forgot! Dryden was also Canada's goalie during this little thing called the 1972 Summit Series against the Soviet Union. You might remember Paul Henderson's legendary goal to seal the game late for Canada, tucking the puck into the Soviet net. The goalie at the opposite end of the rink, standing tall and victorious: Dryden. It's ridiculous to think that Dryden's role in Canada's historic victory during that series is so vital to hockey historically, but his NHL resume is so undeniable on its own that he would find his way into this conversation even if he had never beaten the Soviets. That being said—he beat the Soviets.

Whether Ken Dryden cracks your Mount Rushmore of goalies or not, nobody can accuse him of living a boring life.

BUT WHAT ABOUT

Now, some of you might be a little upset with me because I've named the seven goalies in the goalie Mount Rushmore conversation and I've left your favourite off the list. I already know some of the guys you're going to name, and they're all incredible, some of the best to ever do it; I just don't think they're in the conversation of top four.

Grant Fuhr is probably the most disrespected Hockey Hall of Famer ever. His save percentage numbers don't hold up to many of his fellow greats, that's true. He played 19 seasons in the NHL and had a save percentage above 90 per cent in just two of them, both with the St. Louis Blues as goals started to dip in the mid-1990s league-wide. It's often held against Fuhr that he got to play behind the Gretzky-era Edmonton Oilers. So? He still won his championships and is still a member of the Hockey Hall of Fame. Grant Fuhr is a legend, he just doesn't squeak onto this list for me.

Two of the greats of the 1970s didn't make my list of seven: Tony Esposito and Bernie Parent. Esposito won the Calder, three Vezinas, and one Stanley Cup, while Parent won two Vezinas, two Conn Smythes, and two Stanley Cups. Both of their resumes are incredible in league history; this is just a very short and nearly impossible list to crack.

Vladislav Tretiak came up in several all-time conversations. After all, his resume is littered with international accolades and all sorts of Soviet/USSR honours. This might be harsh, but an argument against him is that he never played in the NHL. That's obviously due to the politics of the time, but it's hard to justify kicking out goalies who played the majority of their professional careers in the best professional league in the world to admit a player who we can only guess how well he would have performed in that league.

Johnny Bower is a tough one to leave off. Beyond being a great goalie, he was a kind and gentle soul I had the pleasure of meeting twice before he passed. Bower spent so much of his career in the minors before becoming a mainstay with the Toronto Maple Leafs in the late 1950s. With a pair of Vezinas and a handful of Stanley Cups, had Bower gotten his big-league opportunity sooner, maybe he would be on the list. The competition is just too stacked.

Ed Belfour and Curtis Joseph fall into a similar category. Both were stupendous, both stole games and even playoff series, and both have their name on the Cup. They just don't quite live up to the outlandish resumes of others from their era. Even Chris Osgood, who also has lots of wins and several championships, doesn't quite stack up. Again, this isn't an insult to them. We're trying to nail down the top four goalies ever.

Roberto Luongo is heartbreaking. As a fan of a Canadian team whose primary colour is blue, who is regularly startled awake at night by nightmares caused by traumatic losses in Game 7 against the Bruins, I have a soft spot for Bobby Lu. Luongo is up there in so many categories, including saves and wins, but never got a Stanley Cup. Whose fault is that? The Vancouver Canucks? No. Well, yes, but the Florida Panthers' end of it drives me nuts. Luongo played six playoff games in parts of 11 seasons with the Panthers. He gave the Panthers a save percentage of .920 or better six times, and that's all they could get him. Unforgivable.

Henrik Lundqvist is a tough one. He was, year in and year out, one of the best goalies of his generation and did basically everything except win the Cup. Like Luongo, Lundqvist played behind some teams that probably wouldn't have gotten nearly as far without him, but that's the goalie's job, unfortunately. He was a fantastic goalie, but he's in the conversation for top four of his era, not top four of all time.

Carey Price is an agonizing one. On top of his Vezinas, Price captured a rare Hart Trophy as league MVP, as well. Remember when the NHL was creating the Covid bubble in 2020? Rumours swirled that the Pittsburgh Penguins wanted no part of the Montreal Canadiens, despite the fact the Habs were nowhere near the Penguins in the standings, solely because of Carey Price. It turns out they were right, by the way, as the Habs beat the Penguins after all, including a 22-save shutout from Price in the deciding game.

Were it not for Chris Kreider crashing into Price's knee, there's a good chance Price and the Habs win a Cup that year. Who knows? Maybe there could have been more, including in 2021, when he dragged an unlikely Habs team to a berth in the Stanley

Cup Final. If Price's career wasn't cut short so prematurely due to injuries, there's a chance he cracks the list. Unfortunately, we can only guess what extra magic he had in him.

Finally, a bit of an asterisk: there's a really, and I mean *really*, good chance Andrei Vasilevskiy ends up on goalie Mount Rushmore one day. He's consistently playing more than 60 games a season when the world isn't in a pandemic. He's consistently winning over 30 games, with a career high of 44. His save percentage is consistently among the league's best. He already has one Vezina, one Conn Smythe, and two Stanley Cups to his name, including back-to-back rings. Vasilevskiy has already passed Dominik Hasek to move into 12th in all-time playoff wins, with 66, and he's barely 30 years old. His story is still being written, so it would be premature to add him to Rushmore now, but we're watching an all-timer in the making.

—

I said I'd give you my four for goalie Mount Rushmore, but understand this: I reserve the right to change my mind about it the next time I go to the bar.

1. **Patrick Roy:** Three Conn Smythes is ridiculous, and his playoff accolades may never be beaten.
2. **Dominik Hasek:** The most dominant goalie I ever watched. Claiming six Vezinas in an era as stacked with goaltending as his was is absurd. Two MVP trophies to boot.
3. **Martin Brodeur:** I know, I know, but his resume is too undeniable. Maybe he hung around a bit too long, but Vezinas in five seasons in a league with 30 teams is too much to ignore.

4. **Jacques Plante:** This one was extremely difficult, but I
   think Plante's resume definitely gets him into the conversation, and the fact that he pioneered goalie masks
   puts him over the edge. Being the first to do something
   is hard, and for whatever reason, even today, being the
   first to do something in hockey takes a special kind of
   bravery.

That's my goalie Mount Rushmore. I'm sure you have your
own, so please type it at me in all-caps on social media, or at very
least scream it at your friends next time you're together. And remember, if your Rushmore contains any goalies not included on
the list of seven here, you're just plain wrong.

9.

Fight Me

When it comes to hockey, there's nothing people fight about more than fighting. Maybe this should have been the first chapter. No self-respecting book about hockey arguments can go far without discussing whether or not fighting belongs in hockey.

Generally speaking, there are two sides of this argument:

1. There should no longer be any fighting in hockey because it serves no athletic purpose in the sport, and there is growing evidence that repeated traumatic blows to the head causes chronic traumatic encephalopathy (CTE) of the brain, irreparably damaging a person at the core of who they are, ruining lives and families in the process.
2. I like fighting.

Before you slam the book shut, I'm not here to take the moral high ground on this subject. I grew up watching hockey in the 1990s and early 2000s, and I loved it. I used to get Don Cherry's *Rock 'Em Sock 'Em* VHS tapes every Christmas, and I would watch bone-crushing hits and slobber-knocking collisions until the VCR got hot.

I'm not about to tell you I lost a certain kind of love for that as an adult, either. When a player gets laid out with a dirty hit or taken out with a two-handed slash, I expect the coach to bring a rag with the offending player's scent on it over to the biggest, meanest, toughest guy on the team and sic that enforcer like a hunting dog on that dirty little rat who hurt our guy. I'm not going to lie, when nobody from the team stands up for the guy who got hurt, I judge them for it. I'm betting you do, too, even if you keep it to yourself.

We should address the idea that fighting is used to "fire up the boys" or "get the bench going." I used to think that was all nonsense. I used to think, *Hey, you're a millionaire getting paid to play a sport in front of thousands of fans. If you're not already motivated and need something external like a fight to light your fire, then maybe you're in the wrong business.* I still think there's a hint of truth to that, but for the most part, now I think it's a bit of an ignorant take. I've listened to countless NHL players say that it's true and watched them all lose their minds on the bench when their teammate dummies a guy. I don't think anybody will deny that fighting brings out the caveman in a lot of us.

What do I want to happen? Nothing crazy. Like, say, somebody to grab a player by the scruff of their jersey and punch them unconscious from behind, like Todd Bertuzzi did to Steve Moore two decades ago. Let's recap what happened there because the Bertuzzi-Moore incident is what happens when it all gets out of hand.

Earlier in the 2003–04 season, Colorado Avalanche forward Steve Moore laid a hit on Vancouver Canucks star and captain Markus Naslund that connected badly with Naslund's head. Everyone expected the Canucks to demand their pound of flesh. They didn't like the hit, and they didn't like who the hit was on.

Naturally, on March 8, 2004, Steve Moore had to pay the piper. He had to fight Canucks agitator Matt Cooke in the first period. They both went to the box for five minutes, and in hockey terms, this is pretty much how it's supposed to go. You cross the line, you drop the gloves, ideally nice and early in the game to get it over with, you take your lumps, and both teams move on. Well, I mean, your teams and fanbases probably still hate each other, which, let's be honest, makes any game more compelling, but that specific issue is dealt with.

But what actually happened? Four fights, including one featuring Steve Moore, in just the first period. There were 20 penalties *before* the infamous Bertuzzi-Moore incident happened in the third period, including eight fighting majors and one ten-minute misconduct. But the score of the game got out of hand, as well. It didn't help that Moore scored to make it 5-0 for Colorado. As a result, Bertuzzi and the Canucks decided there was more to work out between the teams.

Bertuzzi followed Moore around the ice, grabbed him by the jersey, and sucker-punched him in the back of the head, knocking him unconscious. Moore never played another NHL game. The argument has been made that Moore's ensuing neck injury wasn't from the punch, but rather the massive dogpile that ensued after it. But the pile happened because of the punch! Did you expect Moore's Avalanche teammates to stand there and do nothing?

So let me ask: Is that what we want in the NHL? Is that what we want in hockey?

"Well, no, I wouldn't go that far," you're likely saying to yourself. "That's insane!" I'm sure there are still people who think that was just a regular game, and sadly, accidents happen. But with a couple of decades of hindsight, I'm thinking most hockey fans on all sides of the fighting debate can look back on that and say, "Yeah, that was a bit much."

But if we, or at very least I, want to see a team stick up for their player with a fight, aren't I asking for the exact same sort of thing as the Bertuzzi-Moore incident to happen? No, of course I'm not. Except actually, maybe I sort of am?

And this is how it all goes in circles.

If somebody on Team A hurts somebody on Team B, and I expect somebody on Team B to get some form of retribution on the offending player from Team A, aren't I signing up for what happened in the Bertuzzi-Moore incident? Maybe even condoning it, directly or indirectly?

"Of course not!" you might exclaim. You're not asking your team's tough guys to run around out there sucker-punching players or injuring them on purpose. That would be ridiculous! You're just asking for clean, one-on-one, mutually agreed-upon combat between two willing professionals.

Except every single time two hockey players on the ice, or two people anywhere, get into a fist fight, there's a chance one of those people could be knocked out, or worse. Maybe it's a bit less likely that somebody's going to be knocked out from a flush bare-knuckle punch to the face than they are to be knocked out by a giant glove-on sucker-punch, but the chance for disaster is still very much there.

One of the most hypocritical things you might hear on a hockey broadcast is when two players get into a fight and one of them gets knocked out cold. That's when you might hear the broadcaster say something to the effect of "You certainly never want to see that."

First of all, that's just not true. Turn the camera back to the stands and you'll find some fans still frothing at the mouth like sick raccoons. Maybe you didn't buy a ticket to see somebody get knocked out tonight, but they sure did. And even if you don't like it, whenever you see a hockey game, you are very much signing up to at least potentially watch somebody get knocked out in a fight.

Obviously, hockey is a contact sport and accidents are going to happen. I've been in the building for players getting a stick in the eye, players taking a slapshot off the helmet, and even players getting stretchered off after a massive hit. All of them were accidents, and it was the negligence of the offending player rather than violence that caused the injury.

Fighting is different. Hockey fans often debate when it will be banned in hockey, if ever. You know what muddies the water? It *is* banned. It's always been banned! You ever notice how whenever there's a fight in a hockey game they drag the players who fought to the penalty box? That's because you're not allowed to do it.

Except you sort of are. It's only half-banned. You get five minutes in the penalty box for fighting because it's a major penalty, but the vast majority of the time, unless it's late in the third period of a game that's gotten out of hand, the two players who fought are allowed to rejoin the game once their penalty has expired.

So many things about the NHL's relationship with violence are made-up nonsense. Fighting is bad enough to warrant a five-minute major penalty, but not serious enough to have you ejected from a game. A lot of major penalties, although not all, involve kicking a player out of a game. Heck, a ref will eject players if there's about five or so minutes left in the game and it looks like you're thinking about fighting. In some instances, the penalty for thinking about fighting is worse than the penalty for actually fighting!

Then there's the instigator penalty. If you happen to be reading this and you're new to hockey, find the nearest Canadian who's about 45 years of age or older and ask them what they think of the instigator penalty, if you need to kill half an hour or so.

The two-minute instigator penalty gets handed out when you instigate a fight. This doesn't make any sense to me, but not for the reason you might think. When there's a fight between two players, and one of them was the instigator, both players still get five minutes for fighting. Why is the player getting attacked by the instigator penalized for defending themselves? If someone skates after you with their gloves off, what are you supposed to do? Calmly ask them to take a few breaths and think this through? No, they're going to defend themselves. Maybe they can take the next five minutes alone in the penalty box to sit and wonder what the hell they were supposed to do other than get repeatedly punched in the face. Hot take: if one player jumps another, the player who's just defending himself should get off scot-free. Tell that one to your uncle and see what he says.

When the instigator penalty was implemented in the NHL, a lot of hockey lifers openly hated it. It would result in the rats of the league, the dirtiest players in the sport, taking over the game.

But when you think about it another way, that's just whining about not being able to attack an unwilling combatant, isn't it?

And yet again, I find myself having a hypocritical opinion on fighting in hockey. If an opponent starts running around and laying chippy hits on my team's players, do I want someone on my team to go after that person and fight them? Yes.

Do I want the player on the other team to agree to fight the guy on my team? Yes, again.

Do I want the player on my team to get an extra penalty if the player on the other team is too much of a cowardly turtle to answer the bell and fight? No. Sometimes an instigator penalty is handed out if there are two willing combatants anyway. Here's one: if you turtle, that should be a penalty, too. Tell that one to your uncle and see what he says.

Do I think that a player should be penalized for attacking an unwilling combatant? Yes! In any other situation in society, you're going to jail for that. Imagine how crazy you would sound if someone bumped into you with their cart at the grocery store, you started wailing on them with punches, and you tried justifying it by saying, "But they bumped me with their cart." They'd add time onto your sentence!

Do I want the guy on my team to win the fight? Of course I do! Why wouldn't I?

Do I want the guy on the other team to get knocked out and stretchered off? Of course I don't! That's barbaric!

My guess is that if we search ourselves, a lot of hockey fans will discover they have conflicting opinions about fighting.

The idea that the instigator penalty could be a bad thing that allows dirty players to run around and do whatever they want isn't completely without merit. It's easier to lay a hit, whether it's clean or dirty, when you know that nobody is allowed to fly over and start raining down punches, and if they do, at least they'll be punished for it and your team gets an advantage.

You can sit there and say, "Well, then it's on the referees to make sure they punish players who lay dirty hits and commit all kinds of cheap shots." That's a beautiful thought. That's the kind of pure, naive innocence I would expect to see in a child's eyes as they tear open presents on Christmas morning. Unfortunately, simply hoping that a referee is going to call the penalty that you want is a fool's errand.

"Well, if the referees can't handle it, then surely the league can. They have cameras, don't they? Why not just hit dirty players with a suspension after the fact?"

Oh, my sweet summer child.

According to ScoutingTheRefs.com, an absolutely excellent

resource if you want to learn more about NHL officials and officiating in general, there were only 20 suspensions handed out
across the entire NHL through the whole 2022–23 season, and
not one of them was more than three games. For reference, that's
about 3.6 per cent of the season.

In addition to the 20 suspensions, the NHL Department of
Player Safety handed out 34 fines to players. Not one of those
fines was over $5,000. Do you know why? Because that's the max-
imum allowable fine under the collective bargaining agreement.
Why is there a maximum fine? To protect the players' bank accounts. Why are those fines there in the first place? To protect the
players' bodies. Which one do you think seems to be the priority
in this scenario?

The NHL is barely going to punish somebody for crushing
you with a knee-on-knee hit that keeps you out of the lineup for
months and requires surgery. Your own players' union bargained
to have a $5,000 maximum fine for somebody cross-checking you
in the teeth. Referees are going to miss guys hacking and slashing
you, and sometimes even when they don't, they might have decided that tonight's a night where they're going to "let the players
play" and put the whistles away.

Side note: There were two $25,000 fines handed out in the
2022–23 season, but they both went against head coaches being
mean to officials with words. Pause for laughter.

So the league probably isn't going to protect you, your own
union is barely going to protect you, the guys in charge of officiating the game aren't going to protect you. Who's left? You. You can
protect you. You and ten knuckles.

Should fighting be taken out of hockey? Yeah, probably! People are going to get hurt if it isn't. Also, if you're an NHL player
and you know nobody except you is going to protect you or your

teammates, would you fight to defend yourself? Yeah, you would! Otherwise, someone might get hurt.

I'm not saying there's a right or a wrong in this debate. If you want fighting to stay in hockey, I don't think you're a knuckle-dragging caveman. If you want to take fighting out of hockey, I don't think you're a soft bleeding-heart. I don't think fighting in professional hockey has an easy answer.

One thing I'm willing to take a harder line on is fighting in junior hockey. I didn't see the big deal when I was the same age as those guys. I only started to understand when I got a little older. Now I'm in my thirties, and the idea of cheering for a bunch of teenagers beating each other up weirds me out. I just can't do it.

In the Ontario Hockey League, one of the three major junior leagues, fighting still happens, but once you reach a certain number of fights, it results in a suspension as of the rule change in 2012. That seems reasonable enough. Maybe that's the way to go. But we all know what that's eventually heading toward: banning fighting altogether. That's already started, by the way. In 2023, the Quebec Major Junior Hockey League made it so that players who fight are ejected from the game, and players who instigate a fight are assessed an automatic one-game suspension.

If kids aren't fighting in minor hockey, and they can't fight in some major junior leagues and in university hockey, you might not even have to officially ban it altogether. Fighting will just fade away. Maybe that's already begun. Let's be honest, it has.

Today, would I ban fighting from the NHL, or at least assess something more than a five-minute penalty? Probably not. What I would consider, though, is kicking players who fight out of the game, because it's wild to me that you can trade punches with a guy, possibly more than once in a single night, get a nice relaxing time out, and stay in the game like it never happened.

If the pro-fighting crowd want to take any comfort, fighting is going to be a part of hockey long after it's finally banned altogether. You can't fight in baseball, but fights still happen. You can't fight in basketball, but it happens there, too. Even in football, another contact sport, fighting isn't allowed but still happens. Sure, the punishments for fighting are far stiffer in those sports, but knuckles still get chucked from time to time.

This is going to end with the eventual banning of fighting in hockey games; it's just a matter of time. I don't know how we'll look back on old hockey fights once we're all a bit older, but we're going to live to see a day when five minutes for fighting is a thing of the past. My guess is it'll be like high school: you'll look back on some moments fondly, but you're going to cringe a lot, too.

Fighting's days are numbered, but rightly or wrongly, there will still be a few bells rung before the final bell rings.

10.

What Kind of Fan Are You?

It's time that we figure out what kind of a fan you are. "But I'm already a Calgary Flames fan," you might say. Whoa, whoa, whoa, now. Settle down there, tiger. Let's walk before we run here.

If you've picked up this book, odds are you've already been following hockey for at least a little while and you probably already have a team. That, or you're the world's most disappointed porch pirate. I know this isn't the iPad you wanted, but that's what you get for stealing somebody's book off their front step.

Before we pick a specific team, let's figure out a little bit more about you as a person. What are your priorities? What are your tendencies? Do you like playing video games on easy mode or super difficulty? On a scale of one through ten, roughly how pissed off would you be if the team you cheer for were to lose a game against one of your team's own employees in their forties?

We're gonna look through your soul, beyond hockey, beyond sports, even, and find out who you really are. You need to ask yourself what kind of things are important to you as a fan.

Here are the types of fan you can be, ranked from easiest to most agonizing.

CHEER FOR THE LOCAL TEAM

One simple way to be a fan on easy mode is to cheer for the home team. Whether you live in or near the city you were born in or you've moved there as a transplant, nobody is going to bat an eye if you cheer for the team that's local to you.

How did you start cheering for this team? You don't know, you just kind of did. Maybe your mom or dad or best friend cheered for them, too, and you just joined the parade. Some people are born to cheer for who they cheer for, and that's you.

The best part? Even if you're a little late to the game and you've spent most of your life without a team to cheer for, you get to bond with fans over stories and what's important to them. No hockey fan can wait to tell you about their favourite memories with the team they love most. A lot of them, myself included, are even more passionate when talking about their least favourite memories with their team. You're finding fans who turn into friends, and friends who turn into fans.

Want to watch your team live and in person? I have great news for you! They're just a hop, skip, and a jump away. The easiest, simplest decision you could possibly make is to cheer for the local team and take it from there.

SUCCESS

This is playing hockey fandom on easy mode: just pick the team with the most wins. That seems like a no-brainer, but you have to ask the right questions.

If you ask, "Who has the most Stanley Cup wins?" you would

think that's an easy path to the best teams in the league. It's a bit more complicated than that. The Montreal Canadiens have the most Stanley Cups in league history by a wide margin, with 24, but they haven't won a championship since 1993. Their most recent appearance in the Cup Final was in 2021, but what has followed can only be described as a full-blown rebuild.

The Toronto Maple Leafs are in second place, with 13 Stanley Cups, and in recent memory they've done very well during the regular season. Has that led them to consistent playoff success? Ah, you must be new here. The Leafs' most recent Stanley Cup win and Stanley Cup Final appearance were both in 1967. Toronto's most recent appearance in the final four was in 2002.

You'll want to walk the fine line between recent success and ancient history with great caution. Ironically, one of the NHL's most consistently successful teams in recent memory is one of its youngest: the Vegas Golden Knights. Vegas made it to the Stanley Cup Final in their inaugural expansion season, to the final four during the Covid bubble in their third season, and won the Stanley Cup for the first time in just their sixth season.

Looking for a team with a successful history does not necessarily mean you've found a team with a successful future. You could find a team with a championship or two over the past couple of decades, but if you weren't a fan at the time, it might not hit the same in retrospect. So many of the teams with winning records over the past decade or so—the Pittsburgh Penguins, the Washington Capitals, the Chicago Blackhawks—are all in varying stages of taking their last gasp at a long playoff run, rebuilding their empire, or tearing it down altogether.

Even if you did find a team that regularly puts together strong squads over extended periods of time, like the Boston Bruins, you never know when that will flip on its head. Whether a team exec-utive's ideas go stale or a franchise legend retires, you can't predict what tomorrow holds and how your new team will adapt.

I'm a Leafs fan, and as such I'm sure a lot of you figure my advice is good for toilet paper. But if you're a new fan, hear this: if losing is a deal-breaker for you, I have bad news about watching sports. You can't win 'em all.

HISTORY

As long as you're okay with your new-found team letting you down on occasion in the present, the past can be a wonderful thing. I know I just argued that past victories that happened before you were a fan won't hit as hard for you, and that's still true. Does it matter, though?

Half of fandom is talking to people, whether you're commis-erating, debating, celebrating, or reminiscing. If you have time to kill, find a fan of your new team, tell them you're new, and start to ask questions. Depending on the fan you find, you could kill a whole work day, go home, come back, and the first thing they'll tell you about in the morning is stuff they realized they forgot to tell you yesterday.

"Who was the best player in franchise history" is a surprisingly different question than "Who was your favourite player growing up?" even if both of those players are the same person. If you ask who the best player in your new favourite team's history was, a fan will tell you about how important that player was to the team. If you ask a fan who their favourite player was growing up, they'll tell you why that player was important to them. That might not seem like a big difference, but it makes all the difference in the world.

A fan's favourite player is their link to their childhood, to their friends, their family, or some of their most cherished memories from any age, young or old. Ask a fan about their favourite player and you can see an ocean of memories behind their eyes like a rising tide. You're instantly transported to moments in time—at home in their living room, out at a pub, or even there in the building as the action is happening—moments when they felt truly happy.

Ask a fan why a particular player was their favourite, and they'll never just say, "Because they scored the most goals" and leave it at that. Odds are they won't be able to give you an answer without a smile on their face. Something that player did resonated with that fan, whether it was their tenacity, their skill, their work ethic, their swagger, their cheek, their style, or their kindness. Whatever it was, it left a lasting impression that will stay longer than any banner.

The best part is you can do this over and over again. Every fan's story, their history with their team, is different from another's.

Ask fans of the Vegas Golden Knights. It doesn't take long for a team to gain a history. It doesn't take long to make memories that last a lifetime.

UNDERDOG

Who doesn't love cheering for the underdog? Everybody loves it! At first.

Underdogs aren't considered as such because they win all the time. If they did, they'd stop being underdogs. No, underdogs earn their name by being the least likely to win, or at very least, disadvantaged for a variety of reasons. These reasons often come down to finances: your team just can't spend as much money as other teams. This tends to be a bigger issue in other sports, like soccer, but even though the NHL has a salary cap, the teams who spend the most still often do the best.

Screw it, though. Who wants to cheer for a team that wins all the time, anyway? You know what a little losing does for a person? It builds character. It toughens you up. It strengthens your resolve. All right, fine, maybe you cry a little bit in the shower. But crying is good for you! I think? A little bit, right? Let it all out. You sweat when you work out, right? Okay, well, tears are just emotional sweat. I didn't google if that's how any of this works, but just trust me.

Why cheer for the Toronto Maple Leafs when you could cheer for the Ottawa Senators, the smaller team, in a smaller city, in the same province? We could even lump the Buffalo Sabres into this conversation, a team that, despite having one of the most passionate fanbases in the league, can barely outnumber out-of-towner Leafs fans during home games.

Why cheer for the New York Rangers when you could simply cheer for the New York Islanders, New Jersey Devils, or basically any other team in the Metropolitan Division?

Why not cheer for Utah's new NHL team, which is technically just the Arizona Coyotes except now they play in a building with seats in it? If you're starting your hockey fandom from scratch, you might as well start with a team that's pretty much starting from scratch, too.

Heck, you could even cheer for the Winnipeg Jets, a market that lost their team to Arizona (who lost their team to Utah), only to get a team back after a couple of decades, in one of the smallest but loudest buildings in the league.

Then there's what we'll call the "Day-Walker" of underdog

teams: Boston. For hockey purposes, I do specifically mean the Boston Bruins, but Boston as a sports market, no matter how often they win championships, has convinced itself it's always the underdog.

You can kind of see where it comes from. Despite having a great metropolitan area of millions of people, Boston proper has less than 700,000 residents. The Boston Celtics' most historic rival is the LA Lakers, a team in one of the biggest cities on the continent, with whom the Celtics are tied for the most championships in NBA history. The Boston Red Sox's greatest rival is the New York Yankees, who have the most championships in the history of baseball. And the Boston Bruins' most historic rival is the Montreal Canadiens, who might not play in the biggest city in the world, but they have the most championships in NHL history. Pretty much across the board, when it comes to sports, Boston has almost always had to punch up at their rivals.

That being said, the Bruins' owner, Jeremy Jacobs, is one of the most powerful people in the sport, and a lot of the Bostonian teams I've mentioned have sizable budgets. Does that matter? Well, that depends: Does your team have to *be* an underdog or is it enough that they *feel* like an underdog, no matter how much they win?

Underdogs aren't supposed to win. When they do, there's a special added rarity to the feeling of winning a championship. Sure, another team might have their championships, but ours are better.

Every Goliath wants to be perceived as David. Have you ever watched that documentary *The Last Dance*? They made that thing so well that even though I knew who won in the end, I spent half the documentary thinking Michael Jordan's Chicago Bulls were going to lose. The storyline of "this team was incredible and simply kicked everybody's ass" isn't interesting. One of the ways to make a victory story compelling is by explaining how they almost lost.

If an underdog team is what you're after, you'll have no trouble finding one. Even if you don't pick one, you might be able to convince yourself you did.

CHEER AGAINST THE LOCAL TEAM

All right, now we're getting into some sick-puppy stuff. Cheering for the local team is easy. Bonding with fans over the local team is easy. Cheering against them? This is fandom on maximum difficulty.

You know sports are supposed to be fun, right? Like, you're getting into the fandom of a certain team for, ideally, an enjoyable experience, aren't you? Then why are you cheering *against* the team that everybody around you loves?

If you've ever been to a bar or pub, there's almost always chicken wings on the menu and there's almost always a sauce flavour called something like "Mouth Arson," "Intestine Inferno," or "You're Gonna Die," and you think to yourself, *Who the hell is ordering that?* Yet it's always on the menu. You know why? Some people just like Mouth Arson.

People like cheering against whatever the local team is for the same reason people like eating chicken wings that might put them in the hospital. There's something about the challenge they find invigorating, about doing something that most mere mortals simply cannot do, that they wear like a badge of honour.

And it gets worse. Cheering for a team that's out of the local team's conference or division is one thing, but cheering for the rival? You've got to love that life the way a raccoon loves digging through garbage. You've got to love getting heckled and bathed in the boos of the masses like a cold shower. Do you like when people like you? Of course you don't! That's why this is the life for you.

Screw those donkeys hee-hawing at you for just walking down the street wearing your favourite jersey. Are they hollering at you because you wore the Captain High Liner version of the New York Islanders jersey, or because you wore it walking out of Madison Square Garden? Who cares? As long as they're mad, they can stay mad.

Would it have been easier to try to fit in and blend with everybody else? Yes, it would have, and that's why you're not doing it. When your team wins it all, it will mean so much more to you. When your team reaches the mountaintop, you're going to be absolutely insufferable. When the local team loses to yours, you want your co-workers to genuinely consider calling in sick just so they don't have to see your face. If they don't call in sick, do you let them have it the second they walk in the door? No. You wait. Their dread sustains you.

By now, a lot of you are thinking one of two things:

1. That sounds like you're describing a serial killer, and I don't like it.
2. That's me.

If you thought the first thing, congrats! You get to experience being a hockey fan with less hassle. If you thought the second thing, congrats! You've found your calling in life.

11.

32 Things to Think About

Once you've figured out what difficulty level of fandom you want for yourself, it's time to pick a new team. That's not as easy as it sounds. Even if you're going for the local team, depending on exactly where you live, you may have options.

Finding a hockey team of your own to love forever is kind of like buying a pair of shoes. You can see them on the shelves, love what you see, and try them on, just to discover they don't actually fit at all. They're just not "you," y'know? I'm sure they're somebody's cup of tea, just not yours.

You could also cram your feet into them and decide, "You know what? This is gonna be a little uncomfortable at first, but we're going to grow together and make this work." If that reality doesn't sound familiar, then you just can't relate to the plight of the wide-footed community. Skate shopping is worse, which is why I've been wearing the same pair since before the last NHL lockout.

Let's be honest: a lot of fans inherited their shoes, or rather fandom, from their dad. I still remember one day, when I was a kid, asking my dad who we cheered for. He told me the Toronto Maple Leafs, and that's simultaneously the best and worst thing he ever said to me. It's too late for me—I'm in this for the long haul. If I stopped being a Leafs fan and they finally won after more than half a century, I'd have to dedicate the rest of my life to rocket science just to Wile E. Coyote myself into the sun.

I should mention: You don't necessarily have to pick just one team to cheer for. Some fans cheer for a couple of teams. Some have a backup or 1A team. And some fans have no idea who the heck they like, but at least they know they love the organized chaos that comes with stick-wielding ice pirates on knife shoes. That's all fine, but let's walk before we can run and start with one team.

Who to choose? You can look at winners and losers all you want. You can dive into decades of a team's history. You can watch players from around the league and decide which ones seem like the best.

There's nothing wrong with picking a team to cheer for based purely on vibes. You're not totally sure what it even is, but this one team simply speaks to you in a way that's hard to describe. Maybe you think a player is funny in interviews. Maybe you discovered a player makes TikToks and some of them are actually pretty good. Maybe there's a player or team who just goes out there with a Wednesday Addams deadpan face, and just wrecks shop without saying a word. Whatever it is, you're looking for somebody or something to cheer for, and it's starting to feel like you've found a perfect match.

But if you're not sure yet—every team has something going for it. Let's take them in alphabetical order so no one can accuse me or you of anything but pure objectivity.

ANAHEIM DUCKS

Sadly, the Disney *Mighty Ducks* films are not a true biographical series about the NHL team's origin story, but you could always pretend they are. The Ducks should absolutely have "Conway" and "Goldberg" hanging from the rafters in Anaheim.

Speaking of the rafters, you'll occasionally see your team's mascot, Wild Wing, descending to the ice from the rafters, which might sound dangerous until you find the video of him trying to jump over a bunch of fire but falling into it instead.

Don't get too attached to that team name, though. The formerly Mighty Ducks of Anaheim dropped the "mighty" in June 2006, then went on to win their first ever Stanley Cup championship a year later. Winnipeg can claim Teemu Selanne as much as they want, but we're the ones who finally got him his Cup.

We love Paul Kariya in this house. Despite injuries, he scored at a 100-point pace in four seasons in Anaheim pretty much smack dab in the lowest-scoring era in NHL history. If you're looking for a jersey, his wouldn't be a bad one to start with. You could also go with Niedermayer. Which Niedermayer? Yes.

The great news about your new-found love of the Anaheim Ducks is that if you don't like the jersey they're wearing on any given night, they always have a better jersey. They've got black, white, the kind of orange you could see from space, teal, and purple. This might surprise you, but the teal and purple ones are the best, although you could always disagree and be wrong.

~~ARIZONA COYOTES~~ UTAH SOMETHING

So, uh, this is awkward. I wrote this part before the team got moved to Salt Lake City, Utah. I don't really feel like deleting this, so I'll just make little notes along the way.

Be warned: fandom of this team is not for the faint of heart. There are lots of things about the ~~Arizona~~ Utah Coyotes(?) that rule, but you should know they don't have a permanent arena yet (or didn't, in Arizona). The Coyotes(?) (used to) play at Mullett Arena, the home of Arizona State University's hockey team. Why is that? Long story (that just got longer). The current fan experience in the much smaller university arena is (or was) non-existent.

The Coyotes routinely made new jerseys that absolutely slap with the force of a thousand suns. A few years ago, the Coyotes said, "Remember that cool jersey we had with the Kachina on it that everybody liked? What if we just brought it back and used it all the time?" And then they did (before promptly abandoning all of the fans who purchased those jerseys).

Without the Arizona Coyotes, once known as the Phoenix Coyotes, there would be no Auston Matthews. Instead of looking down their nose at you, Leafs fans should worship the ground you walk on.

Winnipeg Jets fans might not like you very much on account of, well, you kinda stole their team. You see, the Coyotes used to be the Winnipeg Jets before they relocated to Arizona (and then Utah). This is confusing because there's a team called the Winnipeg Jets right now, only they stole their team from Atlanta. The Flames also stole their team from Atlanta. And there might be a new team soon in Atlanta. Get it? Of course you get it! All you need to know is that old Winnipeg Jets records technically belong to your new favourite team, the ~~Arizona~~ Utah Coyotes, and nobody is mad about it at all.

I hope you like soda pop.

BOSTON BRUINS

No team and fanbase will more consistently kick your ass and then ask if you're gonna cry about it than the Boston Bruins. Bobby Orr is the best player to ever play the game, followed closely by Patrice Bergeron, Zdeno Chara, and whoever else you want to name, as long as they're a Bruin. Most fanbases hate Brad Marchand for his mischievous antics, which include licking people on the face. But if you cheer for the Bruins, his shenanigans are hilarious and anybody who doesn't like them can, you guessed it, go cry about it.

You absolutely despise the Montreal Canadiens. Maybe you'd hate the Toronto Maple Leafs more if the Bruins didn't beat them all the time. Most importantly, Boston won the Stanley Cup in 2001 by proxy when Ray Bourque won with Colorado, so the official number of Cups for Boston in the record books is actually wrong.

The Bruins have a rich history, true league-wide and local legends, and TD Garden boasts some of the best fans in the entire league. We know we're the best, and soon you'll know it, too.

BUFFALO SABRES

"No goal!"

Did you know that the 1999 Stanley Cup Final has been going on for a quarter of a century? That's because the overtime of Game 6 between the Sabres and Dallas Stars was never properly decided, and I'm excited to see who wins!

If you like wearing a pair of swords, a big scary-looking goat, or both, then the Sabres are the team for you.

While few teams in the NHL look better on the ice, even fewer teams can boast that they sound better. Even though Rick Jeanneret, the legendary voice of the Buffalo Sabres, passed away in August 2023, few broadcasters in the history of hockey have left behind the same quality and quantity of electric calls throughout their career, from "La-la-la-Lafontaine!" to "May Day!" to "Now do you believe? These guys are good—scary good!" If you've never heard Jeanneret's voice before, merely reading his words could never do him justice. Once you have, and fall in love with this team, you'll hear his greatest hits replaying in your head like they happened yesterday.

Dominik Hasek is the best goalie of all time. This isn't up for debate.

Jack Eichel sucks. Sure, he held out for a trade because the Sabres wouldn't let him get the neck surgery he wanted, so he got traded and won the Stanley Cup with Vegas. He still sucks and you'd much rather have Alex Tuch.

We're still waiting on our first Stanley Cup victory, but we've got a bright future. If you want to hop on the bandwagon right now, it's not too late. We've got tickets sitting here waiting for you. Just know that if you sell those tickets to Leafs fans, we're sending Rob Ray after you and you're gonna have a bad time.

CALGARY FLAMES

You look good with a splash of red, but you'd look even better in a *C* of Red.

If you start cheering for the Calgary Flames, you'll be instantly walking into one of the best and most fierce rivalries in all of hockey: the Battle of Alberta. Why? Because Calgary is in Alberta. Unfortunately, Edmonton is also in Alberta. Oilers fans will tell you that Connor McDavid is the best player on the planet, but that loser doesn't even shovel his own driveway because it's heated because he's rich. Boo and hiss.

Leafs fans can claim Lanny McDonald all they want, but

never let them forget that he won it here. Actually, speaking of stolen items, our entire team is stolen from Atlanta. They also didn't win until they got here, so what can I say? Calgary is simply the City of Champions. That is its nickname. Just trust me and do not google it.

Now that you're a Flames fan, it's important for you to know that your favourite thing about Jarome Iginla is everything, because he's perfect and he is quite literally the only cool thing Edmonton has ever produced. If you want to make fast friends with a Flames fan, ask them where they were when they saw "the shift" from Iggy in 2004.

Speaking of 2004, the Flames won the Stanley Cup in six games, except the NHL didn't agree and the Tampa Bay Lightning "won" it in seven. The term "parallax view" is fighting words around these parts, buddy. Google it, get mad, then never google it again.

CAROLINA HURRICANES

Do you like teams that don't give a damn what anybody else thinks? Then you might enjoy the Carolina Hurricanes.

When their head coach, Rod Brind'Amour, was younger, he got locked out of the gym for working out too much. One time both of Carolina's goalies got hurt during a game in Toronto so they had to use the Maple Leafs' 42-year-old emergency backup goalie who also drove the Zamboni and they friggin' won. Have you heard of the Storm Surge? After wins, Hurricanes fans stay behind and do a kind of Icelandic thunder clap while the players stand at centre ice before doing some sort of coordinated stunt. Hockey's grumpy old guard hated it a whole big bunch, so the team started doing the Storm Surge even harder, using basketball nets and even Evander Holyfield that one time. Don't forget to grab your "Bunch of Jerks" T-shirt, which is a thing they actually sold after Don Cherry called them that because of their on-ice post-game shenanigans.

As goofy as the Hurricanes can be, they've pretty consistently had one of the more clever front offices in hockey. That doesn't mean they're just number nerds. The Hurricanes are a smart blend of old and new mindsets in the sport.

The Hurricanes are great if red is your colour, but don't be weirded out when every now and then they bust out bright green jerseys. Why do they do that? Because the Carolina Hurricanes used to be the Hartford Whalers before moving in the 1990s.

If you like funny chaos or your last name happens to be Staal, maybe the Carolina Hurricanes are your vibe.

CHICAGO BLACKHAWKS

Hey, Siri, play "Chelsea Dagger."

I've been cautious not to mention too many active players in these little snippets. After all, players get traded all the time. The Chicago Blackhawks, on the other hand, are a very special situation. Why?

Connor Bedard.

Sometimes, you catch the wave at the right moment. If you picked 2005 to become a Pittsburgh Penguins fan or Washington Capitals fan, then you were there at the very beginning of Sidney Crosby's and Alexander Ovechkin's careers, including all the downs and the highest of ups. If you latch onto the Chicago Blackhawks right now, you've only missed Connor Bedard's rookie year, and you could catch yourself up on those highlights in one afternoon.

The Chicago Blackhawks aren't entirely one kid. Alex Vlasic is six-foot-six every time he takes the ice, Frank Nazar is a seventh overall pick who scored his first NHL goal on his first NHL shot in his first NHL game the day I wrote this, and they have approximately forty billion draft picks.

Chicago, a historic Original Six franchise. The highs in recent memory are obvious, including Stanley Cup championships in 2010, 2013, and 2015 and parades with millions in attendance. The lows . . . oh boy. It's dark, and I'm not even sure where to start. We'd need a whole book to unpack all of that. To put it gently, the Blackhawks' lowest lows happened off the ice.

The Blackhawks are starting over in more ways than one, and Connor Bedard—a true young superstar in the making—is at the forefront of it all. He's just a happy-go-lucky mostly-child with Popeye forearms, and he gets grumpy when you tell him he maybe shouldn't play with a broken jaw. Connor Bedard treats pucks like they cut him off in traffic, and the kid is gonna be a problem for everybody else in the league for two decades.

COLORADO AVALANCHE

One day the Avalanche started playing "All the Small Things" by Blink-182, and whenever play resumed and the song ended, fans kept it going through the next verse and whole chorus. It rules very hard and you should put down this book and look up videos of it at the end of this sentence.

At the beginning of the 1995–96 season, the Quebec Nordiques decided to move to Colorado, call themselves the Avalanche, and win the Stanley Cup immediately. The Nordiques brought a solid team to Colorado but weren't complete until absolutely fleecing the Montreal Canadiens for all-time great goaltender Patrick Roy in what is straight up one of the most lopsided trades of all time. I guess what I'm saying is if you're from Quebec and don't care if your family hates you, this might be your team.

Whether fans love or hate the Colorado Avalanche, it's impossible to not shed a tear at even the thought of the legendary call "And after 22 years—Raymond Bourque!" If you don't know what that is, the Avalanche won the Stanley Cup again in 2001. The Cup was first handed to team captain Joe Sakic. In one of the most selfless acts in sports, and an incredibly underrated flex, Sakic said to himself, "Meh, I've already won this thing before" and immediately handed the Cup to Ray Bourque, a legendary defender who had been playing in the NHL since 1979 and had finally won his first Cup.

If you love winning enough to try chickpea pasta, the Colorado Avalanche are for you.

COLUMBUS BLUE JACKETS

"For those about to rock—fire!"

The Columbus Blue Jackets have a cannon, and it goes off every time they score. Is your hearing too good? A quick trip to watch the Columbus Blue Jackets in action should fix that. Head on down to the game and grab a program, some snacks, and a lifetime of tinnitus. The mascot is named Stinger and is a giant green bug, which makes sense when you consider all you'll hear after a Blue Jackets goal is "eeeeee."

How many playoff series have the Blue Jackets won? It depends who you ask. Some say one, some say two, and they're both kind of right. They did pull off one of the funniest upsets ever in 2019. The Tampa Bay Lightning had just won 62 out of 82 games, an all-time NHL record, en route to winning the Presidents' Trophy as the NHL's best regular season team. Their first-round opponent was the Columbus Blue Jackets.

Most people thought the series would be a massacre, and after a 3–0 Tampa lead after the first period, it looked like those predictions would come true. Not only did the Blue Jackets come back and win that game, but they also swept the Tampa Bay Lightning in four consecutive games. What happened after that for both teams? Listen, man, we're just trying to have a good time. Stop asking so many questions.

Columbus is an underrated hockey market, and the Blue Jackets' best days are ahead of them, if you're in the mood to buy low.

DALLAS STARS

Green looks good on you, and having a toe in the crease rules, actually.

Is there another team in any sport that can say they once had a logo that was nicknamed the Mooterus because it was supposed to look like a constellation of a bull but instead it just looked like a uterus? No, no there isn't. Is it the best jersey Dallas has ever had? Also no, but we all have our history.

Despite whatever Sabres fans say about Brett Hull's toe, the players from the 1998–99 Dallas Stars will have their names carved into the Stanley Cup forever. For at least that one series, even the Dominator was no match for Eddie the Eagle.

If you're looking to make a toothy grin bigger, show somebody the Dallas Stars' adorable mascot, Victor E. Green. If you're looking to make a toothy grin toothless, just point at the guy and tell Derian Hatcher they're on the opposing team.

Although Brett Hull played for the US internationally, he was born in Canada, which makes Dallas Stars legend Mike Modano the highest-scoring American-born player in NHL history. But why split hairs? Both guys won the Cup with Dallas. Oh, and Mike Babcock can kick rocks.

DETROIT RED WINGS

Have you ever heard of the Teddy Bear Toss? It's adorable. Sometimes, teams will have nights when fans are encouraged to bring teddy bears to the game. Once the home team scores their first goal of the game, everyone throws their teddy bears over the glass to be donated. Super wholesome, right?

Anyway, the Detroit Red Wings basically have that, with the tiny caveat that their fans throw real, actual octopuses, or octopi, onto the ice. Does the team's staff get mad about it? You'd think so, but no, some guy comes out, picks the thing up with his bare hands, and flails it around in a circle above his head like a battle-axe, spraying octopus juice absolutely everywhere. Does that sound like a good time to you?

The Red Wings boast some of the greatest teams and players of all time. How is beloved Red Wings legend Steve Yzerman doing as GM? Shush. Don't be a buzzkill. Give him time, even though he's already been at the helm for five years.

The new international bridge that, upon completion, will connect Detroit, Michigan, to Windsor, Ontario, is called the Gordie Howe International Bridge. This is where Mr. Hockey played, and Detroit is Hockey Town.

EDMONTON OILERS

The Oilers have been an NHL team for 44 seasons, and between Wayne Gretzky and Connor McDavid, you could argue they've had the best player alive for a third of that time.

Oilers fans don't have to look up their players on NHL.com, they just go straight to the Hockey Hall of Fame, because that's where half of them ended up. You can guarantee Connor McDavid and Leon Draisaitl will join those ranks, too, whenever they're all said and done.

Connor McDavid is legitimately one of the greatest hockey players ever, and he's still in his twenties. He's one of the fastest players, he's got some of the most disgusting hands, and his face reads like every moment he's not setting the opposing team's defence and goalie on fire is a moment wasted. Whether the Oilers win or lose, it's never a bad time if you came to watch Connor McDavid play.

If defence wins championships, then why does the team with the most goals win? I'm here for a good time, not a long time, so give me games that end 8–7 in overtime every day of the week and hook it up intravenously. If you wanted decaf, you would have asked for it! The Oilers are three shots of espresso dumped into a Red Bull and lit on fire. Except then you blow the fire out because you hate the damned Flames.

FLORIDA PANTHERS

If you like teams that will maul opponents at any and every opportunity, you'll love the Florida Panthers. Like, it's not even done in an angry way, either. Just standing there with a neutral expression, casually chewing a mouth guard, and smacking dudes repeatedly in the noggin.

The Florida Panthers came into existence in the early 1990s and, despite an appearance in the 1996 Stanley Cup Final, had precious little to celebrate in terms of playoff success. Hilariously, one of the final edits I made to this book was this sentence right here because the Panthers just won the Stanley Cup! It's not too late to hop on the Florida Panthers bandwagon now; you're hopping on during what is truly the Panthers' golden age, led primarily by Matthew Tkachuk and Sasha Barkov.

If you want to go and see a Florida Panthers game, whether you live there or you're just visiting, you can relax and have a beautiful day at the beach for a few hours before throwing on a sweater and walking into a frozen blood feud against the Tampa Bay Lightning, who you hate *a lot*, by the way.

Roberto Luongo could run for governor and you'd probably vote for him, and honestly, there's pretty much no shot he'd be the worst option on the ballot. The headline would read, "Montreal Man Becomes Lead Florida Man."

LOS ANGELES KINGS

Do you like seeing Will Ferrell wear face paint at hockey games? Then you'll love the LA Kings.

Up until somewhat recent memory, the Kings didn't have

much to brag about. They had Marcel Dionne, who is considered by many to be the best player who never won the Stanley Cup. After that, they pulled off the biggest trade in NHL history when they got Wayne Gretzky from the Edmonton Oilers in the block-buster of all blockbusters; but even then, the farthest they got was a loss in the 1993 Stanley Cup Final. What kind of narc calls a penalty for a funny stick curve, anyway? In the Stanley Cup Final, of all things? Phooey!

Forget going out and getting the best player ever! The Kings' first Stanley Cup came about when they acquired Jeff Carter in 2012, barely squeaked into the playoffs as the Western Conference's eighth seed, demolished the Presidents' Trophy–winning Vancouver Canucks and basically everybody else in their path, before finally hoisting Lord Stanley's Cup for the first time. The Kings decided that was so fun they did it again a couple of years later, in 2014, when they re-enacted every kid's dream by winning the Stanley Cup on home ice in overtime.

Most other fanbases don't like Dustin Brown. Ironically, that's one of the things you love about him the most. Nerds don't like him much, either, but that's why they're nerds and Dustin Brown is a two-time Stanley Cup–winning captain. You also have one more Cup than the Ducks now, and two more than the Sharks, and you should make sure to let their fans know at every opportunity, including Christmas cards and funerals.

MINNESOTA WILD

A bunch of states have hockey teams, but only one has the *cojones* to call itself the State of Hockey.

Just like Winnipeg, Minnesota is one of those places that used to have an NHL team, lost it even though they never should have, and then thankfully got it back. Sorry, did I say just like Winnipeg? I meant nothing like Winnipeg, because screw those dusty pigeons.

The Minnesota Wild have a scrappy history as an underdog team that's never really out of the fight. After all, the Wild ended the career of Patrick Roy in the overtime of a Game 7.

Your most hated rivals are the Winnipeg Jets and the salary cap. The Wild's cap is currently eaten up by a few things, some good, some bad. The bad is from buyouts and paying players not to play in Minnesota. The good is Kirill Kaprizov, basically a hockey-playing bear made in a lab somewhere in Novokuznetsk who relishes obliterating pucks.

If you like a loud atmosphere and sweater weather, maybe you should take a walk on the Wild side.

MONTREAL CANADIENS

Vingt-quatre.

You're not interested in all this babble about how cute these teams are, or their mascots, or their little songs. You're interested in wins, winning, and winners. Well, the Montreal Canadiens have the most championships in NHL history by a country mile, with 24. If your criterion is "just win, baby," these are your guys.

Our pre-game ceremonies are the best. Sure, they're 45 minutes long, but that's because Habs fans have a lot to celebrate. Lesser teams like the Leafs couldn't possibly relate, and that's why they don't like it.

Carey Price isn't God, but they follow each other on Instagram.

Take your pick through any of the legends that have played for the *bleu, blanc, et rouge* over the past century, and you'll find so much to celebrate. Maurice "Rocket" Richard was the greatest goal-scorer ever before the greatest goal-scorer ever. Jean Béliveau is one of the most revered men in the history of Quebec, and even his signature was handsome. Heck, Jacques Plante basically invented the goalie mask, and he had to fight his coach for permission to wear one.

As for now, our young core is the envy of the league and every other team knows they're in so much trouble once these young guys start reaching their full potential. It won't be long before that 24 turns into 25, and as a new Habs fan, you'll be there for it.

NASHVILLE PREDATORS

Do you like buildings that are loud as all hell? The Nashville Predators might be the team for you.

The Predators' party-animal fans and flat-roof arena make for one of the loudest barns in the league. Even better, whenever the Predators score, all the fans shout, "Thank you!" at the opposing team's goalie, then ask for another before chanting, "It's all your fault!"

Speaking of goalies, the Predators needed one pretty badly. One day, a Predators fan was out for a walk when suddenly they came across a tall yet stunningly handsome giant. Just when the fan thought the giant was going to grind his bones to make his bread, the giant said, "Hi, I'm Pekka Rinne. Do you know which way the arena is?" Then he played like 700 games exclusively for the Preds and was really good!

Want to know why the Predators' mascot is a sabre-toothed tiger? Because when they were digging up the land to build their arena, they found the bones of a freaking sabre-toothed tiger. If you want to enjoy an incredible hockey game then walk out and straight into the bachelorette-party capital of the galaxy, maybe Nashville is your town.

NEW JERSEY DEVILS

Can the New York Rangers kiss your ass? Then the New Jersey Devils might be for you.

Of course, the Devils have an identity outside of the Rangers, like being three-time Stanley Cup champions, for example. Imagine going 54 years without winning the Cup? That's humiliating, and as a Devils fan you simply can't relate.

There's a lot of debate over who the second-best goalie of all time is, behind Martin Brodeur. The correct answer is, who cares? Marty was one of the winningest, most dominant goalies in league history. Forget Marty's mountain of trophies—the league had to change the rules because Brodeur was better at handling the puck than half of the league's defencemen. Then, after that silly little trapezoid showed up, Brodeur still won the Vezina Trophy as the league's best goalie and led the Devils to the Stanley Cup Final. You know what you can do with your dumb little trapezoid.

As a Devils fan, you're honoured and privileged to watch the best American-born hockey player currently living and breathing air: Jack Hughes. Some Leafs fans mistakenly think it's Auston Matthews, but they're obviously wrong. What is it about half-century Cup droughts that rots the brains of fans of Original Six teams?

One time, Devils fans chanted, "Fire Lindy!" at head coach Lindy Ruff before the team got hot and they changed the chant to "Sorry, Lindy!" If you're about admitting your mistakes and growth, maybe the Devils are your angels.

NEW YORK ISLANDERS

Are you completely out of your mind? Do I have the team for you.

If you've ever seen an Islanders home game, you'll know that fans here make Metallica look like Bob Dylan. A few years back, former Islanders captain John Tavares left the Islanders to sign with his childhood team, the Toronto Maple Leafs. During Tavares's return game, fans ran over Tavares jerseys in the parking lot, pelted players with plastic snakes, and chanted, "We don't need you!" at Tavares loud enough that the sound of it could've been picked up by the Mars rover. If you like cheering for a team that basically plays in Arkham Asylum with ice, you might feel at home in Long Island.

How many different jerseys do we have? We have so many jerseys! Are all of them good? . . . We have so many jerseys!

When Wayne Gretzky, the second-greatest hockey player of all time behind Mike Bossy, finally won his first Stanley Cup, he had to go through the Islanders. Sure, Gretzky eventually won four Cups, but he never won four straight like the Islanders did from 1980 to 1983. If you consider a true dynasty to be at least three championships in a row, then the Islanders were the NHL's last true dynasty.

If you want to join us, then great. If you don't, then we don't need you.

NEW YORK RANGERS

If you can make it here, you can make it anywhere.

You should become a fan of the New York Rangers just so you can visit New York City, home of the NHL's head offices, and of course the legendary Madison Square Garden. I once bought tickets to a Rangers-Panthers game at Madison Square Garden. I remember it like it was yesterday, because the tickets were fake so I didn't get to go in. So I guess step number one for your new fandom is don't be a dumbass and buy tickets off some guy on the sidewalk in New York.

The Rangers are a part of the NHL's storied Original Six, but their time in that era was a struggle, with teams like the Montreal Canadiens and Toronto Maple Leafs running the show. In 1994, the New York Rangers won the Stanley Cup for the first time in 54 years. At the game, a fan famously brought a sign that read, "Now I can die in peace."

It is, underratedly, one of the most hardcore signs ever taken to a sporting event, because it was Game 7 of the Stanley Cup Final against the Vancouver Canucks. What if they made that sign, took it to the game, and the Rangers lost? Did they have a backup sign that said, "Now I can die miserable"? Who cares, because they won!

You're not sure Henrik Lundqvist is the greatest goalie of all time, but you are sure that he's the handsomest. That dude has a twin brother, too, which seems unfair and makes rival goalies seem twice as ugly.

Oh, and remember: Potvin sucks. Denis Potvin, of course. Felix Potvin is a flawless angel.

OTTAWA SENATORS

If you think the Toronto Maple Leafs are garbage and you hate them, give the Ottawa Senators a try. So what if Montreal is closer? I mean, definitely screw the Habs, too, but the imaginary lines demarcating Ontario, Canada, mean you hate the Leafs with a fiery, burning passion. The good news is those blue-and-white blowhards never run out of new and exciting ways of humiliating themselves, so the schadenfreude is always piping hot. Besides, who cares about those elitist clowns anyway? We have an identity outside of that tire fire in the big smoke.

Michael Andlauer is the new owner of the Senators, and that's fantastic because after years of being a team with a shoestring internal budget, you can spend to the salary cap. Heck, you should be getting a new and improved arena in short order, too. What's not to like about that?

Our youthful defence corps is the envy of the league, Tim Stützle is our razzle-dazzle star, and our captain, Brady Tkachuk, is like a video-game-created player who's going to shoot a million shots, score a bunch of goals, knock you on your ass, and if anyone has anything to say about it, he'll kick it, too.

Daniel Alfredsson is your team's most cherished son, and he's always been a Senator ever since he won rookie of the year in 1996. Whoa, sorry, were you just googling where Alfie played during the 2013–14 season? Don't do that. It was Ottawa. They wore a red-and-white alternate jersey all season.

PHILADELPHIA FLYERS

If the Philadelphia Flyers had a slogan, it would be "Screw you, we're the Philadelphia Flyers." That slogan usually wouldn't be directed at their own fans, but it *is* Philadelphia, so you never know.

Philly hockey has a brand: tough. The Broad Street Bullies earned their nickname in the 1970s by being the toughest hockey team on the face of the planet. Would they get away with those kinds of antics today? Hell no. Were those antics allowed in the

1970s? Also hell no, but who on earth was going to tell Bobby Clarke to knock it off? If you tried, you'd end up with even fewer teeth than he had.

In 2016, the Flyers held a pre-game tribute for the passing of their long-time owner, Ed Snider, and gave out bracelets that would light up. Later that night, the visiting Washington Capitals scored more goals than the Flyers, and fans starting throwing those bracelets onto the ice.

It's easy to learn how to be a Flyers fan. Fans of other teams don't know who to be mad at, but for you, it's almost always the goalie. Like, for several decades it's been the goalie. One time the Flyers hired one of their former goalies to be their general manager just so they could fire him.

Other teams wear orange, but you're the orangest. Just don't wear black and yellow around here. The Battle of Pennsylvania is real, and the Flyers and Penguins hate each other, players and fans alike.

Some teams match their city's attitude perfectly, but none more so than the Flyers.

PITTSBURGH PENGUINS

Lots of teams have superstars, but only Sidney Crosby is in bread commercials.

A lot of people will tell you that Wayne Gretzky is the best hockey player of all time, which is confusing to you because Mario Lemieux lives and breathes on this very planet we call Earth. Gently reminding them that Gretzky can kick rocks should set them straight.

Between Mario Lemieux, Jaromir Jagr, Ron Francis, and

Sidney Crosby, four of the top ten highest-scoring players in NHL history spent a huge chunk of their careers on the Pittsburgh Penguins, if not their entire career.

As far as Canada is concerned, you love Cole Harbour, Nova Scotia, because that's where Sidney Crosby is from. Hamilton, Ontario, on the other hand, can screw all the way off forever because the guy who owned BlackBerry tried to buy the Penguins and move them there that one time.

Kyle Dubas is your team's president, which technically makes Pittsburgh a colony of Sault Ste. Marie, Ontario. This makes Pittsburgh's front office one of the youngest, tallest, and handsomest per capita in the entire league. Once Dubas arrived and was named president, he also named himself general manager because it's awesome and pisses off your uncle.

My friend, you'd look good in black and yellow. Oh, and powder blue sometimes.

SAN JOSE SHARKS

The Sharks are your team if you like no-nonsense teams who cut straight to the chase.

Who are they? The Sharks. What's their mascot? A shark. What's its name? Sharkie. What do the players skate out of? A big ol' shark head. What's the nickname for the arena? The Shark Tank. The Vancouver Canucks are simultaneously a whale, a flying skate, an angry lumberjack, and a big colourful *V*. Who has time for all that? Pff, not you. What are the Sharks? Sharks. They're the Sharks.

The Sharks, who are the Sharks, do some non-related Sharks things. Historically, they love a big frontier-style beard. Go look up pictures of Joe Thornton or Brent Burns, or that time they both posed naked for a photo with a couple of fake beards that were only slightly exaggerated. Or maybe don't. Are you reading this at work?

Have the Sharks ever won the Stanley Cup? No. Have they come close? Yes. Are they close right now? Extremely no. That's actually good news, believe it or not. Because of the draft, almost every great team in the league had to be awful for a while in order to get there.

Your rivals are easy: the Kings and the Ducks, your Californian neighbours. Have they won the Cup? Yes. Will they remind you that you haven't? Yes. Do you care? Sharks can eat Ducks and also Kings.

Sharks.

SEATTLE KRAKEN

The Kraken are the perfect fit for you because you just got here and so did they.

The Seattle Kraken joined the NHL family in 2021 and they already made the playoffs, which is apparently a thing now! If you're a new hockey fan, I guess that's the standard these days, but it used to be that expansion teams had to stink for years and years before even getting a sniff at the dance.

Because the Kraken are new, pretty much everything about them is, too. The building is new and a lot of the team's hockey ops folks are relatively new or at least new in their role. The jerseys are fresh as heck, too. Some other teams around the league wear navy blue, but the Kraken are pretty much on their own when it comes to seafoam. And don't say the Sharks—they're teal. How dare you. Please learn your greeny blues.

You don't *really* have a rival yet, but when you do you're pretty sure it's gonna be the Canucks.

And Kraken fans are just the best. This is a true story: On the day of the Kraken's first ever home game, a Kraken fan named Nadia Popovici, who was going into medical school, spotted something strange on the skin of Brian Hamilton, the Vancouver Canucks equipment manager, from her seat. She was able to relay this information to him, he got it checked out, and it turns out the mole was a malignant melanoma. Hamilton would later say in a news conference, "She saved my life."

I know that last anecdote wasn't about the team, but you're not on the team, you're a fan. If that sounds like the kind of fan you are or want to be, the Kraken are your new team.

ST. LOUIS BLUES

"We went Blues!"

If you're ever strolling through St. Louis and looking for something to do other than eat toasted ravioli—that's a real thing—then why not enjoy the 2019 Stanley Cup champions, the St. Louis Blues?

Every time the Blues score, they ding a bell in the arena. If they score twice, the bell goes twice. If the other team gets pumped for seven goals, it's gonna sound like the hunchback of Notre Dame is getting in some cardio. It drives other teams nuts, and we love it.

For years, the Blues were known as a team that would have great regular seasons, making the playoffs every year and even breaking a record while doing it, but never accomplishing their ultimate goal. In their early years, they lost repeatedly to Bobby

Orr and the Boston Bruins—screw that guy, am I right? Then, during some of the Blues' greatest seasons, in the 2010s, they kept running into the Chicago Blackhawks or LA Kings, two teams that combined to win five Stanley Cups in six years.

Finally, in 2019, the Blues combined the goofy with the incredible. After beginning 2019 in last place in the league—straight-up last place until January—they got red hot and never cooled down, blazing through the rest of the regular season and grinding it out in the playoffs. The best part? The Blues beat their oldest nemesis, the Boston Bruins, in the Stanley Cup Final—in Boston.

Say, you know what's a pretty great song for no reason in particular at all? "Gloria." If you're a Blues fan, that's your new favourite jam. It's Brett Hull's favourite song, it's probably Keith Tkachuk's favourite song, and one day, it's only a matter of time, Matthew and Brady Tkachuk will finally come home to St. Louis and admit it's their favourite song.

Side note (this has nothing to do with the Blues): Don't go up the St. Louis arch. I hate that thing. It might be for you if you like cramming into a dinky pod and riding up a rickety contraption inside a building that's probably not made of papier mâché but you're not totally sure. Go to a Blues game instead.

TAMPA BAY LIGHTNING

You're not big into math, but you're pretty sure that the salary cap is more like a salary suggestion.

Tampa has three Stanley Cup championships, and big diaper-filling babies like to pretend they don't. Tampa won in 2004, but haters will say the Flames actually won the Stanley Cup Final in Game 6 that year. You ask how before being sent a grainy picture of a puck that might have been taken with an old disposable camera and definitely doesn't show the puck fully crossing the line.

Tampa won the "Bubble Cup" in 2020, when the playoffs took place in a Covid bubble in August and September. Haters will say the Bubble Cup isn't real, like it was easier to win than in other years. Yeah, that makes perfect sense. That playoff format had more teams in it. Tampa's first game in their first series went to five damn overtimes. Everybody was shut up in the same hotel for weeks on end before being flown to the other side of the country to be shut up in a different hotel for weeks. Oh, and they won with their captain injured basically the entire time.

Then, in 2021, less than a calendar year later, mind you, the Lightning won the Stanley Cup because they were "over the cap." In reality, the Lightning just finessed their salary cap better than your whiny little team did. Be sure to come up with a better excuse for next time, because the Lightning are gonna win it again.

Besides winning, which the Lightning do often, Tampa has an excellent development pipeline, a raucous fanbase, and a giant Tesla coil that goes all buzzy when the Lightning score.

TORONTO MAPLE LEAFS

Oh, man. OKAY. This is the team I cheer for, so I feel an added pressure with this one.

I guess we'll start with the fact that if you cheer for the Toronto Maple Leafs nobody will like you, and you have to be good with that. Just because you don't have beef with another fanbase doesn't mean they don't have beef with you.

Listen, the history of the Toronto Maple Leafs is rich; they've won the second-most Stanley Cup championships in NHL history. The unfortunate asterisk there is that their last championship was in 1967, which was a long time ago. How long ago was it? Everybody has their own favourite way of describing it. Mine is that the Leafs haven't won a Cup since man landed on the moon. That's also my least favourite.

Being a Leafs fan makes you an extremely easy target. Your team was the first in NHL history to blow a three-goal lead in the third period of a Game 7—that comes up often. Your team also lost to its own 42-year-old Zamboni driver. That also comes up often.

Here's the great thing about being a Leafs fan: there's lots of them, and they're everywhere, especially in Ottawa and Buffalo, which are essentially just part of the Greater Toronto Area anyway. Sure, that's part of the reason why other fanbases hate the Leafs, but you don't need any other fanbase's approval because you can just be friends with other Leafs fans because there's a billion of them. Are we all friends who agree on everything? Oh dear, oh heavens, oh no, my sweet summer child. We're more than happy to have a filibuster about the team's fourth line at five a.m. on a Sunday, and also that Sunday is Christmas morning. Can't imagine why anybody would hate us.

That's what nobody can ever take away from us: we have The Passion.

VANCOUVER CANUCKS

Luuuuuuuu!

Have you ever been to a sporting event and realized, "Oh no! I'm wearing the wrong colours!" No worries, because over the years the Canucks have had basically every colour scheme in the book. You could wear black, white, blue, green, yellow, or red, and folks will say, "There goes that Canucks fan!"

The Canucks don't have a championship yet, but they've come extremely close, losing in Game 7 of the Cup Final twice. What happened after both of those losses? You guessed it: nothing happened, that's what. Everyone said, "Aw shucks," then went home, peacefully. Do not google it.

It's often talked about, but we still don't make a big enough deal out of the fact that the Canucks drafted identical twins back to back on the same day. They both played on the same line, they both scored a billion points, and then they got inducted into the Hockey Hall of Fame together, too. Their names are Daniel and Henrik Sedin, they're better than everybody else's favourite player, and there's two of them.

One final thing you should know: uttering the name Mark Messier in this house is like saying Voldemort. We must never speak of he who must not be named.

VEGAS GOLDEN KNIGHTS

Maybe you just really like Vegas. I have great news for you: there's a hockey team there now!

The Vegas Golden Knights showed up in 2017, started kicking an abundance of ass, and kind of just forgot to stop.

The pre-game shows will make you want to show up to every home game an hour early. There's always some kind of spectacle that's basically a customized diss track against the team they're playing that night. And guess what celebrity is there that night? You guessed it: all of them! Every celebrity ever is there, and everyone's having a great time, because it's Vegas.

For all the glitz and glamour, Vegas has one story in particular that I love: General Fanager. You see, in 2005, the NHL instituted a salary cap. In basically no time whatsoever, it confused people. After a few years, different websites began to pop up trying to explain how the heck the cap works and keeping track of every player's cap hits and salaries. General Fanager was one of those sites, run by an ordinary hockey fan named Tom Poraszka. Tom ran General Fanager so well that when Vegas was assembling its staff about a year before they took the ice, they hired Tom. Vegas is now the league's top salary cap wizard, which everybody complains about, and in 2023, Tom Poraszka and the Vegas Golden Knights became Stanley Cup champions. If he didn't live the dream, then who did?

The Golden Knights also have one of my favourite dumb stats ever: when Vegas won the 2023 Stanley Cup, every single player on the roster was at least six feet tall except one guy—and he won playoff MVP. His name is Jonathan Marchessault, if you're wondering who to get on your first jersey.

WASHINGTON CAPITALS

You might be right on time for this one!

The Washington Capitals have a siren for a goal horn, and it goes off all the time. Alexander Ovechkin is the greatest player in franchise history and has been torturing the best goalies in the world since 2005. As I'm writing this, he's edging closer and closer to the all-time career goals record in the NHL, which is 894, scored by none other than Wayne Gretzky himself. If you're reading this after Ovechkin broke the record then, uh, I'm sure his record-breaking goal looks great on YouTube.

If you need one core memory to familiarize yourself with, the Capitals finally won the Stanley Cup in 2018 and proceeded to have one of the best Cup celebrations ever. During that tour, one player on the team bus saw a fan with a shirt he liked, so the fan just took it off and gave it to him.

But the best part of that Cup run, maybe better than beating Vegas in their inaugural year, better than Braden Holtby becoming the Holtbeast in Games 6 and 7 against Tampa, was finally beating Sidney Crosby and the Pittsburgh Penguins. Once Evgeny Kuznetsov called game, you knew the Caps were up to something special.

Quick question: Do you have any friends who like the Pittsburgh Penguins? Your options are "no" and the wrong answer.

WINNIPEG JETS

They're back!

Years ago, TV execs took *Family Guy* off the air, even though a lot of people really liked it, because it didn't make enough money. It was then replaced with other shows that people didn't like as much and made even less money. Years after *Family Guy* was cancelled, its underground cult following brought it back to life and back on the air.

That's basically what happened to the Winnipeg Jets.

The 1995–96 season was the final year of the Winnipeg Jets franchise before they moved to Arizona to become the Phoenix Coyotes. Did the Coyotes leave Arizona to return to Winnipeg? No. Was it because the team was too successful in Arizona? Also no. Listen—the old Winnipeg Jets ended up in Arizona before eventually moving to Utah, and the new Winnipeg Jets that arrived in 2011 used to be the Atlanta Thrashers, but it doesn't matter because they're both the Winnipeg Jets. You can argue that banners stay with franchises, but Jets fans know banners belong to the fans who cheered for them, and you know damn well nobody in Arizona cares about the Avco World Trophy, which the Jets won thrice.

Jets fans scream the "True North" part of "O Canada" because of their ownership group, True North Sports & Entertainment. Just wanted to let you know that before you go to a game and crap yourself when they scream it. Also, Jets fans do "the whiteout" for home playoff games, when absolutely everybody in the arena wears white. It looks super cool in person and on TV. Being a Jets fan might not be the choice for you if you're clumsy and love mustard.

One more thing: never throw popcorn on the ice.

"SUCKS TO SUCK"

There's no bigger whiny crybaby tactic in all of sports than complaining about a team running out their top powerplay in a blowout loss. I suppose I could understand it at the level of kids' hockey—after all, they're kids. As you start climbing up the competitive ranks, however, it becomes a lot more whiny.

Why did we all show up tonight? Was it to win? I'm pretty sure it was to win. Don't you want to win? Well, we're winning.

When you get up to the professional ranks, it's completely embarrassing and unacceptable. One of the things the NHL keeps promoting in their own statistics that they release to the public is that comebacks are on the rise. Here's something from an official press release that the NHL sent out in March 2024 for the 2023–24 season. The NHL is averaging 6.2 goals per game, with 42 per cent of games ending as comeback wins. Did you catch that? They're promoting that 42 per cent of games end as comeback wins.

In recent memory, we've seen teams erase countless three-goal leads, some four-goal leads, and even five-goal leads. Why am I going to spare your feelings—at the professional level—just so that you can leave feeling good about yourself?

Am I all of a sudden in charge of you feeling good about yourself? Isn't this professional hockey? Isn't this the most rough-and-tumble game that there is? A contact sport that psychotically has an 82-game schedule instead of whatever the NFL does?

Comebacks are on the rise, and me sending out my good players, who the team pays very handsomely, by the way, is my way of doing my job and trying to prevent you from winning. It's not my fault you didn't do a very good job doing your job of trying to win yourselves. Here's my solution for preventing head coaches from complaining about this going forward. If any coach or player is caught complaining about the other team using their first powerplay unit in a game that their team is losing, not only does the game automatically end in a defeat, the team that's winning has the option to play on the powerplay for the remainder of the game. Not only do you automatically lose the game, you forfeit a point in the standings. Additionally, you have to wear a diaper on your head for the entirety of each game and practice for the remainder of the week.

It's one thing to complain about it in games when there are kids involved. After all, they're just trying to have fun. The higher up the ranks we go, the waters get a little muddy. There's no muddy water at the professional level, and it's perfectly clear in the National Hockey League, the best hockey league in the world. You can complain about so many things; look at me, this book is full of my complaints. But if your complaint is simply that the other team is better than you, then enjoy a week's worth of diaper-hat, because it's what you deserve.

12.
GOATzky

You can walk into pretty much any bar or coffee shop anywhere in Canada and have the same argument every day of the year: Who was the best hockey player of all time?

I love the "greatest of all time" conversation in basketball because it gets so heated. Depending on what you value and how well you've studied the sport's history, you could probably drop a Ph.D.-level thesis paper on who you think basketball's GOAT is.

Is it Michael Jordan? Going six-for-six in the NBA Finals is pretty wild, and *Space Jam* was iconic.

Is it Kareem Abdul-Jabbar? He was a 19-time all-star, six-time league MVP, and, like Jordan, also won six championships, not to mention his appearance in *D2: The Mighty Ducks*.

Is it LeBron James? A man who was given impossible expectations to live up to when taken first overall in the 2003 NBA Draft, yet somehow surpassed every one of those expectations? He was in a *Space Jam* movie too, but I think that's one category where Jordan beats him decisively.

What those three athletes have in common, besides all three having an IMDb page, is that the conversation for the greatest basketball player of all time could start with any of them. Maybe with a few others, too.

I used to think that's how hockey's GOAT conversation was. As a hockey fan born the winter before the Edmonton Oilers traded Wayne Gretzky to the LA Kings, I grew up in a world where almost everybody called Gretzky the greatest player to ever live. I accepted that as gospel.

Then I got a little older, and I started learning about how ridiculously high-scoring hockey was in the 1980s. Have you ever watched "classic" games on TV? For me, those games are from the 1980s. No disrespect if that was the era of your fondest childhood memories, but if you watch those games with anybody who's under 40 years old, they might burst out laughing as the goalie goes to soccer-kick the puck from a standing position and—you're not gonna believe this—the puck soars through him effortlessly. It made me think anyone could have lit up these goalies, and maybe the Great One benefitted too much from that era of hockey.

I started looking into "era-adjusted" stats that take numbers from any era in hockey's history and either boost them or dock them based on how abundant or scarce scoring was at the time. For example, if you look at the 92 goals Gretzky scored in the 1981–82 season, HockeyReference.com adjusts that number down to 68 goals because scoring was so astronomically high that season. On the other side of the coin, if you take the 52 goals Jaromir Jagr scored during the 2000–01 season, the site adjusts that number up to 57 because that season was in the prime of the low-scoring dead puck era.

Because of these era-adjusted stats, for a while I was a contrarian fart-sniffer completely convinced that Gretzky's numbers were inflated and anybody who still thought he was the best hockey player ever simply wasn't looking hard enough.

Then I woke up. Unlike the conversation in basketball, when it comes to the GOAT in hockey, the conversation starts with one guy: Wayne Gretzky.

Do you have another player you think is better? That's fine! But let's try something. Let's compare their stats to Gretzky, their awards, their impact on the game, their entire career, and everything they accomplished. Gretzky is the benchmark of benchmarks in hockey. Don't believe me? Prepare to lose an argument.

WAYNE GRETZKY

STATISTICS
Goals: 894 (record)
Playoff Goals: 122 (record)
Assists: 1,963 (record)
Playoff Assists: 260 (record)
Points: 2,857 (record)
Playoff Points: 382 (record)
Points Per Game: 1.92 (record)
Playoff Points Per Game: 1.84 (record among players with
   more than seven career playoff games)
Plus/Minus: +520
Playoff Plus/Minus: +91
Scoring Titles: 10 (including 7 straight from 1981 to 1987)
Hart Trophies: 9 (including 8 straight from 1980 to1987)
Stanley Cups: 4

Pretty silly, right?

As you can see, Gretzky doesn't have statistics so much as he simply holds records. Rather than give you the full list, I'll take you through some that will most make you question whether Wayne Gretzky is from Brantford, Ontario, or another galaxy.

Records are made to be broken, and over time, some of his

have been. If you give Alexander Ovechkin until the end of his current contract, there is a very good chance he will beat Gretzky's all-time goal-scoring record, and it's possible he might even do it in fewer games. However, Ovechkin will wind up with something in the neighbourhood of 1,000 fewer points than Gretzky.

Gretzky has 382 career playoff points, which is 87 more than the man with the second most, Mark Messier. Of course, Messier spent a huge chunk of his NHL playoff career as Gretzky's teammate. The guy in third is Jari Kurri, another teammate of Gretzky's and his long-time linemate in Edmonton. The guy in fourth is Glenn Anderson, yet another teammate of Gretzky's. For the NHL player with the most all-time playoff points who wasn't ever one of Gretzky's teammates, it's a tie between Jaromir Jagr and Sidney Crosby, 181 Stanley Cup Playoff points back of the Great One.

During the Edmonton Oilers' reign of four Stanley Cups in five years between the 1983–84 season and 1987–88 season, Gretzky had 960 points in 377 games, which is just over two and a half points per game (2.55). The next closest was Jari Kurri, with 583 points, and after that it's Dale Hawerchuk, with 558. Before you ask, yes, Gretzky also holds the record for points per game in the Stanley Cup Playoffs, with 1.84, at least among players who played in more than seven career Stanley Cup Playoff games. My editor has asked that I put some respect on the name of Newsy Lalonde, who put up 15 goals and 19 playoff points between the 1918 and 1919 playoffs, a half century before the first moon landing.

Gretzky has the NHL record for points scored on the power-play, with 890, which is 129 more points than Ray Bourque, who sits in second. If you took away every point Gretzky ever got on the powerplay, he would still have 1,967 career points, which would still make him the NHL's all-time leading scorer by 46 points over Jaromir Jagr.

If you're going to argue somebody in hockey history was better than Wayne Gretzky, that's the kind of superhuman mutant they have to surpass. Good luck.

The Mount Rushmore of men's ice hockey, excluding goalies because they're quirky cats deserving of their own mountain, is four guys: Bobby Orr, Mario Lemieux, Gordie Howe, and of course Wayne Gretzky. There's more room for debate with the goalie question, even though I more or less settled that already. And for players, outside of those four titans of the sport, there are many legends. None of those legends, however, crack this group of four.

Can any of Gordie Howe, Bobby Orr, or Mario Lemieux take the number one spot from Gretzky? Let's find out. You'll notice that for these players' stats, I'm listing them as compared to Gretzky, in terms of goals, assists, points, playoff performance, individual trophies, and championships.

One thing I would like to point out: international achievements at something like the Winter Olympics are obviously worthy of note. The problem is that because of the inconsistent inclusion of professional players in international men's hockey, a direct comparison is virtually impossible. Some pros played at the Canada Cup, others didn't. Some pros played at the Winter Olympics, others didn't. There's a World Cup of Hockey—oops! Never mind, it's gone again. The international accolades will be mentioned, but they're a tie-breaker at best, in my humble opinion.

This isn't to take away from their many impressive accomplishments. It's just that the gaps between them and the Great One are so telling. Just thank me for doing the math for you, and enjoy.

GORDIE HOWE

STATISTICS

Goals Behind Gretzky: 93

Playoff Goals Behind Gretzky: 54

Assists Behind Gretzky: 914

Playoff Assists Behind Gretzky: 168

Points Behind Gretzky: 1,007

Playoff Points Behind Gretzky: 222

Points Per Game Behind Gretzky: 0.87

Playoff Points Per Game Behind Gretzky: 0.82

Plus/Minus Behind Gretzky: 360 (13 seasons of Howe's
    career were played before the NHL tracked plus/minus)

Playoff Plus/Minus Behind Gretzky: 86 (with a heavy
    asterisk)

Scoring Titles Behind Gretzky: 4

Hart Trophies Behind Gretzky: 3

Stanley Cups ~~Behind Gretzky~~: tied with Gretzky at 4

Other Accolades Include: WHA Avco Cup Trophy in 1974
    and 1975, WHA MVP in 1974

First and foremost, "Mr. Hockey" is a better nickname than
"The Great One," so there's one department where Gordie Howe
has Wayne Gretzky beat right off the bat.

And there is no Wayne Gretzky without Gordie Howe.
Mr. Hockey was one of Gretzky's childhood idols. The two famously took a photo together when Gretzky was still just a kid.
Incredibly, Howe, whose first NHL season began in 1946, got to
play against Gretzky in his rookie year, 1979–80.

The lesser longevity of some of the people in the "greatest
hockey players of all time" discussion hurts their case for the top

of the podium. Especially when compared to Gordie. His legendary resume is a combination of short-term dominance and long-
term staying power. The guy did play professional hockey on the
same team as two of his adult sons, after all, which is a wild accomplishment in itself.

Patrick Marleau recently passed Gordie Howe's record for all-
time NHL games played, narrowly exceeding the record by just
12 games when he reached 1,779. But there's an asterisk. Howe
played an additional 419 games in the WHA during the 1970s,
before rejoining the NHL when the WHA folded and some teams
were absorbed by the NHL.

Between the NHL and WHA, adding up both regular season
and playoff totals, Gordie Howe played 2,421 professional games.
If you include the one game he played in the IHL in the 1997–98
season, nearly two decades after his retirement (yes, you read that
correctly), it's 2,422.

In case you're wondering, Jaromir Jagr has played in more
games than that, but there are a few important things to note.
The first is Jagr's totals are across more than half a dozen different
leagues, including leagues in Italy, Germany, and Czechia's second tier. The other important caveat is that for the vast majority
of Gordie Howe's NHL career, a full season was only 70 games.
For most of Jagr's career, seasons were 82 games. Over three decades, that difference adds up in a big way.

NHL players weren't always as big as they are today. During
Howe's rookie season of 1946–47, only 13 skaters in the entire
league weighed 200 pounds or more. Five of those 13 players
made their NHL debut that season, including Howe, tied for the
fourth heaviest in the league, at 205 pounds. During the 1954–55
season, he was one of just eight players weighing 200 pounds or
more, a group that included the mighty Jean Béliveau.

I point out things like that because if you were too young to watch Howe play, and I'm among that group, you might hear legends of how big and mean he was on the ice. Then you might look up how big he was and think people were exaggerating. Trust me: he might not be big by today's NHL standards, but during his prime, Gordie Howe was a freight train.

As my pal and fellow hockey author Ken Reid often says: "Room!" Howe's presence commanded room. That's room to think, room to move, room to do whatever he wanted with the puck, and good luck to any man foolish enough to try to take it off him.

So how on earth do we figure out what Gordie Howe's prime was if he played basically forever? I'll admit this is arbitrary, but let's take the chunk of time between Howe's first Stanley Cup–winning season (1949–50) and his final Hart Trophy and scoring title (1962–63).

In that time, Gordie Howe led the NHL in games played (962), goals (505), assists (604), points (1,109), even-strength goals (363), even-strength points (735), powerplay goals (129), powerplay points (353), and game-winning goals (90). In most of those categories during that time span, nobody was particularly close.

The only player who approaches Howe's level in those years was Jean Béliveau, who matched Howe's points-per-game total of 1.15. Béliveau's career began a bit later than Howe's; otherwise, he might have been closer to Howe's numbers.

Even if you move the beginning of the time frame to Howe's rookie season in 1946–47 and stop at Maurice Richard's final season of 1959–60, Howe's 411 goals beats Richard—who scored the second most with 337—by a whopping 74 goals. What all four of Wayne Gretzky, Gordie Howe, Bobby Orr, and Mario Lemieux share in common isn't just dominance, it's dominance over time, even if some dominated for longer than others. During the 1950s and early 1960s, Gordie Howe was a wrecking machine who could fill your net, and if you tried to stop him, he could fill the local dentist's office with your patronage. Howe was known for his elbows. A June 2016 Sportsnet.ca article quotes Gordie's son Marty as once saying, "You don't hook him around the ribs from behind, or he will most likely take the elbow and knock you out. It's an elbow that goes from the waist and comes up. It's pretty scientific."

While it's obvious that Howe dominated his peers, and it's obvious why Wayne Gretzky idolized him, how do Mr. Hockey's numbers compare to Gretzky's?

I was completely shocked to find Gordie Howe scored 100 points in the NHL just once, in the 1968–69 season. Then I discovered the first three players to break the NHL's 100-point barrier were Phil Esposito, Bobby Hull, and Gordie Howe—all in the 1968–69 season somehow!

As for 50-goal seasons, I was shocked once again that Gordie Howe had zero. He got extremely close with 49 goals in 1951–52. Context matters, though. When Howe scored 49, it was the second-highest single-season total in NHL history, behind Maurice Richard's 1944–45 record of 50. At the time, Howe also had the third-highest single-season goal total in NHL history with the 47 goals he scored just one season before.

Gordie Howe was great. He was well beyond great. We know this. But the question is: Was Gordie Howe better than Wayne Gretzky? No disrespect to Howe, who I can't say enough times is a complete legend of the game, but there really isn't an argument.

Gretzky smashed through Howe's points record by over 1,000, and in nearly 300 fewer games. The only offensive stats Howe has that Gretzky never surpassed are powerplay goals (211 vs.

204) and game-winning goals (121 vs. 91). In nearly every other measurable way, there just isn't a legitimate argument that Gretzky didn't pass Howe during his career on the ice.

In my opinion, there are two players who are better comparisons for Gordie Howe. The first is Jaromir Jagr, who matches up well with Howe in so many ways because of his combination of longevity as well as individual success and team success. Maybe I shouldn't talk about Jagr in the past tense, since he may never actually retire. Howe edges Jagr in goals, Jagr edges Howe in assists. It's a close race for scoring titles, with Howe's six to Jagr's five. Howe does crush Jagr in league MVP wins, though, by a margin of six to one.

While it might seem strange, the other legend I would compare to Howe is goaltender Jacques Plante. There was a time in history when each of those players could be considered the best to ever play his position: They both won Stanley Cups, individual trophies, and served as standard-bearers in the sport. It's easy to argue that both players probably belong on the Mount Rushmore of their positions: Plante for goaltenders and Howe for skaters, or at minimum for forwards. But were both players eventually passed? Yes. Maybe that's a good thing.

Sometimes greatness isn't measured by personal accolades or even team accomplishments. Sometimes greatness lies in inspiring future generations of greatness, even if means being surpassed.

Gordie Howe gave more to the game of hockey than he took. In many ways, Mr. Hockey gave us the Great One. The man who was once the greatest hockey player of all time paved the way for the new greatest player of all time. No matter where you rank him, Gordie Howe was, and still is, a legend. But there's only one at the top.

BOBBY ORR

STATISTICS

Goals Behind Gretzky: 624

Playoff Goals Behind Gretzky: 96

Assists Behind Gretzky: 1,318

Playoff Assists Behind Gretzky: 194

Points Behind Gretzky: 1,942

Playoff Points Behind Gretzky: 190

Points Per Game Behind Gretzky: 0.53

Playoff Points Per Game Behind Gretzky: 0.6

Plus/Minus ~~Behind Gretzky~~: +62 better than Gretzky

Playoff Plus/Minus Behind Gretzky: 31

Scoring Titles Behind Gretzky: 8

Hart Trophies Behind Gretzky: 6

Stanley Cups Behind Gretzky: 2

Other Accolades Include: 1976 Canada Cup Champion and
   Canada Cup MVP

Bobby Orr's career was so much more than one great flying photo. But it was so short. He played 657 career NHL regular season games. Add in 74 playoff games, and we only got a little over 700 games featuring Bobby Orr. It's just not fair.

Bobby Orr played in less than half as many regular season NHL games as Wayne Gretzky did. Had Orr's career not been cut short by injuries, possibly by as much as half, there's a really good chance he'd be the unanimous best hockey player of all time.

Three Hart Trophies and two scoring titles might not sound like a lot for a player to be in the "greatest of all-time" discussion, except you have to remember Orr was a defenceman.

Actually, no. Bobby Orr was *the* defenceman, no question

about it. The list of defenders not named Bobby Orr to win the Art Ross Trophy for the NHL scoring title is nobody, because Bobby Orr is the only dude to do it.

Let's put it into modern context: during the 2022–23 season, Erik Karlsson put together a healthy 82-game season and went absolutely buck wild with 101 points, which was the first time a defender had scored 100 or more points since Brian Leetch in the 1991–92 season.

Bobby Orr also put up 101 points, during the 1972–73 season— and it was the sixth-highest point total of his career. He put up totals of 117, 120, 122, 135, and, in 1970–71, the still-standing record for points in a season by a defenceman: 139. A decade and a half later, Paul Coffey fell just one point shy of the record. The record for points in a single season from a defender not named Bobby Orr or Paul Coffey is held by Al MacInnis, with "just" 103. So 139 in 78 games is madness.

Orr also owns the single-season record for plus/minus with a preposterous plus-124 during his legendary 1970–71 season. Larry Robinson got close at plus-120, while Wayne Gretzky became the only forward to reach the century mark, with exactly plus-100.

During Orr's shortened career, spanning from the 1966–67 season to the 1978–79 season, he had a plus/minus rating of plus-582. The next-closest guy was Serge Savard at just plus-487, while Guy Lafleur sat third at plus-388. Once again, nobody was even remotely close to Bobby Orr.

There is one category where Orr completely mops the floor with Gretzky: Orr has eight James Norris Trophies as the NHL's best defenceman. Gretzky of course has zero Norris Trophies, because he wasn't a defenceman. But check this out: Orr won the Norris Trophy in every single season where he played more than

20 games, except for one. The one full season Orr didn't win the Norris, he won rookie of the year instead. I can't shout this loud enough: Bobby Orr won eight straight Norris Trophies. Essentially, Bobby Orr showed up, instantly became the best defender in the league, and then simply was that for eight years before leaving.

If you want to knock Bobby Orr's complete and utter dominance, his highest-scoring seasons came during the first years of the NHL's expansion era. After Orr's rookie season, the NHL exploded from the Original Six teams to 12. With a league that doubled in size overnight, the talent level in the NHL had been watered down.

For example, during the St. Louis Blues' three straight appearances in the Stanley Cup Final from 1968 to 1970 as an expansion team, they played the Montreal Canadiens twice before famously playing Bobby Orr's Boston Bruins. During those three straight Cup Final appearances, the Blues won zero games and lost 12. Probably worth mentioning that the NHL's playoff format at the time guaranteed that one of the league's six expansion teams would earn a spot in the Stanley Cup Final by default, and it showed.

If you hate that argument, I don't blame you. Maybe it isn't fair. If you're Bobby Orr, you can only play against the opponent across the ice from you. The timing for the start of Orr's career might have been fortunate, but no defender on any of the other Original Six teams was putting up the numbers Orr was.

To give you an idea of how preposterously ahead of his peers Bobby Orr was, Orr had 915 points in his career, and the defender with the next-closest point total over that time span was Brad Park, with 616. In other words, Orr was nearly 300 points up on the next-closest guy. Want to know the guy in third? It was Carol

Vadnais, with 521, nearly 400 points behind. In case you're wondering, the goal leaders are Orr with 270 and Guy Lapointe with 158, over 100 goals behind.

No defenceman Bobby Orr played against was remotely close in terms of two-way dominance. Orr played against slam-dunk Hockey Hall of Famers who couldn't hold a candle to him. There isn't much of an argument against Orr as the most dominant defender because of how absurdly ahead of the pack he was compared to his competition on the blue line. And I'd be willing to hear the argument for Bobby Orr as the most dominant player ever.

But longevity is a killer.

It's impossible to compare Mario Lemieux to Wayne Gretzky, however close you think their resumes are. You just can't say the guy who only played about two-thirds as many games as the other guy is the best ever. It's not fair that it worked out that way for Lemieux, but it would also be unfair to discount the fact that Gretzky dominated his competition for longer.

Unfortunately, Bobby Orr's career is an even more extreme example. Between regular season and playoffs, Orr played 731 NHL games. Gretzky played 1,695. How do you argue that Gretzky is the runner-up to someone with nearly 1,000 fewer games played?

The argument that Bobby Orr was the most dominant defender in hockey history is completely set in stone. Even though his career was severely shortened, Orr still sits 11th in all-time NHL scoring among defencemen, sandwiched between Chris Chelios at tenth and Scott Stevens at 12th, two guys who played nearly 1,000 more games than Orr.

There's room for others in the "best defenceman of all time" conversation: Bobby Orr's greatness sometimes causes us to overlook other great blueliners. We don't talk enough about the NHL's all-time scoring leader among defenders, Ray Bourque, whose

1,579 points is actually good enough for 11th all time among all players, not just defenders. If you want to fantasize about which players of yesteryear would kill it in today's game, Nicklas Lidstrom is a good pick, with over 1,100 points, mostly in an era with decreased scoring, all while barely ever throwing a hit because he always had the puck. Larry Robinson holds the career NHL plus/minus record at plus-722, while Orr, who sits second, was well behind at plus-582. That's a record that won't be beaten anytime soon; the closest active NHL player is still 400 behind Robinson.

If you could stuff the best versions of all the top 100 players of all time in a time machine and have them play each other in a tournament, would Bobby Orr be the best player in attendance? There's a good chance.

But for everything Orr accomplished, flip back a few pages, and go check out Gretzky's resume again. If Gretzky and Orr played the same number of games, whether Orr found a way to get up to Gretzky's nearly 1,500 games, or Gretzky got knocked down to Bobby Orr's 657, would Gretzky still come out on top?

If you only look at Gretzky's first 657 games, which is how many Bobby Orr was limited to due to injuries, Gretzky still put up 1,577 points during that span. That's 2.4 points per game. If they could have invented a league better than the NHL so Gretzky could have had a challenge in the 1980s, they would have. The closest thing we got to that was the 1980s New York Islanders, and he beat them, too.

What if Bobby Orr had stayed healthy and was able to play for longer? That's one of hockey's all-time questions. Consider this: Orr had 915 points in 657 games. If Orr had stayed healthy and maintained his offensive clip of 1.39 points per game, which is the highest average by any defender in history, he would have put up 1,392 points.

For a moment in time, there's no question that Bobby Orr was the best in his day. For all time, it's still the Great One.

MARIO LEMIEUX

STATISTICS
Goals Behind Gretzky: 204
Playoff Goals Behind Gretzky: 46
Assists Behind Gretzky: 930
Playoff Assists Behind Gretzky: 164
Points Behind Gretzky: 1,134
Playoff Points Behind Gretzky: 210
Points Per Game Behind Gretzky: 0.04
Playoff Points Per Game Behind Gretzky: 0.23
Plus/Minus Behind Gretzky: 406
Playoff Plus/Minus Behind Gretzky: 71
Scoring Titles Behind Gretzky: 4
Hart Trophies Behind Gretzky: 6
Stanley Cups Behind Gretzky: 2
Other Accolades Include: Canada Cup in 1988, Olympic
    gold in 2002, World Cup of Hockey in 2004

In terms of offensive greatness and pure dominance, Mario Lemieux is the only forward who can hold a candle to Wayne Gretzky. Lemieux's and Gretzky's points per game are head and shoulders above the pack, with Gretzky at 1.92 on his career and Lemieux at 1.88. The next-closest player with at least 200 NHL games under their belt is New York Islanders legend Mike Bossy, at 1.5 points per game, which is hugely impressive and yet somehow not even close. Other than Lemieux and Gretzky, only ten other players with at least 200 NHL games played are even at 1.2 points per game or higher.

It can be easy to overlook, but Gretzky actually played five full seasons in the NHL before Lemieux even made his NHL debut. Those years include ridiculous feats like Gretzky's still-standing record of 92 goals in a season and his eclipsing of the 200-point milestone twice.

Of course, Gretzky also retired (once and for all) before Mario Lemieux did. What if we only counted stats from Lemieux's rookie season (1984–85) until Lemieux's first retirement from hockey, at the end of the 1996–97 season?

GRETZKY VERSUS LEMIEUX STATISTICS

Regular Season Games played: Gretzky 942 vs. Lemieux 745

Playoff Games Played: Gretzky 156 vs. Lemieux 89

Regular Season Goals: Gretzky 506 vs. Lemieux 613
   (advantage Lemieux)

Playoff Goals: Gretzky 83 vs. Lemieux 70 (advantage
   Gretzky)

Regular Season Assists: Gretzky 1,285 vs. Lemieux 881
   (advantage Gretzky)

Playoff Assists: Gretzky 190 vs. Lemieux 85 (advantage
   Gretzky)

Regular Season Points: Gretzky 1,791 vs. Lemieux 1,494
   (advantage Gretzky)

Playoff Points: Gretzky 273 vs. Lemieux 155 (advantage
   Gretzky)

Regular Season Points Per Game: Gretzky 1.90 vs. Lemieux
   2.01 (advantage Lemieux)

Playoff Points Per Game: Gretzky 1.75 vs. Lemieux 1.74
   (virtually identical)

There is, as I'm sure you've noticed, a glaring discrepancy in games played during this period. A large reason for that is injuries, Lemieux's back in particular, not to mention his diagnosis of Hodgkin's disease during the 1992–93 season. Despite that limiting Lemieux to 60 games in 1992–93, he still won the league's scoring title with 160 points that season by a margin of 12 points.

That season, Lemieux's 69 goals and 160 points put him on pace for 96 goals and 224 points if he'd played the full number of games. That would have shattered Gretzky's single-season goals and points records. And Lemieux's Pittsburgh Penguins were reigning back-to-back Stanley Cup champions at the time. It was quite possibly the greatest season any player has ever had in the history of the NHL, only to be interrupted by a terrifying battle.

If he'd returned to hockey and just been average, it still would have been incredible. But this is Mario Lemieux. After two months away, he returned to the Penguins lineup and scored 30 goals in 20 games, including a five-goal game and back-to-back four-goal games, and 56 points.

There's a strong argument for Mario Lemieux being the best player of all time, ahead of Wayne Gretzky, because there was a time when Lemieux was clearly head and shoulders above him, despite the Great One still being in his prime, or at least the tail end of it. Take the first four seasons Wayne Gretzky spent in LA with the Kings. Steve Yzerman and Teemu Selanne each scored 1.57 points per game. Gretzky crushed them with 1.89 points per game. Mario Lemieux had 2.31 points per game, nearly half a point per game more than Gretzky. For that period, even though Gretzky was still very much the Great One, Mario Lemieux was the best hockey player on Planet Earth by a wide margin.

By now, you might be convinced into crowning Mario Lemieux as the best player in hockey history. The sheer number of times he took time off due to injury, illness, or straight-up retirement only to return as the best player in the sport is a feat in itself. Out of all the players hockey has been robbed of prematurely, Mario Lemieux is at the top of the list. He is eighth in all-time NHL scoring despite being tied for 502nd in all-time NHL games played. Read that last sentence as many times as you need to.

All of those magnificent achievements aside, there is a gap of 204 goals, 930 assists, and 1,134 points between Gretzky and Lemieux. For reference, neither of the Sedin twins reached 1,100 career NHL points, meaning the gap between Gretzky's and Lemieux's point totals is larger than the total either Sedin twin scored in his entire career, and both of those guys are in the Hockey Hall of Fame. Basically, the gap between Gretzky and Lemieux is an entire undeniable Hall of Fame career and then some.

It all comes down to this: You could easily argue Mario Lemieux absolutely *could* have been better than Gretzky. It's incredibly hard to argue that he definitively *was*.

Gretzky played 572 more regular season games than Lemieux, and if Gretzky had done nothing with those games, then maybe things would be closer. That's not the case; he completely tore the sport limb from limb.

During the 393 NHL games Gretzky played before Lemieux's debut, he had 356 goals. That gave him a 62-goal gap on Mike Bossy over a five-season period. His 558 assists gave him a 219-assist gap on Bryan Trottier. His cartoony 914 points over—and I can't stress this enough—five holy smoking seasons gave him a 320-point gap on Mike Bossy, who was second. For the first five years of his career, Wayne Gretzky averaged 64 more points per season than the man in second. Truly, deeply goofy.

If Mario Lemieux had better luck with health, it's entirely possible that he would have been breaking Wayne Gretzky's records while Gretzky was at least in the tail end of his prime. Unfortunately, that's a big if. You can't just give a player 500 or 600 games that never happened and add that to their resume.

There were times when Mario Lemieux was the greatest hockey player on the face of the planet, taking that title directly out of Gretzky's hands. But the best of all time? We'll never know what could have been.

THE GREATEST OF ALL TIME

If you had to make a Mount Rushmore of hockey, I think Gordie Howe, Bobby Orr, Wayne Gretzky, and Mario Lemieux is a pretty fantastic group of four, don't you? To me, this is the undisputed quartet. Sure, there's room for other players to challenge, some of whom I mentioned, and I'm sure some guys who are still playing have a chance to get on the mountain. What if Sidney Crosby finds a way to add a fourth or fifth Stanley Cup? What if Alexander Ovechkin breaks Gretzky's all-time goal-scoring record? What if Connor McDavid keeps being, well, Connor McDavid? Time will tell, but for now, I've got my list.

At the top of that list, however, is a list of one: Wayne Gretzky. No other player in the history of the NHL has put up the same single-season dominance. The list of players to score 200 or more points in a season is only four guys long, and Wayne Gretzky is all four guys.

No other player has dominated his own peers in his own era the way Gretzky did. During a five-season span from the 1981–82 season to the 1985–86 season, Gretzky scored 1,036 points in 394 games. His goal totals were 92 (the still-standing single-season record), 71, 87, 73, and in 1985–86, when he decided to go easy and only score 52 goals, he set the all-time record for assists in a season, with 163, and points, with 215.

No other player's entire body of work, including awards, championships, and records that may never be broken, stands up to Wayne Gretzky's.

If you weren't convinced before, you should be by now. If you were already convinced, then I hope you enjoyed reading about some of the truly mind-bending things Gretzky pulled off, some so silly that they don't even seem real. Like, 1,036 points in 394 games? Get out of here!

He's one of one: The Great One. The Greatest One.

Since this book is about having fun with hockey rants, how about I leave you with a thought exercise: Would a team full of Wayne Gretzkys win a tournament against a team full of Orrs, Lemieuxs, and Howes? If that's the next thing you and your buddies argue about for two hours, I'll feel like I've done my job.

HYPE TRAIN

Nobody wants to admit the hype train was right.

Every time hockey has some hot new prospect, the next big thing, experts will talk about how absolutely incredible this kid is going to be, and a big bunch of party-poopers have to take your good time and tell you, "Alas, no."

Don't get me wrong, there's no shortage of prospects who media and experts alike grossly overhype. These would-be superstars are foisted into the limelight at the ripe old age of a grade ten student, we're sold that this person will become an unstoppable monster while they're a literal child, and then if they don't quite live up to those lofty expectations, they're called a bust.

For those reasons, it's okay to question the hype machine and be skeptical about it.

That being said, the hype machine is often right.

Let's distinguish one thing right away: there's a difference between hockey, the fun pastime that kids play when they're younger and maybe get to continue with their buddies into adulthood, and professional hockey.

Can hockey parents be overbearing? Yes. That's pretty well-documented and not limited to just hockey. Is minor hockey too political, fraught with handshake agreements, nepotism, and egos? Of course it is. Do we often forget that the whole point of kids playing organized sports is so that they can have fun in an environment that gives them tools to grow as people? All the time.

Then there's professional hockey (and this extends to all professional sports).

Professional hockey sells seats to the games as well as jerseys, shirts, sweaters, sweatpants, jackets, hats, stickers, beer openers, novelty giant plastic chain necklaces, and multi-billion-dollar TV rights deals. Professional hockey can't sell a single one of those things if you don't care about professional hockey.

Part of selling professional hockey is saying, "Hey, these players are really good!"

I still don't think of myself as old, and I'm gonna cling to that notion until the arthritis makes it too hard to cling on to, but one thing I'm definitely old enough to remember is the entirety of both Sidney Crosby's and Alex Ovechkin's entire careers. That means I remember the beginning of their careers and the leadup to them.

Crosby and Ovechkin played for two genuinely terrible—I'm talking reprehensibly awful—NHL teams. If that sounds weird to you, go look up how bad the Pittsburgh Penguins and Washington Capitals were before Crosby and Ovechkin showed up.

Despite the weak teams those kids were joining, the NHL was coming out of the 2004–05 full-season lockout. With the league set to return to the ice for the first time in a year, the NHL wasn't about to ignore the gift it was handed in the form of these two generational talents being plunked into its lap at the same time. The hype machine marketed the ever-loving hell out of the Sid vs. Ovi show.

Was that manufactured rivalry overhyped? At the time, yeah, it seemed like it was. You couldn't turn left or right in the hockey world without having that rivalry shoved in your face. Even though these two were putting up highlight after highlight every night, it was like "Uncle! Enough is enough!"

Now Crosby and Ovechkin are grizzled greybeards nearing the end of their respective careers. At minimum, the hype machine was 100 per cent right about these two, and you could strongly argue the hype machine didn't hype these two up enough.

Crosby is already top ten in point-scoring in NHL history, while Ovechkin is closing in on the all-time goal-scoring title, keeping in mind that both guys played most of their careers in one of the lowest-scoring eras in NHL history.

Since the start of the 2005–06 season, Crosby and Ovechkin's rookie season, both players have over 1,500 points. Nobody else has over 1,300.

Since the start of the 2005–06 season, Ovechkin is obviously first in goal-scoring, and Crosby is second. Crosby is also first in assists over that time span with over 1,000, while Ovechkin is still in the top ten despite being a notorious sniper.

Crosby is second in playoff goal-scoring since his career began, while Ovechkin is third. Who's first: Joe Pavelski. I know, right? Speaking of guys who don't get enough hype!

Crosby has three Stanley Cups in a league that has never had fewer than 30 teams during his career, and Ovi finally managed to grab one of his own in 2018. Both players went head to head in the playoffs many times, each player's team getting the best of the other's en route to Stanley Cup victories.

Sidney Crosby and Alexander Ovechkin were never overhyped. Never, not once.

Crosby will likely retire in the conversation as a top five player in NHL history, or a top five forward at minimum. Ovechkin is already regarded by many as the best goal-scorer in NHL history, and the second he beats Gretzky's record of 894 career goals, there will be no disputing it.

Want to know something crazy? At 27 years old, Connor McDavid has already had three seasons with more points than either Crosby or Ovechkin ever put up in their careers.

How does Connor McDavid factor into this? People said he was overhyped, too!

McDavid's rookie season was my first at Sportsnet, and I couldn't believe the amount of moaning and groaning people did about all the coverage McDavid had gotten as an 18-year-old. Now here he is, the best hockey player on the planet, with multiple MVP and scoring titles to his name, consistently putting up the kind of stats we haven't seen in the National Hockey League in three decades.

I could get killed for telling you this, but I'll let you in on a big secret that all the huge media companies don't want you to know: the *real* reason Connor McDavid got so much hype is because he's ridiculously, unfathomably good at hockey. Keep that between us, okay? Don't tell anybody else, I'm serious.

You might look at my little rant earlier about the hype machine and the NHL selling itself and think, *If the NHL is trying to sell us on something, aren't we right to be skeptical?* Honestly, I don't think that's a bad instinct. The world needs more media literacy like it needs oxygen.

All I'm saying is even if the hype machine is always in motion, when somebody truly special comes around, you'll know. Everybody who winds up being the first overall pick comes with some fanfare, but when somebody truly game-changing comes around, the NHL won't be shy about letting you know about this.

On another note, have you guys heard of Connor Bedard?

13.
Let Them Play

We've been around a long time. Not necessarily you and I; I'm talking about people in general. We've been walking around for thousands of years, talking for a big chunk of those years, and we've said all kinds of stuff.

Since ice hockey arrived a little over a century ago, we've invented even more things to say. It's healthy, however, to revisit some of our old sayings and ask if they even make sense. When it comes to sports, we need to spend some time discussing the phrase "let them play."

One of the most exhausting things is watching a fun game, whether it's hockey, basketball, football, or soccer, where the referees get too involved. It's one thing to have to call a penalty or a foul here or there, it's another to make erroneous calls that tilt the game in one team's favour and make it an uphill battle for the other.

This isn't about bashing referees. Ice hockey is a uniquely difficult sport to play and to officiate. As ref or linesman, you're flying around the ice, stopping, starting, hauling ass in all directions, desperately trying not to bump into or get freight trained by players who are bigger than you and wearing double the equipment, while dodging vulcanized rubber zipping by at highway speeds and scrotum height. Shakespearean, I know, but all that is to say: refs have a tough job.

Of course we would like officials to get everything right all of the time. Make sure you catch the big trips, the hooking, the slashing, the chippy stuff behind the play, all while judging off-sides and icings, and protecting your nethers. It's just not reason-able. Mistakes are going to be made. Calls are going to be missed.

Refs are human! They make mistakes. Sometimes they order chicken wings that are too hot and pay for it for most of the next day. Sometimes they pull up to a red light and get caught picking their nose by the guy in the car next to them. Sometimes they're gonna blow a penalty call. If you're getting more calls wrong than you are right, then yeah, that's a problem, but if you're trying your best and making the odd mistake, most reasonable people will forgive you. Hockey can make us a touch unreasonable (and even ranty), but you get my point.

As much as screaming at the TV is practically a national pas-time, the referees and linesmen in the NHL don't have their jobs by accident. They're the best officials in the world, so I can forgive honest mistakes.

What I can't forgive is just "letting the players play."

First of all, what does "let them play" even mean? The idea is that refs decide to stay out of the way, generally ignoring minor infractions. If the game gets too chippy, or there's a bit of a scrum after the whistle, you don't have to send anybody to the box, just break it up. If an attacking player has the puck and gets hooked or slashed, but it's not too egregious, you don't need to go blowing the play dead and giving a powerplay.

Besides, someone on the other team just did the exact same thing last shift. There! Now you're even. That's another aspect of "letting them play" that drives me nuts. While trying to keep things even is well-intended, it starts to get messy. So you let this guy's slash go because you let that other one go. That's okay, I guess. But the blue team has tripped the red team three times and the red team only tripped the blue team once. Are we still keeping score here? I'm a bit confused. Does the red team automatically get two freebies? Why are we evening things up if one team is clearly good, has the puck more, is moving their feet and making their opponent do things to take a penalty?

Hockey is a hard enough game to officiate without mandating that every official has to become a chartered accountant, keeping track of who's tripping who and arbitrarily deciding they're only going to call every third trip, like it's a Boxing Day sale on stick infractions. "Let them play" is the worst, most extreme version of that.

Here's another expression I hate: "Refs don't want to decide the game." As in, late in the third period or in a tight playoff game, especially in a game with something on the line, refs sometimes develop a tendency to swallow their whistle. A defending player slashes his opponent near the end of the game? Well, I'm not calling that. I don't want to put the other team at a disadvantage. Except by not calling a penalty, you *are* putting somebody at a disadvantage—the team of the guy with a newly half-broken wrist.

When an officiating crew decides to "let the players play," they're agreeing to not involve themselves in the game so the players alone can decide the winner. I actually think that's a lovely, noble, romantic concept. My only problem is it makes absolutely no sense.

When refs "let the players play," they're basically, uh, not doing their job.

"I don't want to get involved." Okay, that's fine—have you ever considered a career in the culinary arts? Perhaps a trade? Maybe go to medical school and see what you're made of, Dr. Ref.

Getting involved is exactly a referee's job. If Player A decides to two-hand slash Player B in the ankle, it's a ref's job to put their whistle in their mouth, blow the play dead, and call a penalty. Every time you blow your whistle for a trip, hook, slash, elbow, punch, knee, check from behind, offside, icing, or puck over the glass, you're getting involved. That's kind of the whole gig.

Imagine going to a restaurant, ordering spaghetti and meatballs, and they bring you a box of pasta, a jar of sauce, and some ground beef. You ask what the hell this is supposed to be, and the chef says, "I'm just letting the food . . . *food*, you know. I'm not getting involved."

Then, after you ask, "Isn't your whole job to actually do stuff with the food?" the chef calls you a whiny baby and tells you, "If you don't like it, just go to another restaurant." That's how it feels to be a fan in hockey who actually wants officials to get out of bed and do their job.

Let's apply "let them play" to this scenario: There's a player flying into the zone with the puck, and he's got a defender staying with them, neck and neck. Before the attacking player can get a shot off, the defending player gets his stick into the hands of the puck carrier, he loses the puck, his scoring chance is ruined, and the puck goes back the other way.

When the refs don't call a penalty on that play, exactly who are they letting play? Is it the defending player who wasn't good enough to take his man without hooking him, or is it the attacking player who did everything he was supposed to do until the guy next to him broke the rules and stopped him from doing his job?

Dudes who don't like this argument tend to confuse valid criticism with whining. Don't get me wrong, almost every sports fan whines from time to time. If all refs make mistakes then so do fans. But if we both see the same thing, and I call it what it is and you don't, and you have a problem with me pointing it out, then I agree with you that one of us is a whiner. We just don't agree on who.

Really letting the players play would be allowing the players following the rules to continue to do their thing and actually calling a penalty on any player who tries to stop them with an infraction. I paid $200 for a seat to see Connor McDavid slice and dice defences like a butcher, not to watch a team's fifth-best defenceman hold on to the back of him like McDavid's a speedboat and they're ripping around on a wakeboard.

People often say "regular season success" doesn't matter. Okay, sure, playoff hockey *is* going to ramp up and be more intense than regular season hockey. That's a fact. It's also a fact that hockey has three rule books:

1. The regular season rule book, where penalties are penalties.
2. The playoff rule book, where penalties are called half as often as they would be in the regular season, especially late in a series, because there's a scrum after every whistle.
3. The late-playoff rule book, which only applies to Game 5, 6, or 7 of a series, along with the third period of almost any playoff game.

The trick is to build a team that's pretty good at playing under all three, with the tie-breaker going to the third.

This isn't a call to take hitting, fighting, or nastiness out of hockey. I love a good, hard-fought battle. Just don't lie to me that "letting the players play" is the way to go. It's a sport. If my team can't play by the rules and beat your team, then we deserve to lose, and vice versa. But there's a pretty enormous difference between allowing for some intensity in a game and just letting everybody on the ice do whatever the hell they want.

This is why I pointed out how good NHL officials are. When they "let the players play," they're not missing calls, they're just straight-up ignoring them. There's an enormous difference between making a mistake and having a mandate. If you earnestly miss a call, then aw shucks, shame on you, I guess. You didn't mean to do it, and even though it hurts, mistakes do happen. But when you make the conscious decision to just let things go, that actually makes you more involved in the hockey game than a mistake does.

If you miss a slash, you miss a slash. If you make a conscious decision to ignore 90 per cent of slashes, you might be surprised to find that everybody's skating around flailing their hockey stick like a battle-axe. Not to mention that letting heaps of calls go makes the penalties you do actually call look completely stupid. You can't let a bunch of identical hooking calls go just to blow the whistle on the fifth one.

This begs a valid question I've been asked many times: How much of the game do we want spent on the powerplay? I wish the answer was simple. The harsh answer could be, "Well, it's on the players to not break the rules and take penalties," but that's not exactly realistic. I've been watching games where both teams were awarded eight penalties each and thought to myself, *If this is the first game somebody's watching, it's also probably their last.*

What drives me nuts is the NHL tried calling more penalties a few years ago before almost immediately abandoning the idea. The 2005–06 season was good for the league. It returned to action after a full-year lockout, and teams were jam-packed with exciting rookies such as Sidney Crosby and Alexander Ovechkin. The return of hockey also came with a few rule changes limiting things like obstruction. Not every player adapted to these rules, so naturally a lot of them started taking more penalties.

The result was that powerplay opportunities per team went from 4.24 per game in 2003–04 to a whopping 5.85 per game in 2005–06, the highest total in NHL history, according to Hockey-Reference.com.

Clearly, somebody is struggling to figure something out here. When that happens, you have two options:

1. Work with them to solve the problem.
2. Say screw it and just make it easier for them.

Rather than have NHL players properly adapt to the new rules, the NHL decided that too many penalties being called meant they should just ease up on how many penalties were handed out. Granted, 5.85 powerplay opportunities per game is unsustainable madness—the league needed to address that. But instead of having players figure out the new rules, the numbers suggest that the league took the path of least resistance. Time to let them play.

Following that season, powerplay opportunities decreased nearly every year until the 2021–22 season, when teams had an average of 2.89 powerplay opportunities per game. Not only is that less than half the number from 2005–06, it's the lowest frequency of powerplay opportunities in NHL history, or at least since 1963–64, when they began tracking that stat.

If the increase in penalties during the 2005–06 season was an overcorrection, what followed for nearly two decades was even worse. There are things you can't do in today's NHL that were generally allowed in and before the early 2000s, and I mean that as a good thing. You might see a gentle hook in the hands get called a penalty, and you'll only have to wait nanoseconds until you hear somebody talk about how everything's a penalty in today's softened game. They can feel however they want about it, but that's objectively, provably untrue.

"Letting them play" is no better than calling every little thing you see. It's probably worse. If the refs are going to "let them play," why stop there? Use two sticks at once, put your right-winger on a snowmobile, and make your backup goalie a vending machine. We're letting the players play, after all. Mandated anarchy is still anarchy. There are rules for a reason, and if you don't like those rules, you can always find another sport.

Ooh, I liked getting to say that for a change. I totally get why people use that all the time, even if they're wrong. That's a staple of hockey talk that goes nowhere: you suggest that something violent might have been bad and, you know, against the rules, and some dummy inevitably tells you to go watch soccer or something instead.

I think every hockey fan agrees that we should let the players play; we just have different definitions for what that means.

14.

Women's Hockey Troll Eulogy

In a book dedicated to rants and raves about hockey, I will admit that there should be more women's hockey content.

I had plans to talk about how wonderful women's hockey is, how incredible the players are, and how important women's sports are on the whole.

Take Hayley Wickenheiser, for example. Let's say you were in charge of writing a Disney movie and it was your job to create Disney's next woman protagonist. If you simply took Wickenheiser's resume, just her honest-to-goodness life accomplishments, and wrote them down as the accomplishments of a Disney princess, people would groan and say, "All right, dude, you're laying it on a little thick."

Wickenheiser won about a billion gold medals as an active member of Team Canada's national women's hockey team. That's not the official number, but honestly it's not that far off. Looking for another challenge, she decided to head to Europe to play professional men's hockey. After returning to women's hockey and winning even more championships, Wickenheiser decided to become a doctor. As if to increase the difficulty in a video game because it's too easy, Wickenheiser also did this during the Covid pandemic. Wickenheiser is now an assistant GM of the Toronto

Maple Leafs, a published author, and if I kept going, this entire book would just be about her.

Then there are those who are still playing professional women's hockey. You could easily wax poetic about Marie-Philip Poulin, who is without exaggeration one of the most clutch superstars in the history of the sport. In Vancouver, at the 2010 Winter Olympic Games, I watched a then-18-year-old Poulin score both goals for Team Canada in a 2–0 win over the United States in the gold medal game. As if to outdo her own brilliance, at the next Winter Olympics, in Sochi, Russia, in 2014, Poulin scored the overtime winner for Team Canada to capture yet another gold medal. Poulin has gold-medal-winning goals at the Olympics in both regulation and overtime, as if to complete the set.

At present, Poulin, the woman known as MPP, is playing professional women's hockey in the PWHL after several years of tumult in the sport. Professional women's hockey was divided into two leagues, and even that would later combine into one league (the PHF) and then the PWHPA, the Professional Women's Hockey Players Association, where many of the best women's hockey players in the world said "enough is enough" and set out to build their own league from scratch.

Now the Professional Women's Hockey League, or PWHL, is here, uniting the best of the best from women's hockey under one umbrella. They're not afraid to try out fun new rules, like "jail-break" goals: if a team scores a short-handed goal, the penalty they're killing is now over. On a regular basis, we get to witness the talents of Natalie Spooner and Sarah Nurse in Toronto, Grace Zumwinkle and Taylor Heise in Minnesota, Hilary Knight and Jamie Lee Rattray in Boston, Alex Carpenter and Ella Shelton in New York, Kateřina Mrázová and Brianne Jenner in Ottawa, and Laura Stacey with the incomparable MPP in Montreal.

Now, so far, this chapter doesn't really fit this book. This isn't a rant about anything; I've been going on and on about how great women's hockey is and that the PWHL is awesome.

This isn't a rant as much as it is a eulogy.

Who died? It's not a who as much as it is an idea. The idea that professional women's hockey can't work is dead.

I'm not talking about legitimate criticisms of the PWHL. It's a professional league like any other in that you're completely allowed to offer constructive criticism. Not everybody has to be on board with the rule changes. Not everybody has to be on board with the 3–2–1 point system in the standings that weighs overtime wins as less than regulation wins. One thing I'm not over the moon about is that none of the original six teams in this league have actual team names yet; they're just called by the name of the city they represent. Of course you can criticize the PWHL. It's a first-year league just starting out, and nobody is perfect. Honestly and critically evaluating your new operation is how you grow and get better. What is dead is that idea that professional women's hockey can't work.

If you ever wondered from a place of legitimate concern whether or not pro women's hockey could work, you're not alone. Leagues launched, leagues folded, leagues launched again, leagues barely paid their players, and leagues folded again. The road to the construction and launching of the PWHL was full of potholes and speed bumps and if, after years and years of watching leagues try, struggle, and fail, you lost faith for a little bit, I'm sure you'll find plenty of people who had the same skepticism you had.

But the people I'm talking about are the trolls. Those dorks aren't going to show up to the games no matter what the league does.

I'm talking about those pathetic, keyboard-clicking, dime-a-dozen donkeys in every comment section of every women's hockey—or women's anything—post you've ever seen on the internet. Those swamp-dwelling, shit-posting pissant pigeons pecking away at every video you've ever seen on TikTok, Instagram, YouTube, or Twitter with the same misogynist, dorky insults every hunk of human trash has hucked about for centuries or more.

On January 6, 2024, in St. Paul, Minnesota, a PWHL game between PWHL Minnesota and PWHL Montreal drew a crowd of 13,316, a record-setting attendance for a professional women's hockey game. Well, at least that *was* the record, until it was passed a little over one month later on February 16, 2024, in Toronto, as PWHL Toronto took on PWHL Montreal in a sold-out Scotia-bank Arena for the Battle on Bay Street with a new record-setting attendance of 19,285.

It's working.

No matter what anybody says, the PWHL is working. No, it's not perfect. No, it's not drawing over 19,000 fans for every single hockey game, but it's working. There's one league to get behind, the best players in the world are playing in it, and thousands of fans show up and support it. The PWHL's inaugural weekend saw over 2.9 million people tune in on CBC, Sportsnet, and TSN in Canada alone.

The best part is that a one-time attendance of over 19,000 paying spectators and 2.9 million viewers across one hockey-loving country isn't the finish line at all. It's the starting line. For every bad-faith skeptic, for every chronically online antagonist, for every dull-bladed edge-lord, the success of women's hockey doesn't depend on you and never has. You hope for its failure—as if the failure of others could ever fill the void deep within you—but what you don't realize is that you're like a kid trying to catch the balloon they accidentally let go. Women's hockey is soaring in the air, soaring higher than you could ever reach yourself, bliss-fully indifferent to your absence.

The trolls will still be there, no doubt. What do you expect from them? That they'll find something else to do? Of course not! They *have* nothing else to do, so they'll continue to play all the hits. They were always dismissible and pathetic, but their whining and whimpering hits just a little bit softer than it did just a few short years ago, when professional women's hockey appeared to be collapsing, leaving yet another generation of some of the most talented women athletes in the world without a proper professional league outside of their national teams.

I should mention—it's okay if you don't like women's hockey. You don't have to like it. Hell, you're not obligated to like anything. As long as you don't like something for the right reasons. I don't like bell peppers. Never have, never will, and no, I can't explain it. But I can still accept that most people actually do like bell peppers and I'm not bothered by the fact that they do. You can even eat the ones I'm not eating; actually, I'm encouraging you to! If you don't like something because it's just not your thing—fine. It's the losers who hate all women's sports because "lol women," or whatever, that I can't stand.

You don't have to love women's hockey because it's "inspiring" or "inspirational" or something that your daughter can aspire to grow up watching and perhaps even playing. All that is totally cool.

You don't have to watch the PWHL, or women's hockey in general, because it means something to others. You can watch it because the product kicks ass and you can watch the best women's hockey players on the entire planet go head to head and maul each other in fierce competition while getting paid to do it. It's what they've always wanted, and it's what they've always deserved.

If you're up for being entertained by it, then you deserve to see it, too.

15.

The Worst Trades Ever

If debating big NHL trades was a renewable energy source, we'd all have flying cars by now. Ask most people what they had for breakfast this morning, and it will take them at least a few seconds to remember, if they remember at all. But ask them to tell you about the worst trade their team ever made, and they'll be deep into it before the words are even out of your mouth.

Getting star players on your team is hard. To draft even a serviceable player, let alone a star talent, you have to stink for a while and get a really high draft pick, scout countless games all over the world, get extremely lucky on a flyer, or a combination of all those things. That's before you even get to develop those prospects and pray they find a way to progress and stay healthy.

You could sign a player in free agency, but that's way easier said than done. I always laugh when people complain about why a certain team didn't sign some guy. A lot of the time that player didn't want to play for that team; there's not much you can do about that. You could offer them a pile of money, but other teams have money too, plus there's this silly little thing called the salary cap.

That leaves trading: a true art form. With so many general managers, assistant general managers, assistants *to* the general managers, scouts, analytics departments, coaches, agents, and contract clauses, you wonder how any trades ever get done.

The bigger mystery is how a bad trade ever gets done. Didn't people vet this? Didn't people have their say and give an opinion? How many arguments went back and forth before somebody finally pulled the trigger on a deal?

If you think you could easily navigate all this—*way* better than your team's GM, naturally—then you've never played fantasy sports. People get itchy feet, or desperate. People feel like their window to win is slamming shut. If you make this move, this one solitary move, you'll be boasting about your victory in a matter of weeks. The reality is, we're human. Humans make mistakes, and humans get fleeced in trades by other humans.

Back when I worked at Rogers Sportsnet, we made blog posts and videos called "trade trees" where we looked at how trades happened, why they happened, and how their outcomes evolved over the years. In my research, I've found some really good ones, and some really bad ones. Before we get to those, we have to ask: What makes a bad trade?

Let's look at a deal that is often considered a bad trade but I think is actually a really good one: the Dallas Stars trading a young Jarome Iginla and depth forward Corey Millen to the Calgary Flames for Joe Nieuwendyk, straight up.

In December of the 1995–96 NHL season, the Dallas Stars acquired veteran forward Joe Nieuwendyk, and why wouldn't they? Nieuwendyk had already won a Stanley Cup in Calgary and was a consistent point producer, fairly equally balanced between goal-scoring and playmaking. To get a player like that, you need to pay the price, and Calgary's was steep. Dallas would have to part with tough forward prospect Jarome Iginla, who Dallas had drafted only 11th overall in 1995, several months prior.

This wasn't just some prospect being used as negotiating leverage. Dallas knew who they had in Jarome Iginla. They'd scouted him and they wanted him. Sure enough, Iginla became the best player selected in the 1995 NHL Draft, bar none. That's not opinion, it's fact. Iginla led the 1995 draft class with 1,554 games played, which is also 15th all time. Iginla also led the 1995 draft class in goals scored with 625, which is 16th all time. Iginla had the most assists in the 1995 draft class, with a gap of 105 more assists than the next-closest player. Lastly, Iginla led the 1995 draft class with exactly 1,300 points, while nobody else from that draft reached 1,000.

Dallas picked the best player in the entire 1995 draft, a true future Hall of Famer, only to trade him about six months later. Under most circumstances, that's pure, unfiltered nightmare fuel for any fanbase or scouting department. And yet no Dallas Stars fan on earth should regret this trade. I doubt their management group did.

Yes, the Dallas Stars missed the playoffs the season they traded Jarome Iginla for Joe Nieuwendyk. The next year they didn't, making the playoffs but falling in round one. The following season, they made it to the Western Conference Final, where they ultimately lost to the Detroit Red Wings.

Finally, at the end of the 1998–99 season, the Dallas Stars would win their first Stanley Cup in franchise history, with Joe Nieuwendyk winning the Conn Smythe as playoff MVP. You can't get more "mission accomplished" than that.

Should Flames fans lament that deal? Of course not! They got their greatest player in franchise history out of it, and got very close to the Stanley Cup in the process. They even won it, depending on who you ask and how clear their TV was in 2004.

One team wanted a veteran player to help win them a championship, and they got it. The other team wanted a young star for the future, and they got it. When both teams get exactly what they wanted, that's a good trade.

Not all trades work out so well, at least not for both sides.

ONE-FOR-ONE: TUUKKA RASK FOR ANDREW RAYCROFT, JUNE 24, 2006

Losing a one-for-one trade creates the kind of regret that haunts not only teams but a fanbase, too. Players who are traded for each other are always going to be compared forever after. When you make a one-for-one trade, it doesn't matter how well your new guy performs, because if the other guy is better, then fans are going to think the player you got stinks. Is that fair to the players? Of course it isn't. Is it fair to the management group that made the deal in the first place? I mean, yeah. You made the deal.

As a Leafs fan, I hate this trade more than I hate stepping in a puddle with my socks on. I hate this trade more than getting a sunburn on my shoulders then having to carry a backpack all day. If this trade stole my car, it would be the second-worst thing it ever did to me. I found out more about this trade while writing this chapter, and I hate it even more now. It's a brutal, smouldering pile of crap, and it always was, even from day one.

We'll start with Andrew Raycroft, who was a fifth-round pick goalie for the Boston Bruins in 1998. In a lot of ways, Raycroft's journey to being a full-time NHL player wasn't easy. After being drafted from the Sudbury Wolves of the OHL, Raycroft improved in each of his next two seasons with Sudbury and then the Kingston Frontenacs. From there, he moved on to play in the Bruins' minor league system with the AHL Providence Bruins.

Ideally, you'd like to let a goalie prospect play at least one full season of pro before they even sniff the NHL, but sometimes throwing a rookie into the fire is necessary when guys are out of the lineup. Raycroft was one of four goalies to play ten or more games with the Bruins that season, posting a 4–6–0 record and .890 save percentage. Unremarkable numbers but valuable experience.

Despite playing mostly in the AHL for three seasons, Raycroft got into 21 games for the Bruins spread over that time. Raycroft's opportunity to become a Bruins regular in the NHL finally arrived in the 2003–04 season, when the Bruins' only other option was an aging Felix Potvin.

Raycroft was spectacular, putting up a 29–18–9 record and dazzling .926 save percentage. Even though this was the fourth season in which Raycroft had played NHL games, he still met the criteria of a rookie because he was under the threshold of games played, and he won the 2004 Calder Memorial Trophy as the NHL's rookie of the year.

Unfortunately for Raycroft, and anybody who liked hockey, the NHL was locked out for the subsequent 2004–05 season. Raycroft, like many NHL players, chose to sign with a European team to keep his skills sharp. He had a 4–5–2 record in 11 games with Tappara in the Finnish SM-liiga, with a decent .912 save percentage.

When the NHL returned in 2005–06, things got tough for Raycroft, to say the least. In a shocking fall from rookie of the year, Raycroft was relegated to third-string Bruins goalie behind young 2002 first-round pick Hannu Toivonen and a relatively unknown journeyman veteran named Tim Thomas, who at that stage in his professional career had played for nine different teams in seven different leagues.

Toivonen had a 9–5–4 record in 20 games with a .914 save percentage. Thomas had a 12–13–10 record with a .917 save percentage. Raycroft had a miserable 8–19–2 record and a brutal .879 save percentage. That was the fourth-worst percentage among goalies who had played in at least ten NHL games. I understand the idea of wanting to "buy low" with a player who had previous success in the league, but a .879 save percentage is barely usable. Who would buy?

In 2006, the Toronto Maple Leafs had two big goalie prospects: Tuukka Rask and Justin Pogge. The Leafs had just picked Rask 21st overall in the 2005 NHL Draft. Just the year before, they had selected Justin Pogge in the third round, 90th overall.

Right off the bat, without knowing anything else about the players and applying common sense, who do you think the Leafs should have valued more: the goalie they picked 90th overall or the goalie they picked 21st overall the very next year? It's obvious which one your scouting staff thinks is best. Also, if the goalie you picked 90th overall the year before is so good, then why are you picking a goalie 21st overall the next year, ahead of guys like T.J. Oshie, Andrew Cogliano, James Neal, and Paul Stastny? It's probably because your organization thinks he's *really* good!

A small caveat: I don't think people understand just how big the World Juniors used to be. Sure, it's still a big event each year, but during Canada's five straight gold medals between 2005 and 2009, it was pandemonium. That can't be overlooked. In 2006, the Leafs organization had both Canada's starting goalie and Finland's starting goalie. Rask, on Finland's bronze medal squad, had won the honour of being named the best goaltender in the tournament, but Pogge had backstopped Canada to a gold medal. The excitement with Pogge was real.

So in theory, the Leafs may have had great goalies of the future, but they thought they needed a goalie now. They weren't exactly wrong. They had Ed Belfour, who was clearly near the end of his career, with a 22–22–4 record and .892 save percentage; a young but perhaps not quite ready Mikael Tellqvist with a 10–11–2 record and .895 save percentage in 2005–06; and J.S. Aubin, who put up a 9–0–2 record and .924 save percentage out of nowhere to help the Leafs make the playoffs. Did you believe that? I'm kidding! They missed by one point. Life is pain.

So, on June 24, 2006, the Leafs traded their best goalie prospect, Tuukka Rask, for their divisional rival's third-string goaltender, straight up, before buying out Ed Belfour. It was an asset-management disaster class.

Raycroft was better in his first season with the Leafs than in his last season in Boston, but they played him a staggering 72 games because Aubin turned into a pumpkin with a 3–5–2 record and terrible .876 save percentage. Raycroft won 37 games, which stood as a Leafs record until Frederik Andersen broke it about a decade later, but the team still missed the playoffs.

The Leafs decided to dig the hole deeper on June 22, 2007, less than a calendar year after the Raycroft trade, by acquiring goalie Vesa Toskala from the San Jose Sharks along with big forward Mark Bell in exchange for first- and second-round picks in 2007 and a fourth-rounder in 2009.

Raycroft's second year as a Leaf saw him play second fiddle to Toskala with a genuinely shocking 2–9–5 record and miserable .876 save percentage before getting bought out. Yes, they did it again. The Leafs bought out his contract two years after trading their first-round goalie prospect for him, and buying out Ed Belfour.

How'd things go for Boston, you ask? Between the 2009–10 season, which was Rask's first season as a regular in the NHL, and the season he basically retired, 2020–21, Rask ranked fifth in games played, with 555; fifth in starts, with 536; sixth in wins, with 303; and third in save percentage among goalies with at least 50 games played, with a sparkling .921. Take a wild stab at the two ahead of him. Give up? Second is Tim Thomas, with .922 in 207 games, and Andrew "The Hamburglar" Hammond, with .923 in 56 games. The closest goalie to Rask's save percentage with 500 or more games played over that span is a tie, at .918, between Henrik Lundqvist in 622 games and Roberto Luongo in 500 games, and both those guys are in the Hockey Hall of Fame.

Rask has a Stanley Cup, a Vezina Trophy, a William M. Jennings Trophy, two additional trips to the Stanley Cup Final, and, maybe best of all, three humiliating and demoralizing Game 7 defeats of the Toronto Maple Leafs. A super-underrated aspect of this trade: John Ferguson Jr. was the GM in Toronto who traded Rask to Boston in the first place, and when Rask was beating the Leafs in the playoffs and going on runs to the Stanley Cup Final, John Ferguson Jr. was working with him in the Bruins organization. It's brutal. Oh, and Andrew Raycroft got a broadcasting job covering the Bruins. Whoever's up there writing this script is laying it on a little thick.

Some trades suck because one team won. Some trades suck because one team lost. Some trades suck right away. Some trades suck later. This trade ticked all those boxes right up until Rask retired more than a decade later.

If you're looking for one of the worst one-for-one trades in NHL history, every conversation has to include Rask for Raycroft.

DEADLINE DEBACLE: MARTIN ERAT AND MICHAEL LATTA FOR FILIP FORSBERG, APRIL 3, 2013

Legendary NHL executive Brian Burke has often said that the NHL trade deadline is when general managers make their biggest mistakes. He ain't lying.

Everyone is out trying to wheel and deal for a number of reasons. They're trying to save their job, they're trying to appease their fans, they're trying to win a championship. Or, most importantly, make their owner some money.

"Hey, Steve, making their owner money isn't the most important thing!" Yeah, well, it's not your job on the line, is it?

Obviously the easiest way to make some money is to maximize your number of playoff dates and win a championship—but I wanted to be cheeky. Some trades are a miscalculation of what you're acquiring. You think you're getting a star who's going to put you over the top, and for whatever reason it just doesn't work out that way. Some trades are a disaster because of a miscalculation of what you're giving up. I'm not just talking about your classic case of a guy playing "okay" for you, getting traded, and putting up a billion points with their new team. I'm talking about finding a diamond, having a diamond, being the only person who can sign and play that diamond, and giving away that diamond for a box of Pop Rocks.

Enter the Filip Forsberg deal.

I debated lots of other trades for this chapter, but this is an underratedly egregious deadline flop that doesn't get enough flack, maybe because of the teams involved—the Washington Capitals and Nashville Predators. Neither is an Original Six team, neither is under the Canadian microscope, and they have one Cup between them. It's the Capitals who have that Cup, and my guess is they'd have at least one more if they hadn't made this deal.

Martin Erat was a playmaking winger with several good offensive seasons under his belt. The lockout-shortened 2012–13 season wasn't really one of them. He had 21 points in 36 games with Nashville that season, which isn't so bad, but only four of the 26 points were goals. In a vacuum, you can understand wanting to add a playmaker to the Capitals' offence, where all roads lead through Alex Ovechkin and that touch of death he calls a shot. Also appealing were the two additional years remaining on Erat's contract. There's an alternate universe where this deal is actually super responsible for the Washington Capitals because they're not getting a player who's merely a playoff rental. If only it worked out that way. Erat played just nine regular season games for Washington down the stretch, putting up a goal and two assists. Once the playoffs arrived, he played just four of Washington's seven games in the first round against the New York Rangers . . . and didn't pick up a single point. Four penalty minutes, though!

You might be able to swallow the pill of that disappointing playoff run, since you have an additional two seasons with this guy. The problem? He asked for a trade less than two months into the next season. The Capitals ended up flipping Erat to the Phoenix Coyotes—yes, they were still called the Phoenix Coyotes then—for defenceman Rostislav Klesla, forward Chris Brown, and a fourth-round pick. All the Capitals had to show for the trade was zero playoff points, 62 total regular season games from Erat, 27 points (only two of which were goals), Klesla (who never played for the Capitals), the fourth-round pick (Callum Booth, who never played for the Capitals), and Chris Brown (who played 12 games over three years for the Capitals).

Now for Filip Forsberg.

Filip Forsberg was the 11th overall pick in 2012—one of the weirdest and most underwhelming drafts in recent memory. It's not the nicest to use the word "bust" to describe a former prospect, but the 2012 draft has an absolute barnful of them. That last sentence is how I discovered the word "barnful," by the way.

Lots of guys from the 2012 NHL Draft underwhelmed considering where they were drafted. Filip Forsberg wasn't one of them. In fact, if you were to redraft the 2012 draft, Forsberg would likely be the first overall pick.

Forsberg, a goal-sniping winger with the kind of moustache that suggests he bikes to work on a penny farthing, is the only player from the 2012 draft with over 600 NHL points. Nobody else from that draft class has reached 500 points. Forsberg is one of just two players drafted in 2012 to score over 200 NHL goals, and he's going to hit 300 several seasons before anybody else does. Forsberg is even second among 2012 draft picks in assists, only behind Leafs defender Morgan Rielly.

Worth mentioning: each and every point Filip Forsberg has scored in his career has been scored with the Nashville Predators. Forsberg is the Predators' all-time leading goal-scorer by a wide margin and is second in points only to his teammate Roman Josi, who is several years older.

Here's a fun one: since his first full season in the NHL, Filip Forsberg has about 100 more goals than any living, breathing human being who has played for the Washington Capitals. "What about Alexander Ovechkin?" you might ask. Yes, Ovechkin does have more goals than Forsberg, but I said living, breathing human being. Ovechkin's more like a Jeep.

A few more notes with this lovely trade for Washington . . .

The Capitals didn't acquire just Martin Erat. They also got young forward Michael Latta in the deal. Latta played 113 games with the Capitals, scoring four goals. Like Erat, Latta played four playoff games with the Capitals and scored zero points. He left the team as a free agent.

Without this turning into too much of a trade tree, let's have a gander at Rostislav Klesla. The Capitals got Klesla on March 4, 2015, in the deal they used to dump Erat. Washington actually flipped Klesla in a deal the very next day, sending him along with goalie Michal Neuvirth to the Buffalo Sabres in exchange for goalie Jaroslav Halak and a third-round draft choice.

Halak was fantastic for Washington, putting up an absurd .930 save percentage in 12 games with the team. Hey! This looks promising! What were his playoff numbers like? Well, despite Halak's solid stats, the Capitals actually ended up missing the 2014 Stanley Cup Playoffs.

Whatever the opposite of having your cake and eating it too is, that's what the Washington Capitals pulled off with this trade. They wanted playoff success; they didn't get it. That sucks, but it happens all the time. You can stomach it as long as the prospect you traded away isn't a home run for the other team. Oops! Turns out that prospect you drafted was actually a grand slam, turning into the greatest forward in Nashville Predators history and the best draft pick from his entire draft class.

The Capitals finally got their Stanley Cup a few years later, in 2018, which is certainly the ointment that heals all wounds. But oh man, imagine Forsberg and Ovechkin together. What a force. Now we'll never know.

THE VALUE OF "IFS": THE ISLANDERS GIVE AWAY ROBERTO LUONGO, JUNE 24, 2000

When you make a trade, you should have a goal in mind. Sure, every trade comes with a bunch of "ifs." You could trade a fourth-liner for the best player on earth and still lose the trade if the best player on earth decides to retire to run an ice cream truck. Is that going to happen? Probably not! There is value in ifs, and you have to pick the right ones.

If I offer you two young second-line forwards, that would probably make your team better, right? What would you be willing to pay for that? Is your answer two guys who were recently drafted third and fourth overall? No, because why on earth would anybody paid to run an NHL team do that?

This might be the most underrated awful trade in NHL history. Some would argue whether this is even the worst trade involving Roberto Luongo. But here's some trivia: Luongo got traded to Florida, they retired his number; he got traded to Vancouver, and they retired his number, too. Who was Roberto Luongo drafted by?

The New York Islanders.

The New York Islanders knew exactly who they were trading when they sent Roberto Luongo to the Florida Panthers, which is why this move by GM Mike Milbury made even less sense. At least the Leafs, for their part, had never seen Tuukka Rask play at the NHL level before they traded him. Sure, they thought Rask was worth using a first-round pick on, but since they had not actually seen him in the NHL, there was still an "if" aspect to Rask's potential.

The Islanders had seen a 20-year-old Luongo play at the NHL level as a rookie, and he was immediately the best goalie they had.

Now, a goalie that young probably shouldn't be playing any games at the NHL level, but if anybody could live up to the task, perhaps it would be Roberto Luongo. After all, the Islanders drafted him fourth overall in 1997, just two years prior to his NHL debut in the 1999–00 season. How many times has a goalie been picked fourth overall or higher since Luongo? Rick DiPietro, Kari Lehtonen, and Marc-André Fleury. That's the end of the list. The last goalie to go top five in the NHL Draft was Carey Price, in 2005. Goalies can be tough to predict and can take longer to develop.

Nobody had a fun time goaltending for the Islanders that season. Felix Potvin had a dreadful 5–14–3 record with a .892 save percentage, and Kevin Weekes fared a bit better with a 10–20–4 record and .902 save percentage, but Luongo managed a still-pretty-bad 7–14–1 record and .904 save percentage. Anybody could look at those numbers and conclude a king-sized bed could have been in net for the Islanders, the team with the second-fewest goals in the league that season, and they still would have found a way to lose.

But then the 2000 NHL Draft rolls around, and guess what? The Islanders have both the fifth and first overall pick. What luck! The Islanders selected goaltender Rick DiPietro first overall.

Wait, what?

With the first and fifth overall pick, the Islanders could have walked into the 2000 NHL Draft and realistically picked two out of Dany Heatley, Marian Gaborik, and Scott Hartnell, who went second, third, and sixth respectively and completely changed the offensive future of their franchises. Instead, the Islanders picked a goalie, even though their top prospect was a goalie.

I won't dump on the Raffi Torres pick, which the Isles made in that fifth overall spot. He ended up mostly being a grinder who could chip in a big hit and some points, but in his draft year Torres had 43 goals, 48 assists, and 91 points in 68 OHL games, finishing with 27 more points than his closest teammate. Besides, that pick, while it could have been better, is not what's on trial here. Trading Luongo is.

With Rick DiPietro in the mix, Luongo became expendable. As a result, Milbury and the Islanders traded Luongo, who was the fourth overall pick in 1997, and Olli Jokinen, who was the third overall pick in 1997, to the Florida Panthers for forwards Mark Parrish and Oleg Kvasha.

It's not even revisionist history to say the Islanders fans hated this trade the moment it happened. I found this excerpt from an article on WashingtonPost.com that was published on June 25, 2000, written by Jason La Canfora: "After Luongo was dealt, fans at a draft party on Long Island booed lustfully. Now the team has almost no depth at goaltender, the most important position." Oh yeah, I forgot to mention, they traded Kevin Weekes in order to get the fifth overall pick.

The New York Islanders had a great goalie prospect but couldn't score, so they drafted a goalie, traded their great goalie prospect along with another good goalie prospect, and threw Olli Jokinen in there, too, a forward prospect they acquired in exchange for 40-goal-scoring Zigmund Palffy, who could score. Are you keeping up? Are you paying attention? This makes sense, right?

Help me with this one: Luongo was 21 years old, the fourth overall pick three years earlier, and coming off an admirable rookie campaign. Olli Jokinen was also 21, coming off his second full season in the NHL, with 11 goals and 21 points in 82 games. Those are the guys the Islanders traded.

The Panthers traded Mark Parrish, who was 23 and coming off of his second straight season of 20 goals or more, and 44 points.

Oleg Kvasha was nearly 22, and had just taken a step back as an NHL sophomore with five goals and 25 points in 78 games. Also noteworthy, Kvasha was six-foot-six. Parrish and Kvasha also combined for one assist in four playoff games like two months before this trade happened.

What's the play here if you're the Islanders? Even if you've made the decision that Rick DiPietro is the goalie of the future, you're giving away the third and fourth overall picks from just three years ago for what? A 20-goal-scorer and a big guy going backward? Maybe you figure you're buying low on Kvasha, but then what about Jokinen, who was younger and, I can't stress this enough, the bloody third overall pick?

By now you know this trade completely stunk for the Islanders and was fantastic for the Panthers. It's not that this trade was bad only in hindsight; the odds of it becoming great for the Islanders were slim to none. It all hinged on Rick DiPietro being the Second Coming. In the same *Washington Post* article, La Canfora said, "Milbury believes DiPietro is ready for the NHL at age 18, something almost unheard of."

There's a reason it's unheard of. DiPietro got shelled in 20 games with the Islanders as a rookie, with an unfathomable 3–15–1 record and .878 save percentage. He didn't fare much better in the minors, with a 4–5–2 record and .880 save percentage.

Just to show that this isn't DiPietro's fault, a few years later, the Pittsburgh Penguins had the bright idea to play an 18-year-old Marc-André Fleury for 22 games. He posted a 4–14–2 record behind an awful pre–Sidney Crosby Penguins team, and a .896 save percentage. When all is said and done, Fleury will be in the Hockey Hall of Fame, and even he got roasted as a teenaged rookie goalie in the NHL.

DiPietro had a couple of decent-to-good seasons but never

quite found his footing, what with overuse, odd development, and frequent injuries. The Islanders signed DiPietro to a 15-year contract in 2006 (back when you could do such a crazy thing); he was bought out of it in 2013, and the Islanders will be paying him $1.5 million a year until 2029, when this book is half a decade old. Mark Parrish was good, topping out at 30 goals and 60 points, while Kvasha's career highs were 15 goals and 51 points. Career high in the playoffs: one point.

Olli Jokinen scored 188 goals and 419 points for the Florida Panthers in 567 games, which stood as the Panthers' franchise points record for many years. As for Roberto Luongo, it's hilarious how instantly spectacular he was. His first season in Florida saw a 12–24–7 record, which obviously stinks, but his save percentage was .920. Luongo's save percentages in Florida were, in order, .920, .915, .918, .931, and .914, all while playing seasons of 47, 58, 65, 72, and a whopping 75 games.

You could argue in the Islanders' defence that the Panthers never made the playoffs with both Luongo and Jokinen in the lineup. That's not a sign Florida lost the trade, though; it's a sign the Florida Panthers were really bad for a long time. One of my favourite "how is that even possible?" stats is Pavel Bure having 59 goals and 92 points during the 2000–01 season while his next-closest teammate had just 14 goals and 37 points. Meanwhile, the Islanders made the playoffs three times with Parrish and Kvasha, though they never made it out of the first round.

I don't care. It doesn't matter. Even if you absolutely have to draft Rick DiPietro first overall, you don't have to trade Roberto to do so, especially when you traded Kevin Weekes on the same weekend. The Islanders gave up elite potential for two guys who were fine.

Trades don't need to have bad players involved in order to be bad, they just need to have bad logic. There will always be "ifs" in professional sports, but when the logic is off, your ifs become whiffs.

THE DANGER OF DEALING FIRST-ROUND PICKS A YEAR AHEAD OF TIME: PHIL KESSEL FOR THREE HIGH PICKS, SEPTEMBER 18, 2009

I don't think there should be many hard-and-fast rules when it comes to making trades in hockey. We're looking for fun, and a bit of chaos provides that, after all.

To rebuilding teams, a first-round draft pick is lifeblood, hope for the future. To a contender, any and every draft pick is just magic beans. The Tampa Bay Lightning traded two first-round picks for Blake Coleman and Barclay Goodrow, two guys who combined for 91 Stanley Cup Playoff games for Tampa over two seasons and scored a grand total of 11 goals. Do you think Tampa cares? No, they won two Cups. Who did those draft picks end up becoming? Who cares? They won two Cups.

That being said—never trade a first-round pick a year ahead of time. Not ever, you absolute maniacs!

Generally speaking, trading draft picks at the trade deadline is pretty easy. You can screw that up too, for sure, but teams willing to spend a first-round pick at the trade deadline are pretty confident they're going to at least make the playoffs and hopefully compete for a Stanley Cup.

But what if you're just kind of . . . a team? What if you're in the middle of the pack or straight-up bad? If you trade a first-round pick, you're probably getting back a pretty good player, maybe even your best player, but is that going to make the difference this year?

Now, if you're a legitimate Stanley Cup contender and you trade a first-rounder one year ahead of time, disaster can still strike. Guys get injured, or slump; goalies lose their minds. The risk increases tenfold when you're not actually a contender.

When I talk about trading a first-round pick one year ahead of time, I don't mean one calendar reel, I mean one full hockey season. If you made a trade in September, for example, and you trade away your first-round pick for that upcoming June, you're making that trade one full hockey season ahead of time.

This is exactly what the Leafs did when they acquired Phil Kessel. On September 18, 2009, the Toronto Maple Leafs got Phil Kessel for three draft picks: their first-rounder in 2010, their second-rounder in 2010, and their first-rounder in 2011. Not only did the Leafs give up their 2010 first-rounder before the first game of the 2009–10 season, but they handed off their 2011 first-round pick, as well. That's madness.

In fairness, players like Phil Kessel don't become available often. Kessel was the fifth overall pick in 2006, just three years prior, and had just come off an impressive 36 goals in 70 games. Yes, Kessel required shoulder surgery when they got him, but he would only miss the first month or so of the season. He'd be back in no time to help the Leafs on their march to the Stanley Cup.

Just one small problem: the Leafs lost their first eight games of the season and put up a record of 1–7–4 in their 12 games without Kessel to start the season. One win in 12 bloody games. The Leafs would have to be superhuman to get back into the playoff picture even with a healthy Phil Kessel, and they didn't. The team was better but ultimately still below .500 the rest of the way, despite Kessel's 30 goals and 55 points in 70 games.

With the second-worst record in the NHL and no chance of a draft lottery saving them, the Leafs surrendered the second overall pick in 2010 to the Boston Bruins, who they should probably stop trading with forever. With that pick, the Bruins drafted Tyler Seguin, who would win a Stanley Cup with them the following year, and in 2013, Seguin would be one of the Bruins on the ice for the overtime winner in Game 7 against the Leafs, along with Tuukka Rask. I threw up three times while typing that sentence.

The good news is that the Leafs were better but still awful the next season, surrendering the ninth overall pick in 2011 to the Boston Bruins. Sorry, did I say good news? I meant cartoonishly bad.

The Bruins used that to draft Dougie Hamilton, a big, offensively talented right-handed defender who's better than literally any right-handed defender the Leafs have had over the past two decades at minimum.

The cherry on the awful cake is the second-rounder the Leafs gave up to Boston in 2010 was a guy named Jared Knight. Knight never ended up playing in the NHL, but because the Leafs finished second last, that second-rounder was actually 32nd overall. Now that the NHL has expanded to 32 teams, the 32nd overall pick is technically a first-round pick. So you could argue the Leafs gave up three first-round picks for Phil Kessel. Is it literally true? No. But it's close enough to true that your Leafs fan buddies will hate hearing that a whole big bunch.

The Leafs aren't the only Ontario-based team to do this recently, either. The Ottawa Senators got burned, too. The main difference between the two is that the Leafs were on a four-year playoff drought when they made the Kessel trade and had no logical reason to think they'd be in the running for the Cup. The Senators, on the other hand, traded their first-round pick in summer 2018, just months after making it to double overtime in Game 7 in the Eastern Conference Final against the team that would go on to win the Stanley Cup that season, the Pittsburgh Penguins.

Still, even though the Senators came tantalizingly close to Lord Stanley in 2017, there were signs that going all-in the following year might not be the best idea. In 2016–17, the Senators finished second in their eight-team division. Hey! That's pretty good! The Senators also finished 12th out of 30 teams in the NHL. At that point, you're pretty much on the good side of bang in the middle. The 2016–17 Senators also had a minus-two goal differential in the regular season, which was 18th in the NHL, or on the bad side of bang in the middle, and the worst among any team to make the playoffs.

The following season, the Senators forked over a package for disgruntled Colorado Avalanche forward Matt Duchene in a three-way-deal with Colorado and the Nashville Predators that included a first-round pick in the upcoming 2018 draft. What makes this different from what the Leafs did is that the Senators had already played a handful of games from the 2017–18 season before making this deal, with a record of 6-3-5 in 14 games. That's . . . fine. It's not great, but it's fine. It's more losses than wins, but with five of those losses coming in overtime or the shootout, you could convince yourself that those were tight games your team should have won.

Hilariously, the Senators' first two games after the Matt Duchene trade were in Sweden, against the Colorado Avalanche. Talk about awkward. The Senators ended up winning both of those games.

What happened when the Senators returned to North America can only be described as disastrous. Seven straight losses and just four wins in their first 21 games following the Duchene trade to close out the 2017 calendar. The Senators' record was 22–40–6 after trading away their 2018 first-round pick. Nothing went right. Erik Karlsson put up points but missed 11 games and went from a plus-10 to a minus-25. The Senators' goaltending tandem of Craig Anderson and Mike Condon went from sparkling .926 and .914 save percentages, respectively, to .898 and .902.

The Senators did manage to give themselves some protection in the trade but it was a double-edged sword. The condition on the 2018 pick was that if it was a top ten, they had the option of giving Colorado that pick or their first-rounder in 2019, wherever it landed. Ottawa chose to give Colorado their 2019 first-rounder so that the Senators could select Brady Tkachuk fourth overall in the 2018 NHL Draft.

The whole point of not trading your first-round pick so far in advance is that you have no idea what the future holds. For the Senators, the future saw them going for a full rebuild, trading star defender Erik Karlsson, star two-way forward Mark Stone, and even Matt Duchene during or just prior to the 2018–19 NHL season.

With Ottawa basically trading any star player they could, they ran a serious risk of giving Colorado the first overall pick in 2019. That's what could have happened, but Ottawa got extremely lucky.

Brady Tkachuk would become not only a star power forward for the Senators but also their young captain. Even better, in a true case of irony, the Senators got the San Jose Sharks to agree to give them their first-rounder in 2020, one year ahead of the draft, in the Erik Karlsson trade. What happened? The Sharks were terrible and ended up giving Ottawa the third overall pick in 2020. The Senators selected talented German forward Tim Stützle, who has been absolutely ripping it up offensively alongside Brady Tkachuk ever since.

The Senators thought they were better than they were, made a mistake, and then hilariously convinced the San Jose Sharks to make the exact same mistake. At very least the Senators had some top ten protection in there. Teams that came before them weren't so lucky.

Including, once again, the Leafs. They fumbled top five draft picks in both 1989 and 1996. In August 1989, Toronto traded their first-round pick in 1991, two drafts later, to the New Jersey Devils for defender Tom Kurvers, straight up. For his end of the bargain, Kurvers had a great first season in Toronto, putting up 52 points in 70 games from the back end.

The following season, the one that mattered for the Leafs' traded-away first-rounder, Kurvers had just three assists in 19 games, and the team around him struggled mightily, as well. It was starting to look like the Leafs might finish last, and in doing so, had traded away the first overall pick.

Who was that expected to be? Eric Lindros, the most highly touted prospect in a generation.

Luckily for the Leafs, who didn't want to be bad, there was a team who badly wanted to be bad: the Quebec Nordiques. Quebec was happy to take a second-round pick in both 1991 and 1992 from Toronto, along with Scott Pearson, who the Leafs had selected sixth overall just two years prior, in 1988, in exchange for three bona fide NHL players to help the Leafs not finish last. And it worked! Sort of.

The Leafs finished second last in the NHL and gave up the third overall pick, behind the Quebec Nordiques and the expansion San Jose Sharks. With the third overall pick, the New Jersey Devils selected Hockey Hall of Fame defender Scott Niedermayer, won several Stanley Cups, and had a very merry Christmas indeed.

In March 1996, the New York Islanders gave the Leafs back former captain Wendel Clark, along with defenders Mathieu Schneider and D.J. Smith, in exchange for Sean Haggerty, Darby Hendrickson, future Islanders captain Kenny Jonsson, and their first-round pick in 1997.

Guess what? The following season the Leafs were bad again and ended up sending the Islanders the fourth overall pick, which they used on Hockey Hall of Fame goaltender Roberto Luongo. As we know, the Islanders would screw that one up anyway. But come on.

Stop trading first-round picks, especially unprotected first-round picks, a full season ahead of time or even more, you absolute madmen.

UNFORCED ERRORS: MONTREAL TRADES PATRICK ROY, DECEMBER 6, 1995

The Patrick Roy trade out of Montreal is born from one of the most mystifying, egotistical decisions in the history of NHL coaching.

Patrick Roy was a good goalie. A really good goalie, actually. So good that you could argue Patrick Roy was the greatest goalie in NHL history. Somebody should dedicate a whole chapter of a book to that.

Montreal won Stanley Cups with Patrick Roy in both 1986 and 1993. Roy won the Conn Smythe as playoff MVP in both of those runs and won rookie of the year, four Jennings Trophies including three in a row, plus three Vezina Trophies, two of which were back to back. All in all, Patrick Roy seemed like the kind of guy you should keep happy because he was really good at his job.

Except at the beginning of the 1995–96 season, the Canadiens hired Roy's former teammate Mario Tremblay to coach, even though he had basically no experience. Did that work out well? It might shock you, but no, it did not.

With Montreal's start to the season being rather *comme ci, comme ça*, the powerhouse Detroit Red Wings came to town. The Red Wings scored once. Then again. And again. And again. And again. Has Roy been pulled yet? You bet he hasn't. Again. And again. And again. For the love of god, just pull the guy! And again.

Tremblay left Roy in net for nine humiliating goals against, including a save for which the fans in Montreal mock-cheered him for doing his job. Roy walked onto the Montreal bench, with Tremblay staring daggers, right past the team owner, who happened to be sitting right behind the bench. Roy informed him that this would be his final game for the Montreal Canadiens, walked away, and sat down.

We call this an unforced error.

The head coach of the Montreal Canadiens thought it would be a good idea to get into a pissing match with his star goaltender—a guy who used to openly have full-on conversations with his goalposts—thinking he'd come out of it looking like Jack Adams himself. This, as it turns out, was one of the worst decisions, if not the worst decision, in the entire century-plus history of the Montreal Canadiens.

And yet somehow, the trade was worse.

The Montreal Canadiens traded Patrick Roy along with their captain, Mike Keane, in exchange for forward Andrei Kovalenko, forward Martin Rucinsky, and goalie Jocelyn Thibault.

The Montreal Canadiens took a 20-year-old Jocelyn Thibault, the tenth overall pick in 1993, who had 57 NHL games to his name, and said, "Hey, buddy, you're going to replace Patrick Roy now." As for the two forwards, unless they were somehow going to retroactively score 12 against the Red Wings that fateful night in Montreal, I'm not sure either was ever going to make enough of a difference.

After that, it's like Roy played mad for eight months straight, which was bad news for anybody in his path. Whereas the rest of his regular season was somewhat below the standard you would expect for one of the best goalies in the league, his playoff run was bonkers: a record of 16 wins and six losses, a glowing 2.10 goals against average, and a fantastic .921 save percentage. Unsurprisingly, the Colorado Avalanche won the Stanley Cup in their first ever season. A few years later, in 2001, the Avalanche would win their second Cup, with Roy securing his fourth career Stanley Cup and third career playoff MVP win with the Conn Smythe.

Listen, the sun has set on every great empire, in sports and out. Perhaps Patrick Roy's days in Montreal had simply run their course and it was time to move on. But on December 2, 1995, when Mario Tremblay and the Montreal Canadiens allowed their superstar goalie to endure nine goals against in about 32 minutes of gameplay, they blew their chance at a graceful exit. No calm process, no cordial goodbye, no build-up to the 1996 trade deadline, when perhaps Roy could have been had for a king's ransom. Maybe, but we'll never know.

The Canadiens won 40 games that season and finished third in the Northeast Division. The next time Montreal would reach 40 wins was the 2003–04 season, and the next time they finished higher than fourth in their division was in 2005–06, when they finished third.

Everyone makes mistakes. People can forgive a lot of those mistakes. The ones people struggle with are those you never had to make in the first place.

Historically, there are so many ways to get bitten in the trade game. After writing this chapter, I'm half-convinced one of those is to simply be the Toronto Maple Leafs. In all seriousness, there are a few certainties. Teams who don't do their homework on the players they want to acquire are going to have a bad time. Teams who don't do their homework on their own guys who other teams are dying to get are going to have a bad time. Teams who bet their entire future on a bunch of "ifs" are going to have a bad time. Teams who trade first-round picks a season ahead of time, *especially if they didn't follow the previous three rules,* are going to have a bad time. Teams who create their own problems are going to be fleeced by Colorado.

Fortune might favour the bold, but there's a fine line between bold and dumb.

16.

You're Never Too Old

Even though I'm fortunate enough to talk, or more accurately rant, about hockey for a living, I never played the game growing up. I had skated before but never really learned how to skate properly. It wasn't until I was 29 that I finally got to it for real.

The first time I stopped on skates on my own, even if it was barely a stop, I felt like I had gained a superpower. It doesn't matter that it's Canada and nearly everybody around me already had that power. It was progress! Finally, at long last, a place to build from.

Stopping with one foot turned into stopping with two feet, which grew into pivoting, then skating backward, then pivoting back to forward. After years of practice . . . well, I still stink, but I'm better, and it's super fun!

Today I can play hockey well enough to be bad at it, if that makes sense. There aren't many sports like it. For example, if you've never played a game of soccer in your life, you could get out there and at minimum run around a bunch and kind of figure it out as you go. With hockey, if you've never been on skates before and try to play, you ain't moving. Think water polo without knowing how to swim. Thankfully, in hockey the water is frozen. So yeah, I get out there and still stink, but man do I have fun. It really is the best game, and I wish I had picked up playing it sooner.

If you've never played hockey before, allow me to be your hockey dad for a second. Hockey is an intricate game with a lot of moving parts, and because of that, you can overcomplicate things super fast. And especially if you're too old to get noticed by the scouts, there really shouldn't be any pressure.

Experienced hockey players have given me a lot of advice over the years, but not all of them agreed with each other. Looking things up on the internet can be chaos, too, with a thousand opinions screaming at you at once. So if you're looking to get into hockey, don't worry. Let me be the guinea pig through this process, one beginner to another. Because trust me, it's worth it.

YOU'RE GOING TO FALL

I'm not saying that because I don't believe in you, I'm saying that because you're going to fall. The more things you try to learn on the ice, the more you're going to fall.

If all you're doing is concentrating on not falling, I have bad news: you won't learn as much, it will take you longer to learn anything, and you're probably going to fall anyway.

"But what if I look stupid?" you might ask. Who cares? In the event some idiot laughs, just brush it off. They're probably not going to laugh, though. You know why? Because they fell, too. It's ice, dude. It's not weird when you fall down on ice. It's slippery. If it wasn't, then we could save a whole lot of money on skates.

You're going to fall, and it's okay. The fun part is that you're going to get right back up.

LEARN TO SKATE WITH PADS ON

Learning how to skate requires leaving your comfort zone, and leaving your comfort zone is a whole lot easier when falling down doesn't mean hurting for a month. Little kids fall down on the ice all the time and they're fine because they're tiny and invincible. You're a grown-up, and as the saying goes, the bigger they are, the harder they fall.

Half of learning how to skate is having the confidence to move around properly—this is huge. Why wouldn't you have that confidence? Because you're wobbling around on ice with knife shoes and could completely yard-sale at any moment.

A lot of my early learning happened at public skates. Luckily this was mostly at indoor rinks that weren't that busy. Learning how to skate at the biggest public outdoor rink around Christmas might not be the best idea.

One time, an experienced friend was showing me how to skate a few strides, stop, and cross over back to where you were, and repeat the process. Things were going okay, and I started to gain confidence. That means I felt more comfortable, and without really noticing, I started to go faster.

Naturally, I eventually tripped over my feet, fell down, and smacked my elbow so hard you would've thought I was giving the People's Elbow to the rink, like the Rock. That hurt for a solid month. That's when I put my pride aside and made the decision to wear pads when I skate.

You might have noticed an obvious flaw in the plan: Steve, if I go out to a public skate wearing full hockey equipment, I'm going to look like an idiot. Correct! You're absolutely right. That's why you don't wear hockey pads to a public skate. Wear rollerblading elbow and knee pads instead. They're not big, bulky, and plastic. They're soft, and if you wear a semi-baggy jersey and some loose-fitting pants, nobody will even know you have them on. You could even wear the knee pads over your pants if you want. It still won't look nearly as ridiculous as full hockey gear. And if you're undecided and haven't bought hockey equipment yet, rollerblade pads are cheaper, too.

As for the helmet, that's non-negotiable. You have to wear it. You might see an older guy out there skating around with a toque, and I'm here to tell you that you're not him. That guy's been skating since JFK was president; you're learning how to skate in a world where kids born in the 2000s are getting drafted into the NHL. You are not the same. I promise you, there's a learning curve full of eureka moments there for you if you stick with it.

YOUR FEET WILL HURT

Unless you train in Muay Thai five times a week, the first few times you get a good skate in, you're going to chew your feet up pretty good. I don't just mean that the muscles in your feet will be sore, although that will probably happen, too. I mean that you're going to have cuts and blisters that are the opposite of fun.

There's no shame in throwing a little tape over the areas that typically get chewed up, like the inside of your ankle. You can try a regular Band-Aid, but I've found those come off in your boot. I've done a Band-Aid on the bottom with some hockey tape on top. "But Steve, I have a hairy foot!" Yep, so do I. You're choosing between two different types of pain, and the one that comes from peeling off the tape doesn't last as long.

Over time, the muscles in your feet and legs will get stronger, and the skin on your feet will toughen up a bit. "Shouldn't I just get bigger skates?" Probably not. You need them tight. Once you take off a pair of skates and experience that euphoria, you'll understand why hockey players basically live in sandals.

PLAYING HOCKEY IS THE FASTEST WAY TO LEARN

Let's jump ahead and say you've gone to the public skates for a while and you're starting to feel ready. You're not a great skater, like, at all, but at least you're moving around instead of daintily putting one foot in front of the other with nothing on your mind except not falling down.

This one is a real chicken-and-egg conversation. How do I learn to play hockey? By playing hockey.

Now, I'm not suggesting you get out there and play full-blown men's league after only a few weeks on the ice. I'm not even telling you to play in games. Getting out there with some friends, whether they have more experience than you or not, and just skating around and passing the puck is a great way to learn. I can't explain how this works in my brain, but the less you have to think about skating, the more natural it gets. When there's a stick in your hand and a puck on the ice, that becomes the focus, or at least more of it.

You'll naturally start shifting your weight, bending your knees, widening your stance, figuring out what to do with your hands, and so on. Public skates are great, but at some point you'll eventually have to make the jump to something that looks a bit more like hockey.

HOCKEY THAT ISN'T HOCKEY

One of the most intimidating things about hockey is the depth of it. You just need so much stuff. There's equipment (we'll get to that), two teams full of people, and available ice. It's a mess!

You don't need a full-on hockey game to play hockey in game-form. Is it just you and a buddy? Play posts. You get points for hitting the posts instead of the mesh of the net. The point isn't to score, it's to work on your aim. It'll help you learn to lift the puck with purpose instead of just sliding it along the ice or ripping the thing into the stands and knocking your grandma's coffee all over her jacket. You could also set up targets, too. You can buy them from a store that sells them or just print off four photos of your boss and tape them to the four corners.

Shinny is also the best. It's super-casual hockey, and in my experience, most really good players aren't going to just torch you because they can. I've been lucky enough that the experienced players I've skated with have always tried to teach ankle-benders like me how to get a little better.

We have a problem, though. We've skipped a step, haven't we? You need equipment.

DON'T BUY TOP-OF-THE-LINE GEAR

Hey, Ovechkin, you don't need $800 NHL game-used skates to learn how to skate. You might think it's like putting Lamborghini wheels on an old car, but it's actually more like putting Lamborghini wheels on a donkey. The donkey doesn't know what to do with them and isn't going anywhere. Plus, now you're out $800.

Elbow pads, knee pads, shoulder pads, hockey pants: this is

all stuff you can get for cheap at Canadian Tire or a used equipment shop. If you're going to splurge on one thing, because who doesn't like to treat themselves from time to time, get nice gloves. Again, don't go breaking the bank, but good hockey gloves are feather-light and feel amazing. The weight difference between gloves you'd find in the store a decade or so ago and newer stuff is wild. Plus, really old gloves can get . . . I don't know how else to say it . . . crusty.

Some NHL teams even have equipment sales at the end of the season, and you can find super high-end equipment for cheaper than you'd expect. At least, that was the case with the Leafs a few years ago until they realized, "Hey, we're not charging enough for this stuff," and jacked the prices. It was fun while it lasted; I still have Tim Brent's gloves.

AIR OUT YOUR BAG

You've finally started playing hockey, and you're working up a sweat! This one's not hard: air out your hockey bag, dude. I'm not telling you to wash all your hockey equipment every week, although you could wash most things that often if you wanted to. I am telling you that you've got to at least air that bad boy out. This can be a problem with experienced players, because they're wearing some stuff they've had since Y2K.

Hey, man, just because you skate like the wind doesn't mean you don't smell like you're passing wind on the way by. I might stink as a player, but you smell like the Dumpster behind a store that just sells cheese and socks. Air it out, go upgrade your gear, bury your gloves in the ground if you have to, just don't add to what is already probably the smelliest sport on the planet.

At minimum absolute laziest, you should be opening your bag. A little bit better, you should be taking most of your stuff out of the bag. If you want to level up further, and you have a garage with a little space on the wall, bang in some hooks, or even just nails, and hang your equipment up. It won't quite be minty-fresh, but at least your teammates won't be gagging when you're on the bench.

As for clothes, don't just air them out. You have to wash them. Hockey is a stinky sport, but it doesn't have to be biological warfare.

TRIPLE-CHECK YOUR HOCKEY BAG

The worst feeling in the entire world isn't missing a wide-open net or accidentally coughing the puck up for a breakaway goal against. No, the worst feeling is realizing you forgot to bring a vital piece of equipment to your team's skate.

While embarrassing, this usually doesn't result in total disaster. I've forgotten my stick before, and someone almost always has a spare. I got super lucky one time when I forgot my hockey pants, of all things, and one dude just happened to bring an extra pair that sort of fit me, although I looked like a toddler wearing his dad's pants.

But you forget your skates? I guess you're going home. Somebody might lend you a glove or two if they can, and apparently even hockey pants. But the odds that somebody brought a spare pair of skates, and that fit you, are slim to none. Sorry buddy, you're screwed.

That's why you triple-check. And don't just leave all your stuff in there from last week. We covered that.

WEAR A CUP

I can't believe I even have to say this, especially to men. You might be thinking, *Who the hell wouldn't wear a cup?* You'd be surprised.

One time—and I mean one single, solitary time—I forgot to bring my cup. I sat there in the locker room and debated not even playing. Your cup is probably your second-most important piece of equipment after your skates. Actually, scratch that, it's first.

But play I did. That night, I lined up across from a guy and I told him I forgot my cup. I'm not sure why I told a stranger that. I guess "Hey, I'm an idiot, please look out for my nuts" would have been worse, and that was the first substitute I could think of. He then enthusiastically said, "Ah, that's not a big deal! I never play with a cup!" He said that to make me feel better, but I've got to tell you, it didn't help at all.

I skated around all night with one hand on my stick and the other hand trying to protect any chance I had at becoming a father one day. What else do I remember from playing that night? Nothing. Absolutely nothing. All I could think about was protecting my junk and never forgetting my jock ever again.

I'll just out and say it: former Winnipeg Jets captain Blake Wheeler ruptured a testicle in a game in January 2023. That guy was wearing a cup when it happened (and was also making millions of dollars). How much worse would it have been if he wasn't wearing that protection?

Wear the cup, you actual nutjob.

WEAR A CAGE

We've already established that wearing a helmet is non-negotiable. The same goes for a full cage.

"But won't I get made fun of?" No, you won't. This is such a guy thing. Why are guys so weird about doing things that are common sense?

Do guys in the NHL wear a cage? No, basically never, unless they're dealing with a serious facial injury. Even then, they're getting constant attention on the bench and after the game from highly qualified team doctors and trainers to help deal with the injury. You know what's better than that? Not getting a puck or stick in the face in the first place.

I knew a mechanic who took a cross-check to the teeth in men's league that required major dental surgery. Do you know what his team doctor told him? Nothing, because his team doctor didn't exist, because he wasn't playing in the NHL.

If experienced players want to go out there and risk their entire face even though they've got work in the morning, fine, that's their business. You? You're not an experienced player. A couple of guys might call you tough, but most people in your life are just going to ask you why the hell you weren't wearing a cage.

Women's hockey at the highest level doesn't have this problem, and this is why women live longer than men. Why are we like this?

Wear the damn cage.

THERE IS A LEFT AND RIGHT

This is embarrassing, but I learned this the hard way.

The first time I ever put on full hockey equipment, I was stupid enough to post a picture of it on Twitter. The problem is that I had mixed up my left and right elbow pads. As is tradition with all things on the internet, I made a mistake, and people pointed it out. One Twitter user was kind enough to tweet, "Sorry to say boss but your elbow pads are on the wrong arm!! No biggie." Unfortunately for me, that nice man who pointed out my mistake was none other than former NHL star and current NHL coach Marc Savard.

There's nothing more humbling than a dude who you collected hockey cards of pointing out you don't even know how to properly put on your equipment. Let my dumb mistake serve as a lesson for you.

THERE'S NO RIGHT ORDER TO PUT ON YOUR EQUIPMENT

When it comes to putting on all your equipment, there's no hard-and-fast rule for what goes on first, second, and so on. Some experienced player will tell you the way they do it is the only way, but it doesn't matter. Having said that, there are some things that make more sense.

The way I was taught: bottom to top.

That might be confusing if you've never put on equipment before. You might be thinking, *Wait, you mean I should put on my skates before my hockey pants? Isn't that like putting on your shoes before your jeans?* That's not what I'm saying, although I've seen guys do it that way a bunch of times. I've even tried it, but I've found it's a pain and I usually chew up my hockey pants doing it.

No, my order is jock, hockey pants, shin pads, socks, skates, elbow pads, jersey, helmet, gloves. You might have noticed I left out shoulder pads. I rarely play with them, because the hockey I play is non-contact. It always feels like a bright idea until someone dings you with a shot right between your shoulder blades during warmups, which has happened.

Since you obviously need your hands to get dressed, bottom to top is just easiest, in my opinion, with the exception of your gloves going on last. Some of that order doesn't matter as much, but if you put your helmet on before your jersey, you're going to have a bad time.

ALWAYS BRING CLEAR TAPE

As the new kid on the block, you're going to forget stuff from time to time, and that's fine. Everybody makes mistakes. Just try to remember to bring clear tape.

You won't always need hockey tape; the tape job on your stick is probably fine to last you a few sessions. But you will always need clear tape for at least your socks. Does it actually do anything? Great question! I wouldn't know, because I always wear it. I have this vision of my socks sagging down below my knees. Some shin guards come with straps, so maybe you won't even need it, but everybody loves a teammate who always has "clear." You can buy bundles of five or six rolls and stuff a couple of those in your bag, and now you don't have to worry about clear tape for months.

Plus, clear tape might be the number one thing players forget or just run out of. If you're the one who always has it, and you're willing to share the love with anyone who might have forgotten, you're a hero.

HOCKEY TAPE DOESN'T MATTER

Honestly, ever since I learned how to do it, thanks to Marc Savard's YouTube channel, I love taping hockey sticks. My toddler has a bunch of mini-sticks at home, and I've taped every one of them.

That said, some people are going to make you feel like there's one correct way for everybody to tape their stick, and that's just not true. Some tape only the middle of the blade. Some tape way up the heel of the blade so it looks like their stick is wearing a sock. Others like to tape every inch of the blade all the way down to the tip of the toe, breaking out scissors and everything.

We haven't even talked about the shaft of your stick! Maybe just a little at the top? Maybe use a lot and have it go down a foot or more. Maybe do what Phil Kessel and a bunch of the USA Hockey guys do: the candy cane all the way down.

Did you know there's different kinds of tape? There are! There's regular old hockey tape in all colours and sizes, some skinny, some wide, plus there's that fancy cloth tape that does . . . things? It looks and/or feels nice, I guess? And the wax! Dudes throughout the NHL lather their sticks up with wax. I'll be honest, I have no idea what that does, but guys seem to like it.

Go look at the tape jobs of NHL players like Artemi Panarin, Tim Stützle, and David Pastrnak. Panarin covers up the toe of his stick and just throws one little strip of tape along the bottom up to the heel. Stützle does something similar, except his little strip of tape is smack in the middle of his blade and stops dead in the centre. Then there's Pastrnak's tape job, which notoriously looks like he haphazardly threw it on in the dark while trying to rush out of the house.

Those three guys combine to make $31,242,857 per year. They might be good at hockey.

There are a thousand ways to tape your stick. Back when he was a humble rookie for the Leafs, gritty forward Zach Hyman told me he doesn't tape the toe of his stick because he's always digging in the corners, and those battles would just ruin his tape job anyway. Now, a few years later, Hyman has a big contract and scores lots of goals, and he still doesn't tape the toe of his stick.

What I'm saying is, don't let somebody chirp you for your tape style, because lots of players have success with all kinds of hockey tape fashion statements. A tape job isn't going to make you good or bad at hockey.

My podcast co-host and SDPN co-CEO Jesse Blake is also relatively new to hockey, and he got some excellent advice from Hockey Hall of Famer and former NHL MVP Eric Lindros at a charity tournament. Lindros told him that, if anything, Jesse had too much tape on his stick and that would just make it heavier, which isn't exactly helpful if you're a new player still struggling to get around. But it's not a bad piece of advice. Hell, hockey sticks can be hundreds of dollars these days; how much difference is a dime's worth of tape going to help your game? It's fine for Mark Stone to use up half a roll of tape on the knob of his stick every night, but something tells me that strategy is going to help the captain of the Vegas Golden Knights more than it'll help someone like me.

If you're interested in learning how to tape your stick, Marc Savard's YouTube channel is still up even though he's now an assistant coach with the Calgary Flames. His series is called *Taping Twigs*, and he shows you how to tape your stick like current and former NHL players. However you do it, or even if you like to go with no tape at all, do you.

SKATE SHARPENING MATTERS

As a massive NHL fan, I try to do what the pros do when I play. Obviously, the skill level isn't quite there yet, but there are other things I can emulate. These guys are constantly having their skates sharpened and even replacing their blades entirely. They also have training and equipment staff, and presumably, none of this comes out of their pockets, but I guess it wouldn't kill me to get my skates sharpened more often.

One day, after not sharpening my skates for months, or maybe even more than a year, I got them done. I didn't think anything of it, and I showed up to hockey like any other day.

As soon as I hit the ice, I noticed two things: I'm way faster than normal, and I can't stop. If that combination sounds bad, that's because it is. Why didn't I anticipate this? It's like growing your hair out for a long time, cutting most of it off, and expecting to look exactly the same.

I told the more experienced skaters about my predicament. I didn't even get past "I sharpened my skates" before they knew what I was getting at. If you're Connor McDavid, maybe sharpening your skates every intermission works for you. If you're just Bambi in rec league like some people I know (me), super-sharp skates might not be for you.

Dull blades don't bite in as much, so your acceleration and turning is worse, but you're less likely to catch an edge when you're stopping, rotating, etc.

Some people like sharp blades, and some people like dull. Anecdotally, a defender might like a duller blade. They generally don't accelerate and sprint as much, and with all the rotating back to front to back again, there's less chance they'll catch an edge and blow a tire.

CHECK YOURSELF BEFORE YOU HIT THE ICE

You'd be surprised how often people will just saunter onto the ice completely oblivious that they forgot something. A common culprit is the dreaded skate guards. It'll look hilarious when you immediately eat it in a crumpled heap the second you step onto the ice, but it can be dangerous. I know a coach and experienced guy who has been around the game for decades who accidentally left a skate guard on, took one step onto the ice, fell, and tore his rotator cuff.

Whenever I hear about the old "clear tape" prank, where guys put clear tape on a teammate's skates, I think of that. But don't worry, if you're playing beginner hockey, you're far less likely to encounter some psychopath willing to do that to you. The thing is, they won't have to, because you might accidentally do it to yourself.

Lastly, this isn't part of your equipment per se, but you won't be happy if you forget it: water bottle. There's always somebody trying to mooch water or Gatorade on the bench. You don't want to use somebody else's bottle, and they might not say it, but they don't really want you using theirs, either. You might say, "Okay, but I won't even let it touch my lips." Say that out loud. Yeah, see? Weird. Sorry to be the water bottle police, but bring your bottle.

Oh, and if you step onto the ice without your cup on, get off, strip down, and get it, even though it means taking off pretty much half your gear. Don't be stupid.

HIT ME WITH YOUR BEST SHOT

Lastly, once you hit the ice, it's natural to want to score a heroic goal in magical fashion before pulling out the marker you hid in your glove and signing a contract with the scout who happened to be sitting in the stands watching your scrimmage. While it might not happen that quickly for you, there's a few things to keep in mind.

First, your stick length. You might have thought I was going to start with your stick curve, but in my experience, this one matters more. I watch a lot of high-level hockey, and I can't believe how ridiculous some players' body angles are, how they bend and how they move. I love hearing about players like Adam Oates, who played with a notoriously short stick, hunched right over, because I could never imagine pulling that off. As someone who is very not an NHL player, I can't take angles like McDavid, and I can't stretch out and steal the puck from you like Cale Makar. I need a longer hockey stick.

Find a stick that reaches up to somewhere between your nose and forehead, and don't forget you'll be on skates. It's obviously possible for a stick to be too long, but for most new players, I find the greater issue is a stick that's too short.

Don't worry much about stick curve; that's completely personal preference. Generally, a big curve is going to help you raise the puck and rip it. A flatter stick is going to make it easier to send and receive passes. You might be thinking, *Well, I struggle to raise the puck, so I'm going to go with a big curve.* The problem is, you might overcorrect and start taking people's heads off. Fiddle around with a few different curves and see what you like.

And lastly, you'd be shocked how different it feels to shoot or pass with your weight on your lead leg vs. your back leg. Practicing on both is going to give your game a little depth, and while you won't exactly be Leon Draisaitl out there, you'll feel like him.

HAVE FUN

Fun is what hockey is all about. Don't worry about impressing anybody out there. Don't even worry about impressing yourself. Good things take time. I promise hockey is worth it.

It might feel like it's never going to happen, but someday, you're going to get a breakaway. Then you'll work your way up to a breakaway where you don't get caught for being hilariously slow. Eventually, you'll build to a breakaway where you take a shot that might actually put a puck through gift-wrapping paper.

And—I swear to you—one day you *will* score on that breakaway. It's an irreplaceable feeling, and the best part is that everybody around you is going to be more happy for you than you are.

I've gained such a deep appreciation for what the pros can do since I started playing. You stop watching players just simply doing things and you start to put more thought into how they do it. We always talk about talented body parts, like a player's hands or feet, and those things are definitely incredible. However, the thing about the pros that I appreciate the most now is their minds. The speed at which these players process what's going on, who is where, and what to do makes them seem like a cross between an alien species and a supercomputer.

If you're a huge hockey fan but you've never played the game, I think you owe it to yourself to at least try it out. Do it to appreciate the game more. Do it for the fitness you'll gain from it. Or do it for the beer—I don't care! I've thought about playing hockey—like, really, really bad hockey—the entire time I've been writing this.

And I can't wait to get back on the ice.

Conclusion
Final Horn

I'm all ranted-and-raved out—for now.

But tomorrow I'll wake up, get caffeinated, and be right back to it. Unfortunately, I've been told I have to wrap this book up eventually, so that's what I'm doing.

We've ranted and raved about the state of the NHL, things I like, things I don't like—and after all of that, I've come to one conclusion: I've always loved hockey, and I've never loved it more than I do now.

It's a truly beautiful thing that even though I'm nostalgic about hockey, I'm also genuinely excited to watch it change and grow. Hockey isn't a bunch of characters in a snow globe, sealed under glass, in stasis. It's ever growing, ever changing, and free.

We've talked about hockey's all-time greats. Maybe the legends we've mentioned will always be all-timers. Maybe, one day, the stars of today and tomorrow will pass them. That's the beautiful thing about hockey and sports overall: there's always a next game.

Sure, there are days where things seem bleak. Every now and then, you go, "Wait a minute—this Andrei Vasilevskiy guy is well on his way to being a Hockey Hall of Famer." You realize that Gretzky's unbreakable career goals record is perhaps one season away from being broken by Alexander Ovechkin. Then you realize that there's a guy who was raised in Arizona named Auston

Matthews who's actually on pace to pass Ovechkin if he can keep it up long enough. You tell yourself maintaining that kind of greatness is impossible, and then you realize that's what so many people said about Ovechkin a decade ago.

When a record stands the test of time, you appreciate it and bask in its seemingly eternal brilliance. When a record falls like a once-great city into the ocean, a new standard takes its place. Maybe you'll even be lucky enough to watch the new record get set while sitting next to somebody who witnessed the old one with their own eyes.

Hopefully, you'll come away from this book knowing that old things are not always irrelevant or obsolete, and new things are not always ignorant or arrogant. I hope I come away from this experience with the same takeaways and keep them with me. Learning isn't always linear.

Man, I keep trying to think of a funny line or wisecrack to end this book with, but I'm drawing a blank. I haven't written about anything this lovingly since I wrote my wedding speech.

I love hockey. It's just the best, even when it's the worst. Maybe it's because I love its speed and its intensity. Maybe it's because I love stories and I love people, and hockey is full of both of them.

My son is four years old and has started to ask to watch hockey highlights with me in the morning. The first time he asked to watch them was better than any cup of coffee I've ever had. My daughter is still a baby, and to think that one day I might be blessed enough to have the same experience with her fills me with a joy I can't even describe.

Then, I'm sure, one day, the Leafs will blow a 4–1 lead, and I'll hear my children say their first curse words. Hockey is like life: you take the good with the bad.

If you opened up this book and made it this far, my guess is that you already loved hockey to begin with. If I've done my job properly, you'll appreciate the game even more now. Whenever you watch a game, you can enjoy it by yourself while watching chaos erupt on social media, watch from the couch with family, watch with friends at the bar, and if you happen to stumble across a $1,000 bill on the sidewalk, then you can afford to experience the game down at the rink itself. Well, that or maybe you just live somewhere where pro hockey ticket prices are reasonable; in that case, lucky you, show-off.

Raving about something doesn't mean you think it's perfect, and ranting about something doesn't mean you hate it. I'll rave about hockey in spite of its imperfections and rant about hockey in the hope it will get even better. Passion is a powerful tool.

I hope you enjoyed this book, I hope your day is magical, and—this is the nicest thing I can think of to say to another human being—may your favourite hockey team win at least one championship in your lifetime.

If you ever want to rant or rave about anything to do with hockey and nobody else is around, I'm not hard to find. It's the future! That means I'm with you wherever you are.

Acknowledgements

The first person I would like to thank is you, the reader, for taking a chance on this book. My genuine hope is that it was much easier for you to read this book than it was for me to write it. Whether you agreed with me or screamed curses at the pages, I would call this book a success if it at least helped you bond with friends and family over hockey. If you bond with somebody because you both think I'm a dumbass, I think that technically counts.

I would like to thank every teacher I've ever had from kindergarten through university. See? I *was* listening, I'm just kind of weird.

I want to thank my book agent, Brian J. Wood. You always found a way to turn a lovely phone call about hurrying the hell up writing this book into a conversation about how the Toronto Maple Leafs are the most baffling team in the Universe. Huge thanks are also owed to Jim Gifford, who approached Brian and me with the idea for this book in the first place.

To the HarperCollins Canada team: you're absolutely fantastic. Brad Wilson was instrumental in pushing this book across the finish line. Justin Stoller really helped sculpt the book into what it ended up becoming. Canaan Chu helped turn the jumbled words I submitted into actual readable sentences. Peter Norman meticulously combed through the manuscript to confirm the accuracy of facts and statistics, a task made even more challenging because a lot of this book was written mid-season and then the Coyotes moved. I'd also like to shout-out the marketing manager of this book, Neil Wadhwa, and my publicist for this book, Lisa Winstanley. Yes, that is her actual name. It takes an incredible number of people to get a book done, let alone to make it any good. You're the bee's knees.

To the entire team at my company, SDPN. To my co-CEOs, Adam Wylde and Jesse Blake. You know what? Yeah, maybe choosing to write a whole book during our first full year full-time at our own company was kind of an interesting choice. Thank you to Drew Livingstone, Kristina Weber, and Maddie Smith for their understanding and willingness to work around my silly schedule. To Justin Fisher and Robert Molloy, who helped me throughout the process of reviewing this book, thank you for being a part of the process. If you'd like to support our business, follow SDPN on YouTube, Apple, Spotify, or all of those platforms! If you like hockey talk, I'd put ours up against anybody else's.

Several other people in and around hockey allowed me to bug them for their thoughts on several topics throughout this book. A few of those names were Chris Johnston, Julian McKenzie, Ailish Forfar, Bob McKenzie, Elliotte Friedman, Jeff Marek, and Allan Walsh, just to name a few. I'm sure you had better things to do than let me bug you with random hockey questions during the offseason.

I want to thank the Toronto Maple Leafs for being the weirdest damn team in the entire world. Would I be happier if you were just a regular team who won a championship every now and then instead of constantly blowing Game 7s and losing to their own employees? Yes. Would I have a book deal? No. So this is your fault. Thanks.

I want to thank my son, Leo, and my daughter, Isla, for inspiring me. Right now, your mom and I are the ones reading books to you. One day, I hope you find this book on the shelf and read it to yourself in your dad's voice. Iggy, you're a dog, so good dog.

To my parents, Tina and Gary, and my in-laws, Cid and Louise. I'm not sure how I would have gotten this book done without your help. Isla was born before this book was even finished, and if you weren't there, I'm positive somebody from HarperCollins would have hit me with a Stone Cold Stunner and I would have deserved it.

To my wife, Sarah-Louise. As I type this, you're in the middle of your 50,000th rendition of "Skinnamarink" as you change Isla's diaper and Leo inserts his own lyrics, mostly just the word "poo." As always, you're the only reason I'm able to accomplish anything. Every day and every year, I admire your strength and who you are more than I did before. Thank you for everything, my everything.